SPINNING THE WARP:
A PERSONAL STORY

SPINNING THE WARP:
A PERSONAL STORY

JUDITH H MORRISON

an ELSIE book

TO
ALL who added experiences
to my incarnation this time,
Thank You.

 an **ELSIE** book
www.enjoylivingcontentedly.com

First published in 2011 by
ELSIE Books, Exeter, Devon

ISBN 978-0-9552819-1-4
Copyright © 2011 Judith H Morrison

The right of Judith H Morrison to be identified as the author of this work has been asserted in accordance with Ss 77 and 78 of the Copyright Design and Patents Act 1988.

All rights reserved. No part of this publication may be reproduced, stored in a retrieval system, or transmitted, in any form or by any means, electronic, mechanical, photo-copying, recording, or otherwise, without the prior written permission of the publisher.

Contents

Preface		vii
1	Catalyst	1
2	Early Childhood	5
3	Schooldays	14
4	Articles	28
5	Spinning	41
6	Out of Control	49
7	Chameleon	63
8	Bolt from the Blue	81
9	University	96
10	Wide Horizons	115
11	Shaft of Sunlight	134
12	Out of the Ashes	149
13	Resonance	165
14	No Diagnoses	179
15	Stuck Grief	196
16	Untangling Threads	207
17	Examining the Yarn	223
Afterword		235
Appendix 1		237
Appendix 2		239
Appendix 3		241
Appendix 4		245
Appendix 5		246
Bibliography		253
Notes		254

Preface

'I cannot go through all my thoughts so as to make them clear to you, nor have I ever dwelt on things, to shape the story of them. I know not where the beginning was, nor where the middle ought to be, nor even how at the present time I feel, or think, or ought to think. If I look for help to those around me, who should tell me right and wrong (being older and much wiser), I meet sometimes with laughter, and at other times with anger'.

R. D. Blackmore in Lorna Doone

My experiences were not unique, and were mild on the scale of what some people have to deal with. But I failed to elicit help which would have ameliorated my family's circumstances.

Although there is more openness now, it is not easy to talk, or hear, about what some adults and children endure in their personal lives, day in and day out. Emotional and psychological scars may survive long after physical injuries have healed. I believe such scars not only damage relationships and rob people of their potential in life, but they contribute to the causes of chronic physical illnesses.

Emotional and psychological scars should be recognised for what they are, part of life's experiences. If this happens, and with the right circumstances, deep transformational healings within a person are possible. My story is worth telling if it makes a small contribution to the growing understanding which is developing in our society.

This is a memoir and the nature of a memoir is the author is selective in what is included. I can only give my perspective; others will have their own views on some of the events I've included. Many names have been altered. I've used letters in place of doctors' and psychologists' names, because I feel changes, both to the structure of the system in which healthcare professionals work, and in attitudes generally, would help those facing complex situations.

JUDITH MORRISON
May 2011

'One problem in much abuse is the tendency of the one who is hurt or oppressed to imagine himself as a victim. I'm not saying that victims are responsible for the situation, but that they don't have to take oppression on its own terms. You can refuse to assume the role and, instead, find strength in yourself, no matter how private and internal, to keep from collapsing into victimhood. The problem is that in entering into the field of victim you make constellate in others the role of aggressor. ... In the most ordinary situations people want to bind you and give you orders, and often this attitude is entirely unconscious and on the surface kind'.

THOMAS MOORE
in *Dark Nights of the Soul: A Guide to finding your way through life ordeals*
p105

1
Catalyst

IT was dark. I was alone in the house. The doorbell rang continuously. I decided someone had come to the wrong house and would go away if I didn't answer. In our neighbourhood Becky was the only teenager who rang doorbells inappropriately. I hadn't noticed her ten years previously when I moved to the small residential estate on the edge of Exeter. Then she was one of the children who played on the green under the two mature trees preserved when the houses were built in the 1980s. A couple of years later she'd been left behind by her peer group when they'd outgrown their games. Becky probably had some form of Asperger's syndrome and only rang neighbours' doorbells in a normal fashion during the day, perhaps when she was lonely.

The continuous ringing of my doorbell stopped only to be followed by loud, demanding thumpings. I picked up the phone in my bedroom and started dialling as I walked towards the window. 9, 9, ... I peeked through the curtains. There was a police car parked in front of my house. I replaced the receiver, went downstairs and opened my front door to find two police officers facing me.

'Are you Judith Morrison? The North Devon police have received a complaint about you from Mr. and Mrs. Reed. We have been instructed to call on you to give you a warning', said the officer holding a piece of white paper.

'Can we come in?' The second officer asked, as they both entered and shut my front door.

'Would you like a cup of tea?' I asked, relieved it was the police and not someone's angry ex-partner.

'No. We've come to give you a verbal warning,' said the more abrupt of the two.

I sat on the bottom of the stairs for twenty minutes and the two officers stood in front of me. One said little while the other aggressively delivered the message from the North Devon police. He made it clear I was to have no contact with, or communications about Mr. and Mrs. Reed, and if I did criminal proceedings could be taken against me.

Any control in me evaporated the second I shut my front door. My body was flooded with rage, fury and disbelief. I was shaking and sobbing. I phoned Pauline, a friend who had been as a sister to me since I moved to Exeter.

'What's the matter? What's happened', she asked.

'The bloody Reeds have gone to the police. I've just had two officers beating my door down. Who do they think they are? I suppose they think they can intimidate me. It didn't matter what I said. The police wouldn't listen.'

A police officer had listened to Ted and Veronica Reed, but had he read between the lines? Ted was well known and regarded as a man of the highest integrity in the market town where he'd lived and worked for more than two decades. He called some of the town's police officers by their first names. They knew him in his professional capacity attending after road accidents if animals were involved or, perhaps, in his surgery looking after their family pets.

The police would not have wasted time visiting me unless the Reeds had been selective in what they'd said and not given the whole story. Had Ted been afraid or ashamed, or even prevented from telling them why he had led a double life? Or was there something I did not know?

The next morning, before going out I phoned the police to

speak with the officer who'd dealt with Ted and Veronica's complaint. He was not on duty so I left a message for him to phone me.

I'd planned to attend the monthly meeting of the local Guild of Weavers Spinners and Dyers held in a school hall five miles from my home. It was more than a decade since I had been to a meeting as I've let my membership lapse when I went to America. Veronica had been a member of the Guild then and I wondered if she would be at the meeting.

At the school I followed the GWSD signs and walked through the open doorway into the school's hall and stopped at the top of the half flight of steps to survey the scene before me. Guild meetings hadn't changed. Spreading from one side of the hall to the other were groups of five or six women sitting in circles in front of humming spinning wheels. Spilling out of bags and boxes littered under and around their chairs were the paraphernalia beloved by spinners; fleece of varying natural shades and dyed hues, carders and spindles, spools and lazy kates, niddy-noddies for making skeins, balls and cones of wool, finished and half finished garments and books and magazines.

Around the edge of the hall were tables. Two ladies were looking after the hot water urn, making mugs of tea and coffee and selling slices of cake made and donated by members to raise funds for the Guild. The Guild's library books were on another table to be browsed before selecting one to borrow until the next meeting. There was a sales table where equipment, fleece and yarns were traded between members.

The registration table was at the foot of the steps. On an adjoining table were a few plants, a couple of books, some chocolates and a packet of biscuits, the prizes for the lunchtime draw. A notice indicated the weavers and their looms were attending a morning workshop in a different room. Veronica was sitting on the far side of the room in a circle with four people I recognised as committee members when I took an active part in the Guild.

I went down the steps to the reception table.

'Hello. I'd like to rejoin the Guild. I was a member about ten years ago,' I said to the lady sitting behind the table.

'Do you know anybody here now?' she asked.

'No.'

'Let me introduce you to Brenda,' she said, leading me to the middle of the room.

I joined Brenda's circle and worked on my knitting project as we chatted. We ate our sandwiches while the announcements were made and the raffle drawn. Veronica won a prize. We avoided eye contact as she crossed the room to collect it. After the raffle it was time to tidy away the paraphernalia and turn to face the stage for the afternoon talk.

My pleasure at being back with the Guild was marred by what had happened the previous night. I had been shocked by the manner of the police visit, but why had the Reeds gone to the police. What I had been involved in? What mistakes had I made? I had been dealing with family bereavements, and over the previous eighteen months trying to recover my health. Had I misjudged Ted? Had he fooled me?

In my fury after the police's warning I vowed to find answers to my questions and to tell my story, and I decided I would be quite willing to be cross-examined if Ted and Veronica wanted to press charges.

 Over the following decade my vow turned into a journey that gave me deeper understanding of my family, the personal impact of some taboo issues prevalent in our society and of myself.

2

Early Childhood

TWO contrasting photographs of my grandfathers capture the different backgrounds of my parents. One photograph, taken in a studio probably in the 1940s, is of a man in his sixties wearing Freemason regalia. The other, taken in the 1960s in a farmyard, is of a man in his seventies in an old coat secured with a piece of binder twine.

My paternal great-grandfather was a hemp and twine manufacturer who emigrated from Scotland in the mid-1800s and settled in Marlborough, Wiltshire. He married a builder's daughter. My grandfather was their youngest son. He was educated at Mill Hill School in north London where he excelled at sports. He went to Cambridge University and qualified as a solicitor in 1905. In 1912 or 1913 he was one of the founding partners of Morrison & Masters, a firm of solicitors in Swindon. There are records of him being an officer in the Territorial Army and of overseas service in the First World War. My paternal grandparents married in 1919.

My father was their only child. He was premature and did not walk until he was three. Two photograph albums document his convivial and comfortable childhood. He went to a boarding preparatory school before going to Radley College in Oxfordshire. He never completed one school term without spending some time in the schools' infirmaries. His secondary education ended in the summer of 1939 when he was fourteen.

Ill-health prevented him from serving in the Second World War, but there are photographs of him in Home Guard and Royal Observer Corps uniforms. He worked in his father's office and started studying for his law exams. He attended the College of Law in Guildford after the war, qualified as a solicitor and became a partner in Morrison & Masters in 1947 a few months before his mother died after a long illness. His father died the following year.

My maternal grandfather was part of a large Yorkshire farming family. In 1912 he married a neighbouring farmer's daughter. My mother was the youngest of their three children. During my childhood Edna, her adored, talented sister, was never mentioned. I only knew of her because we had her piano, the piano my grandfather was criticised for buying and spending money they could ill afford in the depression at the end of the 1920s. When she was sixteen Edna contracted tuberculosis. My mother, then aged eight, was sent to Blackpool to stay with an aunt. When my mother returned home she was met at the farmhouse's seldom used front door by my grandfather, who was wearing his black Sunday suit. The rest of the family was gathered in the front room after Edna's funeral. Only then did my mother realise something was wrong. It was a loss that affected the family then and my mother for the rest of her life.

A couple of years after Edna's death the family moved to a farm south of Doncaster which was my mother's home till she married. My mother went to weekly boarding school. Like her sister she was bright but did not have any exceptional musical talents. After leaving school she worked as a hotel receptionist. During World War II she was driving army vehicles with the ATS, Auxiliary Territorial Service. Any comments from me about her driving would bring the retort, 'I was handling trucks and ambulances before you were born.'

My mother was working as a hotel receptionist in Oxford when my parents met. They married in 1949. My mother moved into the home my father had shared with his late parents, and into a life and social world very different from her farming roots, and one she was not entirely comfortable with.

My mother was a homemaker, having all the skills needed to provide a comfortable home for her family. Andrew, my brother, was eighteen months older than me. Our mother took pride in our appearance. She made me hand-smock dresses with puff sleeves, which were fashionable for young girls in the 1950s. In winter I was often dressed in a green Morrison tartan kilt and a hand knitted oatmeal-coloured jumper with a Fair Isle yoke bought direct from the hand knitter in Scotland. My mother had a knitting machine and was a good hand knitter too. I remember my early attempts at knitting and struggling with dropped stitches until my skills improved and I acquired her love of knitting, sewing and making things.

Andrew and I enjoyed sitting at the large wooden table in the kitchen watching our mother cook and bake, and we vied to lick out the bowl when we had been baking buns. We'd help shell peas and broad beans before they were blanched and canned. There were plenty of children's books, dressing up clothes, board games, jigsaws and toys in our bedrooms and in the playroom which was on the top floor of the house next to our father's study. In the garden we played in and around the summer house and large sandpit. Frogs lived in the sandpit and I loved finding the tiny, tiny ones.

When we were very young our parents employed a nanny to help look after us. I have no recollections of her, but I have loving memories of May Williams who helped look after us when we were a little older. Andrew and I called her Billy, and her husband, Mr. Billy.

Andrew did not want to go to school without me, so when he started school I went too but initially just for the mornings. We attended a small, private two-classroom school in a village three miles from our home. The images that stuck in my mind are the daily crocodile as we walked up the village street to have lunch in a cafe, making round woven raffia mats, playing 'I sent a letter to my love and on the way I dropped it' in the playground, and I fell in love with a dark haired boy called David who had polio and wore callipers.

My father's work took him to London frequently. Once or twice a year my mother, brother and I went with him. We'd all stay in an apartment and be joined by my grandparents from Yorkshire. We always visited Hamleys toyshop when in London. I still have the big-eared pink elephant my grandparents gave me when I was four. I remember seeing Buckingham Palace, not because it was the monarch's residence, but because a policeman helped extract Andrew's head from the railings.

The family's favourite holiday destination was the far end of the beach at Exmouth in Devon. My father was an enthusiastic sand-castle builder. We'd explore shallow rock pools exposed at low tide and searched for baby crabs hiding under seaweed awaiting the incoming tide, which also filled our castle's moat. We'd rescue our flags from its battlements and watch our monument collapse. Then, shaking sand from our sandals, it was off to the seafront attractions of crazy golf, a tiny zoo and a boating lake.

Other holidays were taken in Norfolk. We stayed at Itteringham Mill, a vegetarian guest house run by Derek and Mary Neville. I was fascinated by the river flowing under the house. I have mostly happy recollections of playing by and on the river with my brother, other children staying at the Mill and with the dogs. A painful memory was when, wearing only a pair of shorts, I was thrown into a patch of stinging nettles by two older boys.

Each summer our mother took Andrew and me to visit her parents in Yorkshire. I have scant recollection of my grandparents' bungalow in the village where they had farmed since the 1930s. Eric, my uncle, and his second wife lived in the farmhouse. Every morning Andrew and I would go with my grandfather when he went to the farm. His first job was to hand milk the house cow, which he did in the field sitting on a three-legged stool with the peak of his flat cap turned to the back of his head. The milk from the pail was divided into two small churns with handles. One was left in the farmhouse kitchen for my uncle and his wife. I never saw her and the house was uncared for. Andrew and my grandfather went to feed the pigs whose high-pitched squeals before the food arrived frightened me. I carried the second milk churn to my grandmother, who gave me a glass of milk still warm from the cow.

Shortly before birthdays and Christmases a square parcel always arrived from my grandmother containing a fruitcake which she'd baked and my mother would ice. The cake was the centrepiece on the dining room table at Andrew's and my birthday parties, which included traditional games of Musical Chairs, Pin the tail on the Donkey and Pass the Parcel.

There were visits to the park to feed the ducks and visits to Savernake Forest. The enormous beech trees made a deep impression on me. I still get a thrill each year from the translucent green of their new leaves. But my abiding childhood memories from the Forest are of the bracken. I'd uncurl new fonds in the spring, in the summer it was as tall as me, and in the autumn it had turned brown and crispy.

It is hard to say when the change began. Frequently after school I went without Andrew to Billy's house and stayed to have tea when Mr. Billy came home from work. There were times when I did not see my mother for a while. On one occasion she had been away for about three months, and gave me a sewing box and a red plaid needle case when she came home. Both Andrew and I left the village school. Andrew was eight when he started boarding at the preparatory school of Wycliffe College in Gloucestershire. My new school was a small private day school for girls four miles from the new family home in East Devon.

For the next ten years our home was a large, red-brick, Virginia creeper-clad, Victorian house that had been a village vicarage. The five bed roomed house was set apart from the village and had five acres of landscaped gardens. My first recollection of the house and garden must have been the visit after my parents had agreed to buy it but before we moved. I was allowed to explore the house on my own and got lost. The house was in need of extensive work to restore it to a comfortable home. We 'camped' upstairs while the downstairs was renovated. The house had an impressive hall, staircase and landing, and a back hall, staircase and landing. The southerly part of the house had three attic rooms. There was a hatch onto a lead lined gully between the east and west roof ridges which was my mother's naturist sunbathing spot, completely private apart from low-flying aircraft.

The garden was a magical place with many secret places for a child, especially within the clumps of laurel and rhododendron. One of my favourite hides was inside the evergreen skirts of a mature leylandii tree that had been given the space to grow naturally to maturity. The tree's graceful branches were like arms of a candelabra reaching down before curving skywards. The dips of the branches made comfortable seats for me a few feet above the ground.

My mother was in her element in the garden. What she could not grow probably wasn't worth growing. Nowadays her methods would be called organic, but then that term was not needed to describe methods that had been used for generations. At the far end of the vegetable garden was a composting area. My mother had compost bins made that were six feet high, six feet wide and six feet deep. In addition to the garden waste, Willie, a local farmer, would deliver trailer loads of manure. My mother's compost heaps really did heat up and have steam rising from them. My parents grew Christmas trees from seed and planted the small saplings in an adjoining field. They were sold to a local greengrocer when three or four feet high.

Before moving I think my father's gardening experience was limited to sitting in one. He maintained the cultivator, lawnmower and various machines for cutting hedges and long grass, and did much of the grass cutting. One of Andrew's jobs was cutting grass; as an adult he said he would never have a property with a lawn. One of my regrets is that, whilst I have my mother's love of plants, I acquired little horticultural knowledge or skills from her.

Bert had worked part-time in the garden for the previous owners of the house. My father offered him a month's trial, but Bert told my father he would give my parents a trial. I think they passed, as a Bert, and later in the house his sister, Betsy, helped my mother for over twenty years. Bert was as much a Devonian as my grandfather was a Yorkshire man. They had both worked on the land all their lives, had respect for the land and a deep understanding of the need to take proper care of the soil to produce good crops. Bert was a strong, steady worker, never to be rushed, of few words and the right garden help for my mother.

Soon after we moved I wanted a cat and it didn't take much pleading for my parents to agree. The mice in the roof space may have influenced my mother's decision. I was given a straggly, tortoiseshell kitten from Willie's farm that looked in need of rescuing. She had one black, fluffy, bad tempered kitten who became the matriarch of our 'cat colony'. I don't know why my parents were so slow in curbing their numbers, perhaps because they were my friends and there was enough space for them.

My grandparents came from Yorkshire to stay once or twice a year until they moved to Devon when I was thirteen. Mr. and Mrs. Billy were regular visitors; their visits always coincided with Wimbledon fortnight. In the mornings they and my mother picked fruit, then all three either watched tennis or went on trips to the seaside.

One visitor I enjoyed seeing was Kitty, a school friend of my mother's. She had dark, curly hair, sharp eyes and a slim, agile body. She was not married and shared a house with her mother in Scarborough. She was not 'the daughter who did not leave home', but an independently minded woman. To me it seemed she and her mother were the best of friends, respecting and caring about each other. Kitty had run her own hotel. When I knew her she lectured in a college of further education on catering and hotel management. I cannot recall ever going out to eat with Kitty without her first inspecting the kitchens. She played tennis with us and was fun and good company. She was someone I admired, and in my teens I would have been happy to turn out like Kitty.

There were two neighbours, Auntie Jeanie and Mrs Harries, who became and remained family friends until their deaths. Auntie Jeanie, in her late sixties when we met, cared for her housebound husband. She delighted in children, and frequently asked me to have tea with her. Visits included feeding her hens and collecting the eggs. I stayed with her once when my parents went to Yorkshire because my grandfather was taken ill suddenly. I caused her considerable concern by disappearing to my usual haunts in our garden.

Mrs Harries, a widow, was twenty-five years older than my parents and lived on her own with a Dalmatian dog. I had little contact with her as a child. My mother often sent me to deliver a book or produce to her and she'd give me a small glass of apple juice and what she described as 'a special biscuit'. She was an excellent knitter and her occasional presents were wearable. When I was older I learned that she was one of the first members of the Vegan Society, campaigned against cruel farming methods and experimental methods that were used on animals. She actively supported the charities Beauty without Cruelty and Compassion in World Farming. She was strongly opposed to fluoride being added to drinking water as she thought it was an industrial waste. She had deep spiritual values and interests which spanned a wide spectrum including Eastern philosophies, Buddhism and flying saucers. She was a member of the Theosophical Society and of The White Eagle Lodge (See Appendix 1) and regularly attended local meetings. Sometimes my parents went with her.

The Bumblies was the nickname Andrew and I gave to a mild, gentle couple who had retired to Devon from Manchester. They would have been in their late sixties when we first met them. Peter had been a tailor. His appearance and manner exemplified neatness and precision. He was of modest height and build, with blue eyes and a moustache. Florence was of a similar height to Peter. She had fine, light brown, curly hair, brown eyes and was very slim. As she aged she looked undernourished and the tendons in her neck and hands became more obvious. The Bumblies' interests were walking, bird watching and photography. Some wild birds in their garden would perch on Peter's or Florence's outstretched hand to eat the seeds or broken pieces of nuts they had in the middle of their palm. Peter took many photographs, but we had to pose forever until he was satisfied everything was just right.

My parents must have met them through the Vegetarian Society. When we had a meal out with them, Peter would announce clearly and for all to hear, 'We are vegetarian.' The choice for vegetarians in those days was generally limited to omelettes – plain, cheese or tomato – but that did not prevent the Bumblies giving long explanations about vegetarianism before a meal was ordered. The Bumblies were frequent visitors, and my parents often looked in to see them when we were in Sidmouth. There was only one family holiday after we moved to Devon. It was a week in Cornwall and the Bumblies came too.

After a year in Devon I changed schools and attended the Convent of the Assumption in Sidmouth.

3

Schooldays

MOTHER John, the convent's junior school's headmistress, picked up I was having problems with reading and writing. I could not pronounce what I was reading. A girl with a stutter also found reading aloud difficult and we were both mocked by our classmates. I had extra writing lessons with Mother John. One summer holiday I had to copy out *Alice in Wonderland*, with weekly visits to Mother John. The only detail of those lessons I recall was having to put tails to the left on 'p's and tails to the right on 'q's. The writing practice was done at home at a second desk in my father's study. Although the extra writing was done under his supervision he did not turn it into a chore. I've used my bad writing ever since to cover up poor spelling and other language problems.

   Miss Courtney was my form mistress for my last two years at junior school. Those years were the best of my school days, apart from the journey to and from school. The reading and writing problems didn't prevent me being interested in lessons. I enjoyed and was good at arithmetic and the beginnings of algebra and geometry. There must have been the usual end-of-term and end-of-year tests, but the only test I remember taking was the eleven-plus which, as predicted, I failed. During the two years in Miss Courtney's class I had been given the joy of discovery and wanting to know more — a lasting gift from a true teacher.

I was nine when my parents decided I was old enough to walk to the bus stop on the main road in the village, take the bus to the edge of Sidmouth and walk the mile to the convent school. Some older boys who lived in the village made taunting comments and occasionally threw stones at me whilst I was walking down the village street or waiting at the bus stop. It was easy to poke fun, as I was the only girl in the grey convent school uniform and wearing a hat with a curled-up brim. It was probably made worse because I lived in 'the big house'.

During the school holidays I had my best friend back. Andrew was as happy as before to do things with me and show me his new interests and skills. I never succeeded in getting a sound out of his trumpet. His table tennis improved to the point where we couldn't play a game together. He taught me chess and always beat me. My father played chess more gently with me and sometimes let me win. Andrew taught me billiards and snooker on our half size billiard table. He usually won, but we were more evenly matched and I could practice in term time.

In the summer we went off on bikes through the surrounding lanes. Sometimes we'd venture far enough away from home that we had to get the train back to the neighbouring village. One cycle trip was to the sea at Budliegh Salterton, with its shelving, shingle beach and the mouth of the River Otter. Andrew had had swimming lessons at school but I had not. We didn't realise the dangers as I followed him into the sea. Suddenly I was out of my depth and in the current of the river, being taken away from the shore. I looked up through water, seeing bubbles and light. I don't know who got me out of the sea as the next thing I recalled was being on the beach and being given something to eat and drink by two strangers. I had come to no harm and cycled home. Andrew made it clear I was not to let our parents know what had happened as we would not be allowed out on our own again.

My childhood would have been idyllic if it had not been for the distress that enveloped my mother from time to time. Then the family dynamics changed until the distress departed as mysteriously as it arrived. I have no recollection of distressed episodes when we lived in Swindon. While the distress was present my mother became unreasonable and it was not possible to talk her out of the distress. Attempts at comfort had little, if any, effect and could even make matters worse. Sometimes she'd keep herself to herself. At other times she made it clear I was the cause of her distress. My father would ask me what I had done to upset her, as she had been fine when he went out. There appeared to be no obvious trigger and over the years we got used to not knowing what we might be coming home to.

When the distress afflicted her, the atmosphere in the house was tense. It was best to lie low and wait. I'd lie on my bed staring at the ceiling, listening, judging when it might be safe to slip down the backstairs to the kitchen, eat a bowl of cereal or cold baked beans out of the tin and return to my bedroom without being detected.

My mother's distress could turn into personal verbal attacks. When I was eight she started telling me vehemently I was not her daughter; her daughter was perfect. Sometimes the verbal abuse was accompanied by mild slaps or punches which didn't cause bruising. That continued until I was in my mid teens. After we moved to Devon she had ceased taking much interest in what I wore, except to make sure it was clean and that I always had the correct school uniform. I ended up believing that I was not her daughter, my parents had adopted me, and were disappointed I was not turning out like my brother.

My father only restrained her when she used physical violence towards me, and at times it seems physical violence was threatened to try to provoke him. Restraining her was difficult as she had extra strength when distressed. Sometimes she'd seek me out to hit me, even waking me at night with a physical attack. The two most dramatic incidents were in my early teens. One Saturday I was watching television when she came into the room with my father in pursuit. She punched me in the face with no warning other than some verbal abuse as she crossed the room. There was no time for my father to restrain her. The punch produced much blood from both nostrils, but nothing was broken. The scariest time was one Sunday when only she and I were at home. She cornered me in the backyard in a full angry, verbal flood, holding the broken end of a bottle an inch from my face. Fortunately, she did not attack me with the bottle.

When her distress departed she was my loving mother again, but appeared to have no conscious knowledge of what we had experienced during the distress. If the 'visitation' had been a bad one, my father, brother and I needed time to get over dealing with it, and feel it was safe to get back to normal until the next time.

By the time I was ten I had worked out that my mother was distressed and not malicious towards me, and that it was totally taboo to talk about what happened, either within or outside the family. There was an element of control over (or perhaps by) the distress. If the doorbell rang, she would flip out of it, deal with the caller perfectly normally and slip back into it almost as soon as the door shut. As an adult I called her distressed episodes 'flipmode'.

During the final stages of the work to renovate the old vicarage, my father considered returning to working in the legal profession. It seemed his age, then in his late thirties, was against him, and perhaps he would have found it difficult not to be his own boss after having been a senior partner in his own firm since his mid-twenties. So he embarked on training to be a stockbroker.

There had been discussions during Andrew's last year at preparatory school about sending both of us to a Quaker boarding school. Sadly, that didn't happen. Andrew was settled at his school and doing well and moved up to the senior school at Wycliffe College. I never felt anyone had expectations about me as they did for Andrew. It was more a case of 'What do we do with her now?' I'm sure my father had discussions with Mother John and looked at other options before arranging for me to remain as a day girl at the convent for my secondary education. The convent's senior school had had a good educational reputation, but a decline was beginning and the school closed in the summer I took my O-levels.

It was rare for my father to be away from home after we'd moved to Devon, but he was away during my final week at junior school. He returned home to find my mother had arranged for me to be a weekly boarder. When arranging that my mother had inadvertently set up a scenario which could have led to bullying, but only resulted in unpleasant comments. I had not eaten meat or fish as my mother had become vegetarian around the time I was weaned. She specified I was not to have meat or fish and had to have wholemeal bread at breakfast. The school could not cater for those dietary requirements. Each Monday my mother gave me a food parcel consisting of five slices of her home-made bread, five slices of cheddar cheese and five slices of Nuttolene, a peanut-based meat substitute loaf that came in a tin. That might have been alright if the food parcel had been put in a fridge. It was kept in a cupboard, and so by Thursdays there was mould on the slices I had to eat.

I found the senior school different from the happy atmosphere I'd enjoyed during the previous two years with Miss Courtney. As a day girl in the Juniors and with a lay form teacher, the convent's catholic aspect had had little impact upon me. I had learnt the catechism by rote, and still remember 'God made me to love, honour and obey him'. All changed in the senior school and by being a boarder I could not ignore I was in a convent. Further, apart from games and PE nuns did the teaching until the fifth year.

Our day started with mantilla and missal and a visit to the chapel at 7:30 a.m. for mass, which was in Latin as it was before The Second Vatican Council's influence. We always knew which saint's day it was. On Corpus Christi we were all given white veils and processed in a crocodile behind a nun carrying a gilded cross on a pole around the convent's grounds singing hymns, saying prayers and scattering petals in front of religious statues. During Lent we went to the chapel and knelt at the altar rail to kiss a splinter of the actual(!) cross which was set behind a little window in a small wooden cross. Fine gritty gravel was embedded into our knees as we said the Stations of the Cross, which were positioned beside the long garden path leading to a large wooden crucifix facing outwards at the crossroads at the top of the convent's site. During Advent we had to go to the chapel in the evenings to say rosaries for the souls in Purgatory to speed their entry into heaven. I had a picture in my mind, similar to ones I'd seen of concentration camps, of souls lined up in Purgatory queuing to get into heaven, and those souls being dependent upon us saying our rosaries properly to gain release and salvation. Every now and then we had a retreat day instead of lessons. My chief recollection of those days was that we were assigned the domestic work usually done by Spanish-speaking lay women in their late teens and early twenties who lived in the convent. I worked in the laundry and recall sorting and folding piles of poorly laundered pants. On retreat days we had extra visits to the chapel.

The Virgin Mary played a big part in the religious teachings. She was to be our role model, and I think it was anticipated we would only be mothers or nuns. That emphasis on the virtues of motherhood and the perfect loving mother did nothing to aid my understanding of my experiences when my mother was distressed. It served to help me think I was the only person with a mother who behaved like that. There was only one time at school when I could not contain my reactions to a bad episode at home. It was on the Monday after the incident with the broken bottle in the backyard. I was sent from evening prep to stand outside the form mistress's room. She told me she would speak with my father. Before the end of the week I was told 'it' would not happen again. 'It' was never discussed. I went home as usual at Saturday lunchtime not knowing what to expect. Nothing was said and nothing changed. The distressed episodes erupted from time to time as before.

I was a weekly boarder for four years and maybe I did not settle because I was used to my own space, company and freedom. I did not experience bullying during the first year in the twenty bed dormitory as that was aimed at the girl whose bed was across the foot of mine. During the second year I was moved to the junior dormitory. A senior pupil usually slept there. During the winter I went to bed in the dark. There were two or three Spanish-speaking girls aged about six who spoke little English. Frequently they cried themselves to sleep. I used to wonder why such young children had been sent to a foreign country. The following year I started off in the third form dormitory, but after a problem between me and a classmate I was moved to the first year dormitory. I was going to bed in the dark again. I fared little better in the fourth year. The dormitory was on the far side of the convent above and adjacent to the nuns' cells. I remember having problems sometimes understanding what was going on around me, and missing the point of, or not understanding, jokes. I was moved into a room on my own adjacent to the dormitory. The room had a second door into the corridor of nuns' cells. Nuns, taking a short cut, silently walked through the room as a ghost would without acknowledging my presence, though they did have to open and close the doors.

For my final year at the convent I was a day girl again. I would be sitting O-levels at the same time as Andrew would sit his A-levels. I don't know why Andrew left school after just one year in the sixth form, would be living at home and studying for his A-levels at Exeter Technical College. When my father told me I asked if I could be a day girl and be at home as well. Without persuasion, he agreed.

French was a compulsory subject in the senior school, and from the second year we had to do a second language, choosing either Spanish or Latin. Only I chose Latin and had one-to-one tuition with Mother Helen, who was in her eighties. She and my English teacher were always complaining about my spelling. I struggled with French dropping it and history as O-level subjects. I enjoyed the needlework classes and learnt basics sewing skills. I didn't like the arts lessons, but am sure I would have if the teacher not been discouraging. I had no natural drawing ability, and my creativity did not emerge until adult life when I enjoyed playing with colour through the medium of wool. Sports consisted of playing netball and hockey in the winter, and rounders and tennis in the summer. I did not enjoy sport and was poorly coordinated. One of my front teeth was damaged by a rounders ball I failed to catch, as I also failed to duck. We went on walks and runs along the lanes and tracks going up the wooded hills on the edge of Sidmouth, and from where I could see both my parents' and grandparents' homes.

There was no academic pressure on me during the five years of my secondary education. I had heard the advice, encouragement, and, perhaps, pressure Andrew received from our parents about the necessity to get good exam results. I think it had no more impact on him than such advice has on most teenagers, but it had a big influence on me. If it was important for Andrew then I too would need some O-levels.

The convent arranged one interview with a careers adviser.

'Have you thought what you would like to do when you leave school?' he asked.

'An undertaker,' I replied.

'No, you can't do that. Only men are undertakers. What is your favourite subject?'

'Maths'.

'Have you considered accountancy?'

Had he enquired further he'd have discovered I regularly transposed numbers, not a good trait for an accountant. I don't know why I'd said undertaker, as the only funerals I'd attended were requiem masses at school for elderly nuns.

We had the option to take Religious Knowledge O-level in the fourth year. It consisted of studying parts of the New Testament. I passed, and so in the fifth year joined the overseas students for religious studies.

I was interested in the subjects I was taking for O-level which were Maths, Geography, Human Biology, Latin, English Language and English Literature. I liked my teachers, and with hindsight was blessed to have an experienced English and Drama teacher, Mrs King, who transformed my failings into seeds which didn't sprout for thirty years. Our set book for English literature was Gerald Durrell's *My Family and Other Animals*, and the Shakespeare play was *Julius Caesar*. I can't remember which part of Chaucer we had to study. The only line I remember is 'Murder will out', which later in life I adapted to 'Truth will out'.

Andrew and I were both living at home and our parents were pleased I passed all six O-levels and Andrew's A-level results were good enough for him to be articled to an accountant.

My father qualified as a stockbroker and became a member of The Provincial Brokers' Stock Exchange. In the 1960s stockbrokers who practised outside London were not members of The London Stock Exchange. He joined a firm of stockbrokers in Exeter and became a partner the following year. He joined the Men of the Trees and became treasurer of the Devon branch. I helped my father with the charity's bookkeeping. I started by entering subscriptions in the accounts ledgers. My father taught me double entry book-keeping and how to balance ledgers ready for audit. At weekends I went with him to tree plantings, which were usually muddy affairs. We finished the plantings after the dignitaries had posed for the press and left. He was a member of Rotary in Exeter, and again became involved with committee work in London, serving on Men of the Trees and Provincial Brokers' Stock Exchange committees.

My mother's main occupation, other than being a housewife, was her garden. She, and sometimes my father, went to meetings of the local Vegetarian Society, which was affiliated to the national Vegetarian Society. I don't know where my mother's strong views on vegetarianism came from. She didn't have any special concerns about cruelty to animals or farming practices, nor was it because she disliked meat. She was happy to acknowledge she was a farmer's daughter, understood about the production of meat and liked beef even though she never ate any. I had not been aware that vegetarianism was generally considered eccentric in the 1950s and '60s. In junior school at lunchtime I had always been given a silver-foil wrapped triangle of Krafts processed cheese in place of meat or fish. It was only when I became a weekly boarder I discovered I was different from other pupils. Andrew was brought up as a vegetarian but Wycliffe College catered for vegetarians. At home my father was happy to be vegetarian and was involved with preparing our meals. He enjoyed cooking and baking. One of his specialities was Dundee cakes.

Two or three times a year my mother went to an open air meeting on Holdstone Down on the coast in North Devon. Often I'd go with her. The gatherings were to pray for world peace. They were arranged by The Aetherius Society (See Appendix 2), to which my mother belonged. In my childhood my mother often listened to a strange voice on a reel-to-reel tape recorder. It was George King's voice. He was the founder of the Society. As The Aetherius Society and its teachings were important to my mother, I read three books by Dr George King whilst researching these memoirs. I knew my mother had some unusual views but I was not prepared for the extent of her awareness of global and cosmic matters, which she viewed from a spiritual angle and not with a Western or conventional scientific perspective.

My mother was a champion of Nature Cure, which is a form of naturopathy. Before we moved to Devon my mother had had an extended stay at Kingston Nature Cure Clinic in Edinburgh. The clinic was founded by James C. Thomson in the 1930s. He also established The Edinburgh School of Natural Therapeutics which, after the Second World War, offered a five-year full-time training course in Naturopathy. The principles extolled by my mother included enhancing the body's own ability for self-healing, that prevention is better than cure, ridding the body of any toxins by natural means, and that what is eaten makes a difference to the body's health, as does plenty of fresh air and exercise. The family's health bible was Harry Benjamin's *Everybody's Guide to Nature Cure*. The author is critical of orthodox medicine, but he is sound on his understanding of Nature Cure. In his book he writes,

> '. . . the cardinal principle of Nature Cure, . . . is that although, . . . the names of diseases are legion, in reality *their basic and fundamental causes are the same in every case*, viz., a body clogged with waste materials and impurities; and no matter *what* the particular disease in question might be *called*, apart from shock, or direct injury, or mechanical interference with the blood and nerve supply, its causes can always be found in disturbance of function due to three main factors:
> (1) Wrong feeding;
> (2) Improper care of the body;
> (3) Habits of living tending to set up enervation, such as worry, fear, overwork, excesses of all kinds, sexual abuse, temperamental and environmental difficulties, etc'.[1]

My mother adhered to the Nature Cure principles and, without me realising it, had brought me up using them. She was a patient of Dr Gordon Latto, who was a naturopath as well as a medical practitioner. His patients included those who felt the orthodox or allopathic system was not helping them sufficiently. One of his most famous patients was Sir Francis Chichester[2] who, when diagnosed with cancer, followed his wife's advice to consult with Dr Latto rather than follow the surgeon's advice, and that was before

Sir Francis sailed around the world in Gypsy Moth IV in the 1960s.

In various places around my parents' house were newsletters and magazines from the societies to which they belonged and other organisations, which could be termed ecological, spiritual or esoteric. There was a new and growing collection of books on food, complementary health, and spiritual and esoteric topics. Whilst the business world was my father's domain and gardening was my mother's, their health, ecological and spiritual interests were shared. But even there they maintained individual approaches. My father was not active with The Aetherius Society, but had a growing and practical interest in Buddhism. He lived it. I was in my thirties before I realised what I had absorbed by osmosis from both my parents and its influence on me.

Once my grandparents had moved to Devon I'd lost the summer holidays on their farm in Yorkshire. My mother never wanted to venture far. She was definitely a person who loved her home. She did like Torquay and in autumn or winter would take a holiday flat for a short break. My father had visited Ireland once or twice. It was a country he was becoming increasingly fond of. He and Andrew had had two holidays in Ireland, and in August 1968 it was my turn.

My father and I flew from Bristol to Dublin. It was my first flight. My pre-flight nerves started the moment we checked in. I spent most of the time before boarding in the ladies' toilets while my father kept dispatching nuns with requests to find out if I was alright. The nerves lifted completely once I was on the plane and strapped into a window seat ready to take off for Ireland. We hired a car at Dublin Airport and stayed in guest houses as we toured. We went to Waterford and Cork and I kissed the Blarney Stone. Andrew and my father had already done that. We stayed a while around Killarney. The lakes made a deep impression on me, and one day I'll return to refresh the image of tranquillity that has stayed with me for more than forty years. We walked on cliff tops above Dingle Bay before visiting Limerick and Galway. Then it was a drive across the middle of Ireland back to Dublin and the flight home, without the need for my father to dispatch nuns to check on me. My father visited Ireland often during the rest of his life. He used to tell me that he did not want me to look after him when he was old as he was going to go live in Ireland.

My mother's distressed episodes continued throughout my teenage years. I was no longer blamed for triggering them. My father, brother and I seemed to have an unspoken understanding that they just happened, but I do not know if my father knew why. In my early teens I decided I would not have children until I understood what had happened to me. I did not want to risk doing the same to my children. By the time I was sixteen that decision had evolved into a decision not to get close to anyone. I did not want to meet someone, fall in love, marry and want children.

There was virtually no discussion or instruction from my mother about puberty and the facts of life, nor was it on the convent's curriculum. There was an embarrassing visit with my mother to a department store to buy my first bra. She gave me a little booklet produced by a company making sanitary towels and told me, '*It* is your badness coming out.'

In my mid teens my mother started telling me repeatedly and forcibly that Andrew did not like me and I was not to annoy him. He was my lovely big brother and the last thing I wanted to do was annoy him, so I kept my distance. He had an active life and friends at school. We became more like cousins than the buddies we had been.

When I was fourteen I listened to a discussion on the BBC's *Woman's Hour* programme about telling children they had been adopted. From the conversation it was clear that if I was adopted I would have been told before I was fourteen. So adoption did not explain the feeling I had of being an outsider.

A feeling of being cut-off in some vague sense also happened when I was with groups of my peers or in class. I did not always know what was going on or grasp what was being said. There was something wrong with me. I did not know what, nor was I able to formulate clearly how I felt so as to be able to talk about it with anyone. It did not happen all the time, and was worse when I was, or thought I was, the butt of jokes or mild bullying. The feeling was strongest during my fourth year of boarding. Our classroom was on the silent corridor by the chapel and next to the headmistress's room. So apart from lessons the classroom was usually empty. It had two south facing windows with wide sills. I spent many hours sitting there doing extra school work to keep up. That was my choice. I was not made to do it. Ironically, the cut-offness resulted in a blessing as I did extra work. Like the extra writing lessons in junior school, it wasn't a chore and probably made the difference between pass and failure in my O-levels.

My mother's sister, Edna, who had died in 1930 at the age of sixteen, was hardly ever mentioned. I can't recall who was visiting my parents, but she commented on the resemblance between Edna and Eric, my mother's siblings, and Andrew and me. Something painful passed across my mother's face. I don't know when I first came across the phrase 'the wrong one died' to describe how parents' natural grief reactions on the death of one child can be misunderstood by a surviving child. The child wrongly thinks the parents wished he or she had died instead. Maybe my mother had experienced 'the wrong one dying' after Edna's death. I'd thought more than once that my mother would have preferred to have her 'perfect' daughter rather than me.

In 1968 my father organised an international conference at Exeter University for the Men of the Trees. It had all the usual trappings of speakers, dinners, a reception with the Mayor in the Guildhall and a couple of tree plantings on the University campus to mark the occasion. Sue, the daughter of another committee member and I were going along to run the bookstall. She was three or four years older than me and we were the youngest at the conference. The majority of delegates were over fifty, and some had been of pension age for a while.

The conference accommodation was in a University Hall of Residence. On the eve of the first day delegates began arriving and gathering in the Hall's common room, which had a bar. My father was busy and never thought someone should keep an eye on his daughter. I was, after all, there to help. Someone had bought the two girls a drink. I had had small amounts of wine, often diluted with water, with meals at home, but never enough to know the effects of alcohol. It was something I was to learn that evening.

Two tree surgeons in their thirties had been sent to the conference by their firm. They bought Sue and me another round of drinks and invited us to go with them into town to find an Indian restaurant as they hadn't eaten. The first two drinks were already having an effect on me before we left the common room. On standing up I misjudged the swing of my shoulder bag and swept some empty glasses off the table to smash on the floor. I don't remember the detail of the rest of the evening. One piece of music that was played in the restaurant was *Young Girl* by Union Gap. I did eat something at the restaurant but not a full meal, and had more to drink. Back in the hall I was lying on one of the men's bed, fully clothed, with him lying partially on me. Thankfully, he must have realised that to interfere or worse with the conference manager's underage, intoxicated daughter wasn't a good career move. I woke up the next morning in my room with my one and only hangover. When I did not appear for breakfast my father came to find me. He told me to drink some water, get something to eat and be behind the bookstall. And under no account was I to let my mother, who would be at the conference's opening session, know what had happened. Pictures of the reception the following night in the Guildhall included one of me shaking hands with the Mayor as the guests arrived. My father, standing next to the Mayor in the welcoming party, was beaming at me proudly. That night's underage drinking was also recorded on camera, a half consumed glass of sherry which lasted all evening.

4

Articles

I WAS glad to have left the convent school. With seven O-levels I was eligible to go to the grammar school but I refused. If I had to do A-levels, I'd go to the technical college as Andrew had done. I told my father I wanted to do A-level law, a reasonable request as both he and my grandfather had been solicitors. The grammar school didn't offer A-level law, so I'd have to go to the College. My mother wanted me to go to agricultural college and study horticulture.

The technical college would only offer me a place on a one-year A-level course, which generally was for those re-sitting their exams. So most students had already done the two-year course and were older than me. I was required to take at least two subjects and had given no thought to a second subject. So when asked what it was to be I chose maths not knowing how different it would be from O-level maths. As I was registered in the General Studies Department, but studied maths in the Science Department and law in Business Studies, I was left pretty much to my own devices. On Wednesday afternoons students either had to do sports or voluntary work. I put myself down to visit a long-stay hospital ward for people with multiple sclerosis.

The law teacher was a retired barrister who always wore a

bow tie. He was a clear, precise teacher. He advised his students to keep a small notebook with them and make one line entries as aidemémoires of legal cases which set precedents. He told us to look at those notes frequently at odd moments so we'd remember the case law and get good grades. I enjoyed studying law and it was likely I would pass A-level law.

Maths classes were a total shock to me. I could sit through an hour-long class, not understand anything, and be too frightened to ask questions. My saving grace was a student from Persia; it was before the Iranian Revolution. After classes we went to the library and he explained the main points of the lesson to me. Somehow I had to maximise my chances of passing maths. The law lecturer had stressed the importance of exam techniques, including reading questions carefully and allocating time in exams appropriately. My only hope with the maths exams was to make the maximum use of exam techniques. I would get some marks if I recognised what the question was testing and start the answer correctly, even if I did not get to the end of it. I spent hours in the library working through ten years of past exam papers. I entered myself with two examining boards to give myself an extra chance of passing.

Andrew was accepted by a firm in Exeter to train as a chartered accountant. The year I was studying for A-levels he was at the College of Further Education in Bristol, preparing for the first set of professional exams. A couple of months before his exams, Andrew confessed to our father he'd been enjoying himself and had not done sufficient work to be able to pass his exams. My father seemed capable of taking things in his stride; there wasn't a crisis or any recriminations. Andrew went to Yorkshire stayed with Eric and his new wife, Peggy, worked on their farm and thought about what he'd do next.

In January of that year my grandmother became ill and was diagnosed with stomach cancer. She had a short stay in hospital and was then nursed at home by my mother with good support and care from her GP. My grandmother died at home two weeks after Andrew had gone to Yorkshire. Only my parents and I went to the crematorium for her funeral as my grandfather was not well and neither Eric nor Andrew travelled from Yorkshire. I missed my grandmother so much. It was the first death I'd experienced of someone so close to me. I cried often in the following months, but I knew she was all right and I was crying for myself. Two months after her death, on my seventeenth birthday, my grandfather gave me her car. I passed my driving test on the first anniversary of her death.

My grandmother's death brought changes as my grandfather came to live with us. My parents decided it was time to sell the old vicarage and its large garden. They bought a detached house in Sidmouth, close to the seafront and a mile from the convent school I'd left the previous summer when it had closed. Andrew was back from Yorkshire and living at home. He was a trainee with a national insurance company, working in an office in Exeter and studying for an insurance qualification.

In the summer after taking my A-levels, which I passed, I had my first job. I'd seen an advertisement in the local newspaper for an office junior's position in a solicitors' office. In my application I said I'd just taken Law and Maths A-levels. I didn't get an interview as I was overqualified. The following week another firm advertised a similar job. Replying to the second advertisement, I said I had English and Maths O-levels and was invited for an interview. At the interview it came out that I was awaiting my A-level results, but I was offered the job.

I had a desk in the reception area alongside an experienced secretary who covered my duties when I was making tea or doing errands in town. I did not make a good telephonist as I frequently got names wrong and transposed numbers in messages to return calls. The photocopier was in reception, and secretaries gave me the photocopying to do. In those days plans in documents weren't photocopied but traced from the Ordnance Survey Map onto blue linen using Indian ink and the property marked with red paint before sewing the plan into the document with green tape. My working day ended by franking all the mail and taking it to the post office. I stayed in that job throughout the summer, and while the formalities were sorted out so I could begin to train as a solicitor.

The Law Society is the representative body for solicitors in England and Wales. It is responsible for training solicitors. In 1970 it was possible to train to be a solicitor immediately after leaving school without obtaining a degree. Those regulations were altered soon after I started my training.

The training fell into three areas, which were assessment of character and suitability to be a solicitor, academic training, and vocational training. The first steps were to apply to the Law Society to enrol as a student and be interviewed by a panel of solicitors. I was interviewed in Exeter by three solicitors who sat at a large, polished table with their backs bathed in the autumn sunlight streaming through the windows. A solitary chair for me was set back from the table and faced the windows. I was too nervous to say I couldn't see their faces, but answered their questions adequately as I received the certificate of enrolment, which was a prerequisite before a solicitor could agree to train me.

I was trained by Michael, the solicitor in whose office I'd had a week's work experience during the summer after I'd left the convent school. The training agreement, or Articles of Clerkship, was for five years during which time I would attend college to prepare for the two sets of Law Society's exams, and spend a continuous two-year period in the office to receive vocational training.

As I didn't have a law degree my training should have started with a year at college, but my father said I was too young and would have to wait a year. My father may have been influenced by my brother dropping out of accountancy training earlier that year, and he may have had doubts about my ability to achieve the academic standard required to qualify. And maybe he did not expect me to last six months anyway. That left Michael with the problem of what to do with me, as I had few useful skills; I could not even be sent to the law library to do research. My first task was to draft my Articles of Clerkship. I was given a precedent book and the oldest manual typewriter in the office.

The letters on some of its keys had been worn away with use. I was allocated a room in the attic of the former Georgian terraced houses that had become offices. I produced a badly typed draft of my Articles, and after Michael corrected it I was told to engross it. I had to type it out perfectly on thick legal paper with red lines around the edges. It was not perfect but was signed by Michael and me, and was also signed by my father as I was not eighteen. It was probably one of the last Articles of Clerkship to be signed by a parent.

All wills and documents relating to property were first drafted and, once approved, engrossed. The final documents had to be proofread against the draft by two people. Secretaries knew I could do that with them and also I could do photocopying and sew documents. My first work that could be called training was in the Probate Department. An experienced legal executive gave me simple estate accounts to draft. I got familiar with how things were done. There were no computers then and I found it satisfying going through files checking all had been done and producing an account that balanced.

Sometimes Michael would ring my extension and tell me to come to his office. When I got there he did not speak with me, but pointed at a chair in the corner of the room. Then he asked the receptionist to send his client up to his room. He greeted the client on the landing, they came into his office, shut the door and discussed the client's concerns. When the interview was over the client left and then Michael indicated I should go. I was puzzled at first; then I realised he was teaching me how to interview and interact with clients. He saw his clients as people, and their problems in the context of their lives. I did not know it at the time, but I was being given something special; an experienced solicitor letting me observe him working with a range of clients, across the social and economic spectrums. As I was also able to see the clients' files, I saw how solutions to problems were found, how negotiations were handled and how laws affected everyone's daily life. Michael was a practical lawyer and looked for a sensible solution to clients' problems, not just the strict legal position.

I had my place to go to the College of Law at Guildford. The

Part I exams were in Land Law, Constitutional Law, Tort Law, Contract Law and Criminal Law. In preparation, I started studying land law and the principal text book, Gibson's *Conveyancing*. References I'd seen on documents to the Law of Property Act 1925, began to have greater meaning for me. The twenty months between sitting A-levels and starting at the law college had not been wasted. I had had a good grounding in what goes on at grass roots level in an office. If there is a good team and it runs smoothly, then those who interact face-to-face with clients will be more efficient and have less stress in their working lives.

My father was still not happy about me going away to college for a year, but had no choice as attendance was compulsory. I acquired the necessities I'd need for my first time living away from home, plus a knitting project. My mother and I were in a phase of knitting Aran jumpers, and I thought I would have a go at a mid thigh-length jacket. My father gave me an allowance, telling me it was sufficient if I budgeted properly. There would not be any more but he would listen to me if I got in a mess. I bought all the set books and was daunted at the height of the pile.

My father asked Philip, a stockbroker friend who lived in a village near Guildford, to keep an eye on me. Philip and his wife, Jackie, both in their late fifties, introduced me to neighbours from whom I rented a flat above their garage. I had my grandmother's car and could easily get to college. Philip and Jackie often invited me for meals and I house- and dog-sat when they were away.

When I did my training, women in the law were a minority of less than twenty per cent and it was noticeable in the make-up of our class. I was probably the youngest in the class and again did not find it easy mixing socially. During the previous year I had occasionally gone to the pub after work or to skittle matches, but experienced the same problems I'd had at school in groups. At college, social activities involved sports or alcohol, neither of which were my thing though I did play squash occasionally.

Classes consisted of an hour one day and two hours the next, and there was plenty of reading. I did my studying at my flat, and was not finding it easy. I thought about what my A-level law teacher had said about passing exams. I bought a cassette recorder, recorded my notes and listened as I knitted. I did a case names notebook and looked at previous papers. Questions about theft dominated the Criminal Law paper. In the exam, I needed to start answers by accurately quoting statute laws, and then argue my case using case law backed up by citing case names. So I learnt the Theft Act 1968 by heart.

I went home for a weekend every four or five weeks, and have little recollection of problems with my mother that year apart from the weekend I was bridesmaid to a school friend. The ceremony was at a village church and the reception at a hotel on the same road as my parents' home. My mother went into flipmode the day before the wedding. I remember the contrast between the atmosphere at home and the wedding ceremony and reception. Marriage is a step into the unknown.

Sometimes after I had been to Philip and Jackie's for a meal in the evenings, Philip would accompany me as I walked back to my flat. It was only a short walk but the lighting was inadequate and the houses were set back from the road, with mature trees and shrubs landscaping the gardens. It seemed harmless at first, but it changed subtly, so subtly it is hard to recall how he manipulated it so he came in and had me masturbate him. He was not interfering with my body nor was I frightened of him. But I did not know how to deal with the situation. My exams were only a couple of months away and I did not want to do anything that would jeopardize them. I would sit it out and be gone.

When I returned to the flat after Christmas it was cold and the heating was inadequate. Jackie suggested I stayed with them until I finished the course. Whilst there I noticed when I had a bath the handle of the locked bathroom door slowly and silently move down and then up. During the last week or so of my stay, Philip started coming into my bedroom early in the mornings and putting his hands under the duvet. A few months after

I'd left Guildford, my father asked why I had no contact with Jackie and Philip. I said little but think my father understood.

I took my exams in Bristol over three days. My pre-exam nerves were terrible, and I seemed to consume more brandy than food during those three days. Once an exam started my nerves were fine. I passed all papers, and gained distinction in three subjects, Contract Law, Criminal Law and Land Law.

The next two years were spent in the office doing vocational training. I would always be working under the supervision of Michael, another solicitor, or a legal executive, to gain practical experience. Much of the work I did was conveyancing, but I preferred probate work and that was the area in which I'd have like to have specialised. It surprised me how many clients of pension age had no family and relied upon a professional adviser to keep an eye not only on their financial affairs, but on their personal well-being as well. Michael had a number of such clients and he was consulted for help on a variety of practical matters, even going to clear a blocked drain for a client one Sunday morning.

I was not suited to litigation work. My introduction to matrimonial work was reading a file about an acrimonious divorce where the parents were manipulative and were using their children as pawns. I'd decided children should be given the legal aid and representation, and parents should be the ones moving in and out of the matrimonial home each weekend, not the children. My introduction to criminal law was short and brief. I was told to go to the prison to interview a man charged with stealing women's underwear from washing lines. I took that to be a joke. Apart from sitting behind counsel at trials I did no training in criminal cases and don't recall even going into a magistrate's court. I didn't like sitting in on court proceedings, as I was never confident I had the complete picture of what was going on. Initially, some of that would be due to courts being a new experience, but there was the same feeling I had when in groups of not fully understanding what was going on around me.

Practical work outside the office on the conveyancing side was often to do with inspecting land and plans, and in a rural area checking the routes of rights of way, water pipes and the position of septic tanks and their overflows.

When a partner in the firm was an executor of a client's will, it was sometimes necessary to register the death and arrange the funeral. Occasionally, the late client's house had to be inspected and secured, and papers and valuables removed. Once I went to the house of a spinster whose fiancé had been killed in the First World War. I found the bank statements and share certificates, and some items of jewellery in her bedroom. Well hidden in the bottom of her wardrobe there was a tin containing letters and mementoes from her fiancé. On another occasion I went to a bungalow in the country that had been neglected by the old lady who had been a widow for many years. Her dining room was filled with two feet high piles of old newspapers. It was impossible to walk across the room. In one pile I saw a £5 note sticking out and, after searching through the piles of newspapers, retrieved a quantity of cash.

With the exception of the Accounts paper the Part II qualifying exams could not to be taken before the vocational training was finished. I went to the College of Law in Chester for a month in the middle of my vocational training to prepare for the Accounts exam, which I passed. I lodged in Chester with a law student from Machynlleth in mid-Wales who was studying for her Part I exams. I spent my weekends visiting Machynlleth and Snowdonia with her.

After I left Guildford I returned to living with my parents. Andrew had been transferred by the insurance company to an office in Norfolk, three hundred miles away, and he rarely visited Devon. My grandfather's health was deteriorating and my mother was spending more time looking after him. My father was on committees in London and went there for two or three days each month.

Looking back, my social life was very restricted. I liked people and generally got on with them, but did not click with any group. That may have been due to the amount of time I spent studying and the decision I'd made not to let myself get involved with anyone plus my dislike of the effects alcohol could have on people's behaviour. And there was the vague feeling I had about not understanding what was going on around me. I liked walking and took myself off on the coastal path or to Dartmoor and was spending more time sewing and knitting.

Maybe the real reason for my limited social life was connected with my mother. I was beginning to notice that after anyone had met my mother their attitude towards me changed. The first time I can recall it happening was after a weekend when one of the fulltime boarders at the convent school had come to stay. There had been nothing that seemed to upset her and we had not had an argument, but back at school our friendship had changed and some of her friends were less friendly towards me. I felt I had been talked about. Andrew had few friends in Devon, and I have no recollection of him ever bringing a friend home after he left school. I knew that for anyone to know me well they would have to know about my mother's behaviour, my commitment to her and to supporting my father, and accept that was how it was with me. But I was convinced no one could accept that, and that too was how it was.

I met Sally when I answered her advertisement in the local paper for someone to share a cottage she had rented on a farm a few miles from Exeter. Sally had just finished her social work training. We did not see much of each other as work dominated for both of us. One breakfast time she was talking about tanks in the war passing her childhood home. During the day I wondered where she'd been living and which war she'd experienced. That evening I discovered it was World War II and she was fifteen years older than me. She thought I was older than I was and would have remembered the war. She enjoyed the cottage's garden and grew a few vegetables. One Saturday we were shelling peas for lunch and did not notice we had no peas to cook because we had already eaten them as we chatted.

Around then, my grandfather went to live in a nursing

home in Exmouth as his care had become too demanding for my mother. The nursing home was a short distance from the flat Auntie Jeanie had moved to when she'd left the village. I'd visited her there until she died the year before my grandfather's move to the home. Florence, one of the Bumblies, moved to the home after Peter died following a heart attack. Florence had Alzheimer's disease; Peter had cared for her so lovingly and thoroughly he'd had kept her illness from us. Later Mrs Harries spent the last ten years of her life in the same home. My grandfather spent his last nine months there.

My mother went into distress mode on the way to my grandfather's funeral. Neither Eric, my uncle, nor Andrew, who still lived in Norfolk, came to his funeral. Shortly afterwards, Andrew successfully applied for a job settling motor insurance claims in Bournemouth. He had taken and passed some of his insurance exams but there were still more to take.

Six months before I was due to go to the College of Law to prepare for the remaining six papers of the Part II exams, I told my father that I'd not want to be a solicitor, I was not going to college and I would have to find something else to do. I don't know what triggered those feelings; perhaps it was having met graduates who had failed all or some of the papers, or knowing someone who desperately wanted to be a solicitor but could not pass his final exams after several attempts. My father pointed out to me I'd only have failure to show any future employer, and I would have wasted the previous three and a half years. I eventually agreed that I would have one attempt at the exams, I would not re-sit and I would not go to college, but I would do a correspondence course and give it the best effort I could.

I'm sure my father and Michael must have discussed the situation. To my utter surprise, shortly before I finished work to prepare for the exams, Michael told me I would be sent my monthly pay cheque. It would have been unusual to be paid while I was at college, but being paid when I had refused to go to college was incredible. Initially I thought the money was really coming from my father. He hadn't offered to finance me, but if he was going to he would have given it to me directly with the usual caution to budget and that there was no more.

Not long before I was to start the correspondence course, Sally received notice to quit the cottage we shared. I went back to my parents' home. Studying there was not possible as my presence at home all day disrupted my mother's life. Luckily, Sally found another farm cottage to rent and I moved there. The cottage was attached to the farmhouse, with splendid panoramic views to the sea in one direction and across to Dartmoor in the other. The price for the views was the cold draughts on windy days that went right through the cottage. I made myself a study plan and worked six days a week, having Tuesdays off. I did the usual examination technique preparation, plus one other thing, although I will never know if it made any difference.

For more than a decade at home there had been discussions between my parents, as well as books and magazines, about the power of the mind, the difference positive thoughts can make, and Eastern and esoteric philosophies. My parents believed prayer, absent healing, and positive thinking were beneficial. Every night just before I went to sleep whilst preparing for my Part II exams, I'd repeat ten times to myself and pictured what I wanted to see printed in the results list, which was my name and passes in six papers.

My final exams were held during a scorching week in August. The examination room was in a listed building and had a glass roof. Luckily, I had a desk at the front within range of the fans. Each paper was three hours long, with the first on Monday morning, then two on both Tuesday and Wednesday and the last one on Thursday morning. It should have been a long holiday after that, and the only question was what to do after my failed attempt at law. On my return home there was a message waiting for me from Michael. His wife had been diagnosed with cancer and was to have an operation. Michael wanted to spend three months with his family. He asked if I would look after his caseload, with the help of his partners and others in the firm, of course. So no holiday, and I was back in the office, thrown in at the deep end.

I stayed with my parents the night before my exam results were due. The notification would be sent by post and the letter was to arrive around 8 a.m. with the first post. My father was more anxious than me. The results list was published in some national daily newspapers. I think, he must have asked someone in London to look at the results list in a newspaper and phone him so he'd be prepared for when I opened the envelope. I opened it in the hall of my parents' house. When I went back into the kitchen both my parents were standing there beaming at me. My father was holding a bottle of champagne. I had passed all six papers, gaining a distinction in Conveyancing.

I had a few weeks left to serve of the five-year articles before I could apply to the Law Society for admission to the Roll of Solicitors, and then I would be a qualified solicitor. My father and Michael had given me good advice, guidance, patience, support and encouragement, and had believed I could do it.

5

Spinning

I HAD not expected to pass my final law exams and I was sure I would be working elsewhere after my five year training contract finished. Apart from two partners who had been articled to their fathers, articled clerks in Michael's firm tended to leave when they qualified. When Michael returned to work, he offered me a job as his assistant, which I accepted. The manner of my return to the office after my final exams had got me up to speed rapidly, and I'd had plenty of contact with clients, which I enjoyed. A few times when meeting a client for the first time, I had to explain I was the solicitor they had come to see and I was not Mr Morrison's secretary. By the mid 1970s there were more women entering the profession, but it was a year or two before another female solicitor joined the firm. I didn't power dress or even own a black suit, and probably didn't look old enough to be a solicitor.

There was an amusing occasion when Jeremy, a new articled clerk, came with me to an auction sale of land where I was representing the seller. Before bidding starts the solicitor reads the legal conditions affecting the land and the terms of the sale and deals with any questions. Jeremy had just retired as an officer in the Royal Marines and was embarking on his post service career. In his business suit and tie and with his military bearing, he fitted the image of a solicitor. The auctioneer did a double take as I joined him at the front of the room to read the terms and deal with questions, and Jeremy observed.

The offices where my father and I worked were formerly Georgian houses adjacent to the city's shopping centre. My father's regular lunchtime eating place was the salad bar at the Ceylon Tea Centre, a short walk from both our offices. I had lunch with him and one or two of his friends from Rotary once or twice a week. Some of Michael's probate and trust clients were also clients of my father's. He could tell the difference in my voice when I phoned him in connection with work. In response to my 'Hello,' he would say, 'Oh, you've got your business voice on, what can I do?' I became used to being introduced as Mr Morrison's daughter, even when he was not present. But we did have a laugh together later, following the first time he was introduced as Miss Morrison's father.

When Sally had completed her probationary period and was fully qualified as a social worker, she moved to Bournemouth to work at a psychiatric hospital. I enjoyed visiting Bournemouth. Sometimes I'd stay with Sally, or go for a day with my mother. We'd spend time in the fabric department of Beales, a department store. I was acquiring her habit of buying more lengths of material than I was using. I enjoyed sewing and made most of my own clothes and bought lengths of high quality cotton lawns and fine wool worsteds.

Andrew seemed settled in his job in Bournemouth dealing with motor insurance claims. He took motoring safety seriously, but then every day he was reading detailed reports of horrific injuries and the resulting life changes. He insisted we always wore seat belts, drove defensively and were not to eat whilst driving.

'People don't realise a car is a lethal weapon,' he would say.

He bought a second-floor flat in a modern block near a large park about a mile from Bournemouth town centre and the sea. Our mother laid the carpets and helped him move in.

I did the conveyancing when Andrew bought his flat and, as there was no chain, all went through quickly. About a month after he'd moved, the deeds of the flat were ready to be sent to the Land Registry. I went down to the strong room in the basement of the office to get them. I was back at my desk with his file and the deeds when I started crying. I could not stop crying. I went to the cloakroom to wash my face, but I was still crying when I got back to my desk. I picked up my handbag and walked out of the office. I was not crying when I got to my father's office and he was there and not with a client. I started crying again as soon as I sat in the chair in front of his desk and again could not stop crying. He said I had better go home and he'd leave a message with my secretary that I was not well.

The next day I did not go to work, but drove to Torquay. What was happening to me? I walked around aimlessly, and at one point was wandering around the multi-storey car park that had a bad reputation as a place where people jumped from to attempt suicide. Late afternoon I went to a colleague's house and she phoned Michael, who invited me to stay in the empty flat in his mother's house. The following day I could see that when Andrew bought a flat it meant he had left home. I was living at home and my working life was now settled. My mother still had distressed episodes, and I felt I would be the daughter trapped at home. Michael said I could rent the flat for a while. My father arranged to take my mother away for the weekend and Andrew came to help me move to the flat. Monday morning I was back at work, having been off for three days.

A few months later I bought my first property, a bungalow on the edge of Exeter with a westerly outlook and views across the valley to the hill and the farm where Sally and I had lived. There was a steep, narrow drive to the bungalow's garage. The pretty front garden had roses and shrubs around a small lawn. The rear garden backed on to a private road and then fields. There was a Devon bank along the rear boundary and two mature oak trees, many of whose acorns sprouted in my lawn. My neighbour was a retired farmer, and Bert enjoyed a chat with him when he came with Betsy and my mother to tidy the garden from time to time.

My parents gave me my bedroom furniture, the cooker from

my grandfather's flatlet and a desk. My sitting room furniture was a sun-lounger and two folding garden chairs. The bungalow needed decorating which I was going to do myself. Of course, my parents helped from time to time and Jack, the husband of Barbara, who worked in the Probate Department at the office, did some of the repairs and building type jobs.

I had not hung wallpaper before, though I had watched my mother do it when I was the one slapping the paste on the paper, then folding it and handing it to her to hang. She must have made it look too easy. I thought I'd start with the hall ceiling! I used twice the amount of paper it should have required. The longest piece started to come down from the far end just as I smoothed the final part into place. There was nothing I could do but watch from my perch on the steps as it gracefully descended to the floor. I did do a satisfactory job in the end and after that, papering walls was easy. As each room was finished it was carpeted. My mother enjoyed attending furniture auction sales and found me a drop-leaf mahogany dining table and chairs with tapestry seats and a second-hand three-piece suite, which was as good as new. The finishing touches were added and I had a comfortable home.

My mother was spending more time with friends who shared her interests in spiritual matters, healing and food. She was seeing complementary therapists as arthritis was beginning and slowing her down. For the first time I could move faster than her which was useful when she was in flipmode. On one occasion she had hold of my arm and would not let go. Andrew was home and it took both of us to free me. Another time she had been shouting and then locked herself in her bedroom. All was quiet for a long time and she did not answer when I knocked and called. That was unusual. I told her that if she did not unlock the door I was calling the fire brigade. She responded and unlocked the door, shouting at me not to be so stupid.

My father went to London at least once a month. He continued to be involved with the Men of the Trees committee and the Provincial Brokers' Stock Exchange. Changes were afoot with the provincial brokers as they were preparing to join the London Stock Exchange. Provincial brokers would have to computerise their businesses if they were to continue once the merger had taken place. As part of that work, my father visited all the provincial brokers' firms to convey to them that it was imperative to computerise their businesses, and in a way that would be compatible with the changes occurring with the London Stock Exchange.

At some point after I left home my father was diagnosed with diabetes. He was not injecting and controlled it through diet. He attended annual dinners of organisations he was connected with and was also invited to others as an after dinner speaker. These dinners did upset the balance he maintained and he put himself on a careful diet the following week. When my father was away I slept at my parents' home. My mother had a dread of being in the house on her own at night. If I stayed she was less likely to be in flipmode when my father returned.

My life was settled. I had a good job, which I mainly enjoyed, a home and hobbies. Those around me seemed to be accepting that I was happy with my single status and settling down was no longer linked with getting married. I was twenty-five and there were no more challenges. I had no ambitions to be a partner in a law firm. I liked working with the clients and with Michael, and knew I would never work for anyone better as a person, boss or colleague.

I had been Michael's assistant for over three years, and one morning in the office whenever I saw a colleague over forty a thought went through my mind. The thought was I didn't want to be the office spinster when I was in my fifties; that person who had given years of loyal service to the firm and would be there until retirement, and who went home to her cat. By the end of the day the thought had changed into 'I want to do something with my life, so I have something to look back on when it is my turn to be left in a nursing home'.

Working in a probate department gives a view of old age that probably is different from those doing the daily care of the elders of our society. From my observations I'd decided that:

- money does not make one happy, but may allow one to be miserable and bad-tempered in more comfortable surroundings;
- some of the kindest care was found in the homes run by local authorities;
- mental illness in old age can affect anyone, whatever one's social, financial or intellectual status;
- there were some problems it was not possible to buy one's way out of;
- it was a good idea to try to manage a smile and to show appreciation to those doing the care work and nursing;
- those who did better into old age were those who made early decisions about what they wanted and were involved in implementing such decisions.

I was not planning my old age at twenty-five, but perhaps I had forty years of active life. What did I want to do with it?

What I did next was not thought out, and had I discussed it with anyone I knew they would have advised against it, and so would I if someone had told me of such a situation. I handed my notice in. I had to work another three months, and then …?

And then nothing. No sympathy or understanding, as I had just given up a well-paid, interesting job and anything else would be a step or two down the ladder. My mother did get a bit agitated and worried about what I was going to do. It was a blessing to have a father who did not get upset whatever, gave good advice, seemed to know all the answers or where they could be found, and was supportive even if he did not approve of what I had done. Initially, I wanted some time when no one wanted anything from me, and there was no phone on the desk whose ring generally was demanding something from me. With hindsight, I realise that I had pushed myself hard for the previous ten years to achieve my qualification.

One morning I called in on my parents. It was a day when my father was not going to the office. He called them non-office days. He would visit some of his private, usually elderly, clients in rural parts of Devon for whom it was difficult to get to his office. That morning I went with him; I'd go for walks while he saw his clients.

After their business chat, Margaret suggested I should be asked in to join them for a cup of tea. Margaret lived in a Devon longhouse, built of thick cob walls, with a thatched roof, and one room leading into the next with no hallway. The first room was filled with a loom and I had to edge round that. One wall in the second room was lined with books, and there was a spinning wheel, fleece waiting to be spun, skeins of different coloured wool, and, to the uninitiated eye, a chaotic collection of tools, gadgets, boxes of many sizes, and a covering of bulging carrier bags. The third room had an Aga with skeins of wool draped over the line strung above it, steps up to the kitchen and a glass door opening into the secluded cottage garden.

After the cup of tea, Margaret placed a spinning wheel in front of me and asked if I knew how to treadle. With some guidance from her I soon got the knack. My father intervened at that stage, as he did not have time for the spinning lesson which was about to begin. My first spinning lesson was the following week, in the sunshine under Margaret's apple tree. It was a little difficult getting everything co-ordinated and the thread kept breaking. Margaret had taught many to spin, so she was patient and we persisted and then I got it. On the next visit I ended up staying the night. In the morning we went in Margaret's Morris Minor to Frank Herring's Art and Craft Shop in Dorchester. The upstairs of the shop was devoted to spinning and weaving equipment, wool and books. Margaret helped me choose an upright spinning wheel and one or two other small bits of equipment, all birthday presents from my parents.

Margaret told me about the monthly meetings of the Devon Guild of Weavers, Spinners and Dyers held in the Friends' Meeting House in Exeter. I joined the Guild and went regularly to meetings. There was a happy, productive atmosphere, and lots of encouragement and advice for the beginners from experienced craftswomen.

I bought my first dirt and lanolin laden, Jacob sheep's fleece, sorted it, carded and spun the wool, plied single yarns into a three ply knitting wool, made and washed skeins and knitted myself a waistcoat. Spinning became a passion for me. I improved my knitting skills to make garments from homespun wool for which there are no standard patterns. I never found time to get into natural dying, but did play with chemical dyes and made small skeins which I used for tapestry weaving.

My father was putting in many hours in connection with the introduction of computers to his and other provincial brokers' offices. The computer revolution was yet to reach solicitors' offices. I thought it might be something I could be involved with if I had some computer training. I saw an advertisement for courses funded by the government for programmers and systems analysts. I passed the aptitude assessments, had an interview, and was offered a place on a six month course in Bristol for analysts. In those days computers occupied a room and programming was done by writing on sheets that went overnight to be converted into a pile of cards, which were then fed into the computer by an operator. I was doing well on the course, but it was essential to secure a programmer's job when the course finished to gain practical experience. I was attending interviews well away from Devon. The interviewer in London picked up that I was unlikely to want to live in London for long. The job I was most interested in was with a firm of solicitors in the north of England who were developing systems in-house. I attended the interview. It was a job I would have loved but other events intervened.

6

Out of Control

THE regular early morning phone calls from my father began soon after I'd been for the interview in the North of England. He was phoning me from his office. My father had never been in the habit of going to work before 7 a.m. even though he was a workaholic. He'd demanded his Dictaphone be brought to him soon after he had been moved out of intensive care after one heart attack. Something was worrying him but he couldn't talk about it over the phone. I decided I had to see him. The next day was one of his non-office days. We arranged to meet and talk as I chauffeured him to his appointments.

On the drive to Woolacombe, my father explained to me he was thinking he would have to live separately from my mother. He told me her behaviour was deteriorating and he thought it would be better if they each had their own home. He made it clear he was not leaving my mother. No one else was involved. He loved my mother; that had not changed. He reassured me he would always make sure she was alright, but he could not continue with things as they were.

I was stunned.

I dropped him off for his first appointment. I had an hour before I had to pick him up. It was a wet, windy day and apart from a lone dog-walker in the far distance I had the long, sandy Woolacombe beach to myself as I walked along the tide line. My tears mingled with the rain as they rolled down my cheeks. There had been many challenges and difficult times over more than two decades with my mother. Up to then, my father always seemed to have weathered the storms and survived.

I drove him to his other appointments and back to pick up his car. There were many questions going through my head as I drove to Bristol. But both my father and I had work to get on with and would talk more over the coming weeks.

I had a week's break for Christmas. I spent three days with my parents. Andrew didn't visit that Christmas which was low key with my mother keeping herself to herself. My father and I had three quiet days together.

I went back to Bristol and successfully completed my course. I'd already decided I didn't want to move from Devon even though I wouldn't get a programmer's job in Devon. I wanted to stay within easy reach of my parents. I was beginning to realise I may have provided both of them, in different ways, with some stability. My mother didn't adapt easily to change. Had some of the problems with her behaviour in the preceding weeks been triggered by my impending move?

At the beginning of January my father was ill and having a problem with his legs. He was away from work for about three weeks and wanted to go back to work before he was fit to drive. As I was unemployed, I became his driver.

'Heart conditions aren't hereditary. The younger generation get worn out by lugging heavy cases,' I teased him, as I carried his briefcases up the two flights of stairs to his office.

By April he was well enough to resume driving. He had two after dinner speaking engagements on consecutive Fridays, the first in Stratford-upon-Avon and the second in Edinburgh. He had meetings arranged in the intervening week. He told me he was taking a few extra days away before the first engagement and would have a few days' holiday in Scotland before returning to Devon. He was going to be away for about two weeks altogether. As I was not working, I did not make any special arrangements about when I'd see my mother. I could be flexible and it would depend how she was.

I received a postcard from Stratford a few days after he'd left there. The next time I heard from him was a very brief and slightly odd phone call the day after the Edinburgh dinner. It was from a call box and the money ran out. I didn't speak with him again until I was in Edinburgh.

My mother phoned me midweek to tell me the police had been to see her. She would not tell me why, though I gathered it had something to do with my father. I drove over to her house so we could talk, and I'd have a better chance of seeing if she was alright. But she was still refusing to tell me what the police had said. The only solution was to go to the police station and ask them. I was told it was a routine matter, as they needed to check my father's identity in connection with something to do with a rental car he had been using. The car had, by then, been returned. There was nothing to worry about and my mother had answered their questions and the matter was closed. I was left feeling foolish and was wondering why my mother hadn't been able to tell me.

Whilst talking more with my mother, I discovered the hotel where my father was staying had phoned her the previous day. But I was no closer to understanding what was going on, except that whatever it was my mother was not coping with it, and perhaps things had got too much for my father. I decided I should to go to Edinburgh and find him. It was more than twenty years before I pieced everything together and worked out what I should have done, but by then I had the benefit of hindsight.

I borrowed my mother's car, as I thought it was more reliable and comfortable than mine, and set off for Edinburgh the next morning. I blindly trusted I would find my father in the same hotel and he would agree to come back to Devon. Then my parents, brother and I would work out what needed to be done.

By late afternoon I was on the M6 motorway approaching Preston and had another hundred and ninety miles to drive, plus finding the hotel once I was in Edinburgh. I decided to stop at a motel overnight and arrive in Edinburgh the next morning. The next morning the car wouldn't start and I didn't leave Preston until lunchtime as the breakdown services couldn't fix the car and towed it to a garage.

I arrived at the hotel in Edinburgh around 6 p.m. hoping I'd find my father. The hotel receptionist told me he was in the lounge. He recognised me, but it soon became clear he was not the competent man I'd known all my life. I was not sure he knew he was in Edinburgh, and he didn't question why I was there. I suggested we went to his room and have a chat to decide what we were going to do. I think he thought we were going to go out, but I was thinking some help was needed. He gave me his wallet while we were in the hotel lift.

We hadn't been in his bedroom long before there was a knock on the door and two men came in. One said he was a doctor. I was surprised, as I had not yet spoken with reception to ask for a doctor.

'Are you his daughter?' the doctor asked.

'Yes.'

'Will you agree to your father being sectioned?'

'No,' I said in utter disbelief. 'My father is diabetic. He should go to casualty.'

The doctor called an ambulance. At the hospital my father was wheeled into casualty on a stretcher. I was told to wait while the necessary tests were done. I didn't know how long the tests would take; he was conscious when we arrived so they might not have been an urgent priority. I phoned my mother to tell her where we were. She told me a solicitor was trying to contact me to arrange an interview about a job I'd applied for.

When I enquired about what was happening with my father I was told he'd been transferred to a psychiatric hospital and I would not be allowed to see him that night. The nurse said they didn't know anyone was with him and he hadn't said he had any relatives when they'd asked him.

I didn't physically collapse to the floor, but I broke down in such sobs that they had to take me off to a side room. The nurse sat me down, brought me some tea and for the first time since I arrived in Edinburgh someone attempted to have a conversation with me. The nurse either did not know, or would not say, and I never did find out, whether any tests had been done, or what information accompanied my father into casualty or to the psychiatric hospital. I was given a piece of paper with a phone number, which I was told I could ring the following morning. Around midnight I was put in a taxi back to the hotel.

At the hotel I asked for a room. The receptionist handed me a key and told me they'd already moved my father's belongings into that bedroom. I ordered some sandwiches to be sent to my room and took the lift. I opened the bedroom door and saw the day had one more shock. There was little I recognised as his in the mound of belongings piled in the room. Uncharacteristically for my father, he'd been on a spending spree. I ate the sandwiches and lay down exhausted.

The next morning, a Saturday, Andrew drove to Devon to be with our mother, and I went to the psychiatric hospital to see our father. I was told he was too ill to be moved but was not told what was wrong with him and, as it was the weekend, I'd have to wait until Monday before I could speak with a doctor.

It was hard to tell how he really was as he'd been well medicated and was too drowsy for conversation. He looked so weak, a mere shadow of himself, lying in a hospital bed in the middle of a side room.

Back at the hotel, I spoke with Andrew. His presence was keeping our mother stable. There was little we could do until Monday, and the priority was to get our father transferred to Devon. Andrew didn't go to work after the weekend but stayed with our mother.

By Sunday, my father was worse. He had had a fall. I was told nothing was broken, but he was bruised. He was well tucked up and I did not see how badly. He didn't seem aware of anything around him or that I was sitting with him. It was so different to when he was in hospital after the heart attacks. Then, nurses were visible, gave information to us, and we did not feel unwelcome as visitors. In the psychiatric hospital, he had no means of calling for any help, and I wondered how often anyone checked on him alone in the side room, incapable of being the tiniest bit demanding. He was looking old, much older than his fifty-six years, and frail. How suddenly one can cease to be an active, competent person and become so helpless, trapped in the hands of strangers.

I had sorted though the belongings heaped in the hotel bedroom. Most of it needed to be thrown away or go to a charity shop. But he had had an extravagant time in Austin Reed. I decided to go to the shop and talk with the manager. He was understanding and agreed to the merchandise being returned and the credit card refunded.

During the following few days I had no meaningful conversation with anyone at the hospital, nothing about a diagnosis other than a Latin name that was meaningless to me (and which I can no longer recall), prognosis, treatment, diabetes, when he could be moved, or any enquiries about his history and circumstances. As our father was physically incapable of going anywhere, Andrew and I decided I should return to Devon. Then with our mother, we could decide what to do. We had the immediate situation to deal with, but there were long term issues to face about our parents' care.

I drove from Edinburgh to my home in Exeter, slept for twelve hours, and then went to my parents' home. I don't remember the detail of our discussions, but it was decided that until our father could be moved to Devon, our mother would stay in Edinburgh. That was what she wanted, and, apart from our mother's dislike of hospitals and doctors, it seemed the most practical option. Whatever problems had been going on between our parents, they did love each other, and the long term care of our father would have to accommodate the intermittent problems with our mother.

My mother had spent a few months in Edinburgh in the late 1950s, when she stayed at The Kingston Nature Cure Clinic. She had good memories of that time and appeared to want to go to Edinburgh on her own and stay in a vegetarian guesthouse until our father could be moved to a hospital in Devon. We did not know how long that would be, but helped her pack for what could be a two- or three-week stay.

Andrew and I stayed at our parents' home for a couple more days until our mother was settled in the guesthouse and had made contact with the hospital. We had some practical matters to deal with, as the house would be empty for a while, and we had to retrieve our father's car. I'd found a Heathrow hotel bill and an airline ticket for the return flight our father never made. The hotel confirmed his car was in their car park.

My mother was happy with the Edinburgh guesthouse, had been to the hospital and seen my father, who was dressed and walking. The hospital still would not say any more about his condition or when he could be moved. The following morning my mother took matters into her own hands. The hospital phoned me to say they had lost my father. Later that day my father's office phoned and told Andrew a bank in Edinburgh had contacted them for confirmation of my father's identity before he withdrew some cash. He had no identity with him as I still had his wallet.

My mother had persuaded my father to go for a walk in the hospital grounds. Having had a pleasant walk, it was perfectly normal for them to get into her car and go home. My father did not know he was meant to be in hospital and was seriously ill. They stayed overnight in a hotel on the Scottish/English border and arrived home in Devon the next day.

Andrew and I thought it was more than likely our parents would be coming home. We had acquainted their GP practice with the situation and our concerns about our father. On arrival at home my father was certainly looking better than when I had last seen him in hospital, but the mental change in him was huge. He knew us, and that he was home, but all his adult knowledge needed to deal with daily life and his business acumen had gone. Basically, he was a lovely four-year-old.

My mother's attitude towards me was dismissive. Why had she had to go to Edinburgh to get him, when I should have done what she did and brought him home? With hindsight, I think her objective had been to remove him from psychiatric care before anyone started asking questions. It was clear that she was embarrassed about the change in him and was not allowing any visitors in the house, other than Betsy to do the cleaning as usual.

Andrew returned to work and visited for one or two nights at weekends. I started work again at the end of May having had a successful interview. The solicitor wanted assistance for a year as he had extra commitments that required him to be away from the office. It was a rural practice and I'd be dealing mainly with conveyancing for private clients. Morning and evening I had an hour's commute through some of Devon's rolling landscape and twisting roads, with few opportunities for overtaking when stuck behind a slow vehicle. But I reminded myself that many people work hard all year for their two weeks to enjoy the beauty around me.

I was surprised my father was not admitted to hospital for the diabetes to be checked, and my mother taught how to monitor and manage it, as my father was no longer capable of doing that himself. I also expected some medical input into his mental state. Soon, I became extremely concerned that my father was not receiving proper care. His GP was not acknowledging even the possibility of my mother having the ability to appear perfectly capable of caring for my father whilst a different situation was happening behind closed doors. I had concerns that my mother was not treating my father properly. She would not let me speak with him when I phoned. A couple of times he answered the phone, but it was taken from him before we had chance to say more than a few sentences. I phoned my father's doctor regularly, asking for him to be admitted to hospital and the whole situation assessed. The doctor did not say it explicitly to me, but I had the feeling that my mother had convinced him I had some mental problem that required my father to be in hospital.

At the beginning of June, I was banned from my parents' house. I knew my mother would enforce the ban through subtle threats of harm to my father. My mother knew I would not risk testing how far she would go. Andrew was still visiting regularly at weekends. He negotiated for me to be able to take my father for a walk on Saturday afternoons. My father and I favoured a short drive to an area of open heath land and small copses with views over the Exe estuary and the sea. We could walk comfortably side by side on the wide tracks and were away from traffic.

The two walks I had there with my father showed me something special. He was in the present; just sunshine, views, trees, birds and wild flowers. I saw the essence of my father now he had been stripped of the identities of husband, father, friend, businessman, colleague, committee member and Rotarian. He did not even see himself as a patient. The business of life was done. He was just being. There was a serenity in him as he stooped down to show me the detail of a flower; stopped and watched the flight of a bird gliding over the heath; listened to birdsong coming from a gorse bush, and then saw the flash of brown feathers as the bird darted to another bush. Those walks were interludes of timelessness we shared.

On the first Saturday in July, Andrew phoned me. It was a brief call to tell me our father was in hospital in Exeter and to give me the name of the ward. I was pleased, and said I'd do my shopping and visit in the afternoon. At the hospital I followed the signs to the ward. It was the cardiac unit.

A trainee nurse took me into an office. We sat on each side of a desk. There was a clock on the wall above her head. She told me my father had had a heart attack, was unconscious when he arrived, was currently in theatre, and would be back on the ward soon, but was unlikely to live. I had the impression she wasn't meant to tell me the last bit. It was ten minutes before I could speak. I kept opening and closing my mouth like a goldfish. I phoned Andrew to say that if he and my mother wanted to see our father again they'd better come right away.

An hour later my father was in a side room. He was unconscious and my brother and mother had arrived. We were told to wait in the corridor opposite one of the nursing bays, which had four patients and lots of bleeping equipment, and two nurses who were chatting about contraceptives in voices loud enough for all to hear. My mother kept muttering about the nurses' behaviour. When the doctor came, we all remained in the corridor while he told us the detail of the medication my father would be on three weeks later, implying my father would be home by then.

We did not stay long with my father. My mother was showing signs of agitation. We asked the hospital to phone me and not my mother before we all left the hospital together and Andrew took our mother home.

I'd wanted to stay with my father, as I believed the trainee nurse had spoken truthfully. I went to eat something before returning to sit with him. Little had changed though he did occasionally say my mother's name. I was glad he was in the quiet side room and not on the ward. I don't know how long I had been sitting beside his bed, but it was the evening when I became aware of two 'figures' at the foot of his bed. These beings had a gentle air about them and 'spoke' to me, reassuring me that my father was alright, they were looking after him and I should leave him with them and go home. All was serene and peaceful. I said goodbye to my father in my heart and left, knowing I would not see him again.

At home I sat and listened to music. I can't remember what, except it was Beethoven. In the early hours of Sunday morning I said out loud, 'It is all over now.' Five minutes later the hospital phoned to tell me my father had died five minutes earlier.

In the morning, I phoned one of my father's business partners. I managed to tell him my father had died before losing my voice again. I don't think he knew how bad the situation with my father had been and was surprised as well as shocked. I tried for a number of minutes to say something more, but had to hang up as I found no voice and could not stop crying.

I don't think any of his partners had been allowed to see him since he'd come back from Edinburgh. The terms about ill health in the partnership agreement did not apply until he had been ill for more than a couple of months. The only thing that had been dealt with due to ill health was his resignation from his roles within the Provincial Brokers' Stock Exchange.

My mother, Andrew and I were all in shock, and my mother had probably been in some form of denial since the events in Edinburgh. As it was Sunday, the formalities that follow a death had to wait a day. My father had left a will with instructions for cremation and scattering of his ashes. What was needed was agreement between the three of us on the detail for his funeral. The only conversation I'd had with my father about his funeral was after he had upset his secretary by saying it would be all right by him if his body was put in a sack and sent to the crematorium. That was all light-hearted and fitted with his Buddhist views about disposal of the body. It would not have been difficult to arrange a suitable funeral if we could trust my mother would not have a distressed or violent episode just before or during the service. My father was well known, and it was likely the crematorium would be full for his funeral service.

By the time I went home it had been decided that, as far as the world was concerned, the funeral was private, for family only. My mother was insistent that no one must know there was to be no service. Both Andrew and I knew our mother didn't cope with funerals and was already distressed. If she went, it would risk turning my father's funeral into something that brought trauma, not solace. She could not go without us and we would neither go with her nor without her. It was agreed I was to instruct the funeral directors no one would officiate, there would be only a period of silence and no one would be attending. That way my mother, Andrew and I could each decide how and where we wished to be at the time of the funeral and be with him in our own prayers and meditations, which would be sad but peaceful.

The next morning I dealt with the formalities. I knew what to do as it was routine work when employed in a probate department. But that was the first time the deceased was a close relative of mine. First, I had to go to the hospital office to collect the death certificate. I was told the certificate had not been signed and I was asked to wait. I sat for twenty minutes thinking a mistake had been made. My father had not died and soon someone would take me to the ward to see him. When my name was called, I was given the signed death certificate to take to the Registrar of Births, Deaths and Marriages.

I knew what happened at the registrar's office and the questions I'd be asked. I lost my voice again when asked to give my father's full name. Patiently, all the necessary information was coaxed out of me and entered in the register, which I signed. I have no recollection of the appointment at the funeral directors later that day. My emotions were so mixed, and I wished my father had left us precise instructions. I did not explain why I was giving the instructions I did. I hoped the roses on the coffin would show any officials who cared to think about it that he was not uncared for or someone whose death did not affect others' lives.

Andrew stayed with our mother that week. I went back to work for three days, taking Friday off for my father's funeral. I went first to see my mother and walked from her house to the wooded paths leading to the ridge between the two valleys where my father had lived for the previous twenty-one years. I sat under a beech tree from where I could see the old vicarage which had been our family home for ten years, and also my grandparents' former home. I cried, prayed, and gave thanks for my father's life.

A few months later, I scattered his ashes under a different beech tree in a copse on that ridge. He had directed that his ashes were to be scattered in a designated area of outstanding natural beauty.

Over the weekend after his funeral, we sorted through the papers in his study at home. I took the papers relating to his financial affairs that would be needed to get the Grant of Probate and transfer the assets into my mother's name. Everything was in order and straightforward. The only thing I discovered that I did not know was that my father was a life member of The Buddhist Society, but this did not surprise me. He had lived, not preached, the principles he believed.

There were some handwritten notes he'd made that probably summed up his approach to life. The notes were headed 'The Supraconscious' (See Appendix 3). I realised how much I'd absorbed from him without knowing it. I had applied 'the night work' religiously when studying for my final law exams, not to learn law, but to keep a positive attitude and the determination to be able to give it my best shot.

I found one of Derek Neville's poems in his desk. For me that poem was a personal message my father had left me. It was then, and remains, a source of strength and encouragement to me.

> There shall be no going back,
> Not for me,
> Not for the world,
> Not for God.
> For the past is already dead,
> Except so far as it lives in the present.
> You already possess the good
> That was squeezed out of its pain.
> Let that be enough.
> Go forward with the rest of life
> Unto your highest good.[1]

In the autumn, as part of National Tree Week, six tulip trees were planted in memory of my father on the verge of one of the routes into Exeter. The planting was arranged by members of my father's firm, the Rotary Club of Exeter, and the Men of the Trees. A photographer from the local paper recorded the Club's President and me with shining spades doing the honours at the ceremony. One tree was vandalised, but the others grew, and for years later they gave me a feeling of warmth when I drove by.

Andrew and I gave our mother as much support as we could during the following months, but we were both working and could only visit at weekends. She was not happy on her own in the family home, and the difficulties she was having were beyond those I'd have put down to the inevitable processes of grieving and adapting to the changes of widowhood and the next phase of life.

The GP practice gave no support in response to requests from us. I know she wouldn't have been willing to take medication, and maybe there was nothing else the doctors could suggest as bereavement services were scarce then.

Six months after our father's death Andrew stopped working to spend an extended length of time with her, which he believed would get her settled and enable her to make decisions about what she wanted to do if she sold the family house. My mother was more likely to respond to Andrew's suggestions and would have found it more natural to prepare meals for him than me, and perhaps that would bring some routine into her life. My work contract ended in May, so we could review the situation again then.

I stayed with Sally for a few days in spring. We visited the New Forest when the beech trees were newly in leaf. While talking and walking among tall beech trees, I became aware that I was laughing with her. Sally and I had the ability on occasions to descend into giggles. I stopped suddenly when I realised I had not laughed since my father's death. It had been as if I had no right to laugh. The spring sunshine, Sally's company, and the majestic beech trees were all confirming that life continues.

7

Chameleon

I HAD settled back into legal work and was kept busy, with conveyancing work. In rural practices, Michaelmas, the autumn quarter day, was a traditional day for farm sales to be completed and when ownerships changed. I was given a book by the senior partner as a token of acknowledgment of the volume of my work that Michaelmas. As I did not want to commute during dark, icy mornings, I decided to rent a holiday cottage during the winter months. I'd return to the daily com-mute at Easter for the last two months of my contract.

Shortly before Easter I was offered bed, breakfast and evening meal four nights a week by Veronica. The thought of no commuting and meals being prepared for me was too good to ignore. I was tired. The situation with my mother and brother was deteriorating. I had done nothing about looking for a job after the end of my contract, and what I did next would be influenced by what was happening with them.

It was a Monday in March when I reversed into the drive in front of Veronica and Ted's house. Ted was in the dining room, sitting at the breakfast bar by the hatch into the kitchen when I arrived. After putting my case in my room, I joined him for a cup of coffee and then went to work. Months later he told me there were two things he'd noticed about me that morning. First, I had reversed my car on to their drive, and second, I could pronounce Machynlleth. Two days later, at breakfast on his birthday, he opened a card from his daughter telling him he was a 'Super Dad'. It choked me up; how I missed my father.

Ted, a vet in a country practice, worked a strict rota with his colleagues of 'on duty' or 'on call' many evenings and weekends which restricted their free time. When Ted was 'on call', all phone calls were diverted from the surgery to his home, and Veronica had to stay at home to answer the phone.

Many of my weekday evenings were spent with Veronica. Occasionally in an evening when Ted was not 'on duty' or 'on call' we'd all go for a walk. One such walk was my first trip to the old coaching road between Woody Bay and Heddon's Mouth on the North Devon Coastal Path, an area which became one of my favourite places for walking or just sitting staring out to sea.

Another walk I remember was on a mild, spring evening in April. After supper Veronica suggested Ted and I went for a walk whilst she cleared up the kitchen. We drove a few miles down the valley from their house to a wood where herons nested. The track was wide and Ted was making small talk.

'A year ago today it was snowing in North Devon,' he said.

I burst into those crushing tears that don't allow words. Ted looked confused and I waved him to walk on as I tried to compose myself. It was twelve months to the day since I had last seen my father as the intelligent, competent, compassionate, generous person he was before the changes during the last weeks of his life.

When Ted and I re-met on the woodland track I explained a little to him, not knowing then he'd trained as a Samaritan. Over the following weeks he gently coaxed my story out of me.

Although their house was within walking distance of the office, most days I took my car and parked in one of the side streets in case I needed it during the day. I started finding notes, picture postcards, and paper bulls on the windscreen, the latter probably from a memo pad left by a rep from a veterinary pharmaceutical firm. Ted had distinctive handwriting, but it seemed innocent enough. He had a reputation for listening to people and giving encouragement. He was fondly known as 'Uncle' in the surgery. Rarely, I'd accompany him if he was called to a farm in an evening. Students and passengers were useful for opening and closing gates. I enjoyed seeing a sick or scared animal slowly relax a little under his touch. When driving past a quarry's warning sign that read 'Blasting Daily', he commented that life at home could be like that. Once in a while he'd make general comments about never knowing what he was coming home to.

Some time during those early summer months I learnt of his sadness over the changes about three or four years earlier in the good relationship he had enjoyed with his youngest child. The way he talked reminded me of my father's feelings over the distance that developed between him and Andrew after he'd left home. Andrew's contact with us then was mainly telephone conversations with my mother. The loss my father felt was aggravated by 'distortions' sometimes created by my mother.

Veronica told me things about her relationship with Ted that would have been better kept to herself. She told me she had lodgers in the house to help modify her behaviour towards him, but also enjoyed the bit of financial independence that lodgers' rent gave her. On one occasion, when we were stuck in traffic, she mentioned about thumping Ted and once threatening him with a knife. Ted had stopped his voluntary work with the Samaritans before I met him, but Veronica mentioned that was yet another thing he neither couldn't nor wouldn't talk about with her.

Shortly before my one-year contract expired, the firm offered me a permanent job. Andrew was still not working, and spent much of his time with our mother, but she not getting better. We and others had contacted her GP, but he offered no help or advice. It was probably Andrew's regular and prolonged visits that were maintaining some stability for her. Andrew and I decided it would be best if I accepted the permanent job and settled myself in North Devon. I liked North Devon, and it was an area to which my mother might be content to move.

She had stayed at Bude on the north Cornish coast a few times before she was widowed, and had friends in the area.

My bungalow in Exeter sold before I found a property to buy. Veronica and Ted invited me to stay with them until I did. Soon after I'd signed the contract for the sale of my bungalow, they were to have a week's holiday in their caravan in North Cornwall. I was to join them midweek on Veronica's birthday. The day before her birthday Ted returned home, saying he wanted to do some oil painting. The next day he returned to Cornwall and I joined them for the day as planned. I was told that Ted had left Veronica alone the previous night so she would know what it might feel like when he was no longer around on her birthday, meaning when she had been widowed.

Veronica knew Ted had spent a night in his own house and I was the only other person there. Although I did not consent to, or protest about, what happened I knew I could not look Veronica in the eye, if confronted, and say nothing at all had happened. At the time, and since, I accounted for what did happened that night not as sexual harassment or love for me, but as an expression of emotion by Ted due to his inability to talk with anyone about deeply emotional matters and the apparent similarities in some of his and my father's families' circumstances. That was my perception of the situation and the perception that influenced me over the following months and years. Whilst I lived in North Devon Ted asked for no more than a cuddle, and sometimes masturbation.

The day after Veronica's birthday I went to work as usual, but whenever I was alone in my office I started crying. That went on throughout the day. It was still bad at the end of the day. I had no chance of making a life in North Devon free from the fear of Veronica doing or saying something that would make my life impossible. It was a small community where everyone knew everyone. Ted was well respected. Both he and Veronica separately had said enough to me for me to know Ted was doing something similar to my father to look after his family and maintain family unity. It was harder doing that in a small community. I knew where his loyalties lay. There would be only so much he'd do if I became the subject of a 'distortion' talked about or initiated by Veronica. The irony was that I would have had no respect for Ted if his dedication to preserving his family's unity had not been strong. I never had any impression, neither then nor later, that he was in the habit of pursuing or harassing women. I also had the professional dilemma that Ted and Veronica were clients of the firm who employed me. At the time, my resignation was put down to not coping with my employer. Though respected in the community, he had a reputation for being a challenging person to work for. It was agreed I'd worked only half the contractual period of notice.

By September, just six weeks after Veronica's birthday, I was jobless, with no family to turn to, no prospect of pulling my mother and brother through their situations, and living in a household where if I said what I thought was going on there would be no help. If I spoke with a doctor it would probably guarantee a mental health referral judging by how my family had been treated since Edinburgh. I was out of resources, other than the survival behaviour I'd learnt in childhood, which was to lie low and wait for things to change. I didn't even know how to move out of Ted and Veronica's house and away from their influence.

The week in the middle of September was surreal. Having no job, there were no work demands, and it was a week when no one phoned me about my mother. Veronica was away. Ted was working as usual. I was to be on hand to answer the phone during his out-of-hours 'on duty' should he be called out. Apart from that, I had nothing to do other than prepare his meals and do a bit of washing and ironing. He was more relaxed than I had seen him before, coming in whistling, greeting me, doing something around the house and then returning for the meal. He spent his free time with me, either at home or out walking. He was good company. I was twenty-nine and it was the first time I'd felt safe to be in my body, and at ease around anyone other than my father, brother, and maternal grandmother. I did not have to explain to them or Ted the unacceptable, unbelievable part of my life. It was accepted as part of who I was. I did not love or fancy Ted, or want a relationship with him. We came to know each other simply because circumstances had placed us under the same roof, and incidentally we'd discovered something about the other's acceptance of their role in their family.

Over the next few months, the pattern developed of me spending time with Veronica on her own, Ted on his own, with Ted and Veronica together, or with friends of theirs. Both Ted and Veronica were different people away from each other and different again as a couple. All 'three' – Veronica, Ted and 'Ted-and-Veronica' – spoke about themselves and their family. It was a strange situation to be in, hearing three angles on the same family. I was a chameleon, adapting to whoever I was with. In one sense, my body was there but I was not, so I probably appeared to be going along with whatever was suggested. No one seemed to question what I was doing there or that I might need outside help of some kind.

Eighteen months after my father's death, matters came to a head with my brother and mother. My mother phoned and claimed Andrew was being violent. I went to Sidmouth. All Andrew had done was slam the sideboard drawer shut, but it was the signal to me that something had to change. Whatever he did we were not going to get our mother settled without help, and it was useless talking with the only GP practice in town. It seemed as if my mother was blacklisted.

When I arrived at the house, Andrew and my mother were hurling verbal abuse at each other. We all went into the room that had been my grandfather's bedsit, which after his death became a second sitting room. My mother and Andrew continued arguing and it was impossible to break in and get them to calm down and discuss what we needed to do. I sat on the sofa watching them. Then I had a strong feeling of my father's presence. It was so strong I felt he was standing behind me, also watching them, and had I turned around I would have seen him. Thoughts came into my head about what I should do. I stood up, left the room, went out through the front door, and walked to a telephone box. I phoned the nursing home where my grandfather had been for the last few months of his life. The nursing home was willing and capable of looking after people whose behaviour could be challenging and still had the same matron whom I liked and trusted. There was a room, and they would take my mother.

Back at my mother's house, I packed a suitcase for her and then told her I was taking her to the nursing home. To my surprise she came with me without a protest. I drove her the fifteen miles to the home and saw her settled in. When I got back Andrew was calmer, and said he wanted to go home. We did the practical necessities around the house so it could be left for a few days. He drove to Bournemouth and I went back to Ted and Veronica's house.

The immediate crisis had been dealt with. I just had to hope my mother would accept being looked after long enough for all of us to get some help. The family had fallen apart without my father. I knew we would be better sorting the problems out together, because neither Andrew nor I would walk out on our mother, even though neither of us knew how to look after her, or what help was needed.

I can't remember if it was the next day or the day after when my brother phoned. He was upset and Veronica said he could come and stay for a few days. He was happy to do that and it would give us a chance to talk and look at our options. I hadn't told my brother the true reasons for leaving my job or the circum-stances under which I was living.

When Andrew arrived we decided we both needed a day's rest before talking about anything. Veronica said she was around and would keep an eye on Andrew while he rested at her house. I took my spinning wheel and went to spend the day with a friend. Spinning was my favourite form of relaxation. The rhythm of the wheel, co-ordination of hands, eyes, and feet, the feel of the fleece, the tension as fibres twist and draw onto the spool all help stop thoughts going round and round as one becomes absorbed in the action and at one with the wheel.

I do not know what happened to my brother after I'd left

Veronica's house. There was a telephone call in the afternoon to my friend, which I presumed was from Veronica. It was suggested to my friend that I should stay the night. It seemed a good idea as twenty-four hours away could be as refreshing as a week's holiday. No indication was given that anything had changed with my brother.

When I returned the following day, I discovered Veronica had called Dr A to see my brother but I never discovered why a home visit was necessary. If Andrew had wanted to see a doctor he was quite capable of going to the surgery himself when I'd left. Did my departure have anything to do with whatever had happened?

Dr A had given Andrew some medication, but for what or why, I never found out. Dr A had made all the arrangements for my brother to be referred as a day patient to a psychiatric hospital in Bournemouth. It was not an emergency referral, and I never understood why Dr A didn't leave any such decisions to Andrew and his doctor in Bournemouth. Then there would have been time for a proper assessment of all the circumstances.

I don't know what my brother had been told by Veronica, what had been said to Dr A or why I was not informed a doctor had been called. I never was to know why Veronica didn't phone me as soon as she'd phoned for a doctor. Andrew never gave me any indication he'd wanted me excluded and an appointment had already been made for me to go with him the next day to see Dr A at his surgery.

Dr A told me my brother was having a 'spiritual crisis' and it would be better if he was in Bournemouth. I have remembered the word 'spiritual' all these years as it was such an odd thing to say. Why was a mental health referral made for a 'spiritual crisis'? Before making the referral did Dr A consider the stigma and employment problems that come with such a referral? The questions went through my mind, but I did not voice them to Dr A. Andrew went to Bournemouth on his own a day or so later. We never did talk properly about our situations or about our mother.

I agreed with Dr A that Andrew would be better away from North Devon. It would not help if he got drawn into the situation I wanted to get away from. I was shocked another mental health referral had been made without prior reference to, or discussions with, a relative. I was slightly comforted when I discovered the hospital to which Andrew had been referred was where Sally worked as a social worker in the alcohol unit.

At the end of Andrew's appointment with Dr A, he arranged for me to be registered at his practice and made an appointment for me to see him the following week. Dr A he told me I had probably been depressed all my life. He hadn't asked sufficient questions of me to know whether that was even likely to be true, nor did he check out any possible causes for his assumptions. He didn't tell me what information he had been given about me. He was acting on incomplete and maybe inaccurate information. He said he could make a mental health referral, give me medication, or support me. I opted for the latter as the former were both unacceptable. I felt very sure that if I began to tell Dr A even part of what was actually going on in my life I would definitely have been referred, and that would not have help me. In fact, it would have been a nightmare; having no capable relative and with Ted and Veronica being seen as a kind, generous couple who were supporting me.

Since the previous summer, when Ted had come home for that one night in the middle of his holiday, I had wondered if Veronica and Ted were fearful I would talk about what I had learnt about them and their family while I was working and residing there temporarily. Had they wanted to ensure that they had some kind of control over me?

My mother had had a quiet ten days at the nursing home. Her return home began another distressing period which I called 'the nursing home and companion stage'. It began for me with a phone call from someone who lived near Holsworthy, a market town in North Devon, to tell me that my mother's car was parked at their house and she was in a nursing home in a village on the North Devon coast. I did not hear the full story of how she got there. I think her friend recognised she needed help and, with the aid of a doctor, got her into the nursing home. She stayed in that home long enough to be seen by a clinical psychologist, to whom the nursing home's GP had referred her.

A month after Andrew's departure for Bournemouth, one of Ted and Veronica's daughters came home having given up her degree course. There were tense emotions in the house, especially between her and Ted, before she returned to the city where she was living.

Ted and Veronica both talked with me about their daughter. If I was in the sitting room and the television was not on I could not help hearing some of Veronica's telephone conversations in the hall. Sometimes I would hear her say, 'Your father thinks . . .' before statements that seemed more like the views she had previously expressed to me than those Ted had. But a fly on the wall only hears snippets. It seemed that whatever her parents' views and disappointments were, much of the emotion was evoked from earlier times.

There were two incidents during the weeks after she'd left that made an impression on me, though I cannot recall the detail. Ted and I were walking on the coastal path near Heddon's Mouth. He talked about his daughter and his feelings for her. Any daughter in her early twenties would have been touched and blessed to have a father who had such regard for her and who wished to support his daughter in whatever she wanted. The other incident involved Veronica. It was the only time I saw her so angry, frighteningly angry. The anger was directed towards Ted. It was hard to say what the rational cause of it was, if there was a rational cause. It did not appear to be Ted. I perceived it to be the kind of anger that could easily slip into uncontrolled physical harm.

During those weeks I gained an insight about my mother's behaviour when I was a teenager. Just because I had the insight then does not imply that the situations were the same. I hadn't realised my mother had exerted a control over my father, my brother and myself by giving us distorted information. It could be either about the thoughts or actions of one of us, or about people or events outside the family. The 'distortion' always contained enough truth for it to seem plausible initially.

Distortions could be built upon so the origins and truth became lost. There is a saying that if you repeat a lie often enough it gets believed as true. It could also set up resentments or misunderstandings. When trying to sort out a misunderstanding, my mother would put down as 'silly' or 'stupid' whichever one of us 'had got it wrong'. It was a form of divide and rule. My mother was not malicious towards any of us, and loved us. So why had that happened?

The crisis with Andrew and my mother had not altered my situation. I was still living with Ted and Veronica, and was still being a chameleon, waiting to see what would happen. My way of using Dr A's offer of support was to avoid him. I read my medical notes in 2005, which showed I saw Dr A only once more that year, about six weeks after the first visit.

Veronica told me that she had seen Clinical Psychologist A privately a few years earlier before she returned to work. Veronica suggested I saw the same psychologist. I complied with suggestions during those months and could see no harm in seeing the psychologist. When I did, we spent most of the time discussing employment options, but it was never checked that I had an occupation I was qualified and capable of doing if I could manage my personal circumstances.

My mother had been referred to Clinical Psychologist A by her GP. I hadn't told my mother I'd met Clinical Psychologist A, nor did I tell the psychologist my mother had an appointment with her. Clinical Psychologist A referred my mother to a psychiatrist at the North Devon District Hospital. At my next appointment with Clinical Psychologist A she told me she had seen my mother and she advised to me to emigrate to Australia. I found that sad advice, as it was in effect saying 'run away'. If I had wanted to run away I would have done so long ago, probably as a teenager. An opportunity had been missed to assess correctly the family situation, treat us as a family, integrate the healthcare and individual needs of my mother, my brother and myself, put bereavement counselling in place for all of us, and establish the means whereby my family, together or individually, would know how to access suitable healthcare and support in the future.

My mother saw the psychiatrist, and afterwards he agreed to meet me. We had a brief conversation in the hospital canteen. He told me there was nothing wrong with my mother, but she did have a difficult mix of dominance and dependence. I thought that was right, and I was relieved she was not given a psychiatric referral. But it did nothing to help get her settled, and there was no further help from her doctors.

Andrew, who hadn't visited our mother, wrote to me:

> 'Thanks for phoning to let me know what the position is about Mother's condition when the psychiatrist saw her. I know we will be able to cope in a way which does not interfere unacceptably in our own lives, although it may seem to be tough at times. I do understand the kind of pressure you were put under as I have had some very bizarre phone calls with Mother myself, especially last year.'

> 'One thing which strikes me about the whole business over the last six months is that mother has seen several doctors, psychiatrists, psychiatric nurses and psychologists, but we do not have any documentation about her condition. . . . What I am coming to is that I would very much like to see a comprehensive medical report from the North Devon psychiatrist. Do you think you could ask him to supply this to you/us? Also is [Clinical Psychologist A] prepared to give us a written report on Mother as a result of her discussion? I am quite happy to pay for the medical reports, although I think in all the circumstances we are entitled to them if the people involved are saying it is not a medical problem. I think this sort of documentation is essential to us in the future. I can promise you I am not prepared to allow the previous situation to reoccur, where Mother's influence becomes a factor which inhibits you enjoying your life in the way which you choose.'

After I had failed to get a written report from any of our mother's doctors, Andrew wrote to me again:

> 'Coming back to your letter this week, as neither [Clinical Psychologist A, the GP or the psychiatrist] will give a medical report of any substance, the conclusion I come to is that none of them really have any understanding of the problem at all and

they would rather wash their hands of the matter. It seems to me that they do not have any confidence in their own opinions and judgement. Have you noticed that they are all apparently able to give vast amounts of verbal advice, opinions and sympathy, but will not put anything down in writing? Imagine a client coming to you for professional advice about a complex legal problem. So you spend a lot of time analysing the problem, advising the client what to do, etc. When you have reached your conclusion and communicated it to the client, surely you would be quite happy to confirm your views in writing if asked to do so. If you refused then the client would be perfectly entitled to assume that you were really quite unsure of what you were saying.

'I think the lesson to be learnt is that we are the only people who see the problem in total and in proper perspective. Other people are just seeing it from their point of view so whilst it is alright to listen to their comments, opinions and advice, it is necessary for us to arrive at our own decisions and take the correct action. So it is just as well that we are jointly able to do exactly that.'

By mid-summer Andrew had been discharged by the psychiatric hospital and was applying for jobs. He attended the unemployment benefit office and had difficulties regarding his National Insurance contributions being unpaid during the time he was not working after our father's death. He was asked to provide independent evidence of his reasons for not working, and requested that from our mother's GP in Sidmouth. Two years after our father's death, the GP wrote to Andrew:

'I can confirm that your mother, during the past twelve to eighteen months, has had certain health problems which may have required considerable family support and attention'.

That was the first indication from anyone in the medical profession that our mother needed help.

By the middle of August Andrew had a job offer and wrote to me:

'I am very pleased about this but it will mean making a big effort, especially at the beginning. I want to put everything into it to prove I can still do the work and after that they should reward me on merit. One disappointing thing is that they checked with the Chartered Insurance Institute about my exam results and I am not now credited with any papers because of the time which has elapsed. So although I had passed about three quarters of my ACII, I will now have to start from square one again on the new syllabus'.

At the end of August I received a letter from him saying:

'The first week at work went very well and I have not felt tired or short of energy at all, despite getting up early and getting home from work quite late'.

My mother remained in the nursing home on the North Devon coast until after my meeting with the psychiatrist, returning to the family home shortly before Andrew started work.

Ted was a keen and knowledgeable birdwatcher. He'd planned a visit to mid-Wales in late spring. He particularly wanted to see red kites, chestnut coloured birds of prey with a wingspan of six feet, which were fairly rare then. He suggested I went with him. We saw a variety of birds but no red kites. On the way we visited his mother, who lived on her own in a village in South Wales.

In my absence, a solicitor had phoned Veronica to offer me a job. I'd met him when I was working the previous year, and he was wondering if I would be interested in working part-time looking after the non-contentious side of his office as he needed to spend more time with his family. I would work three days a week and do overtime as required. That job offer was the turning point for me; being part-time, I would still have sufficient time to attend to my mother's affairs.

One month later I was house-hunting. The house I bought was a Victorian terrace house, five minutes walk from the office. It was close to the park and playing fields beside the river in Barnstaple. Although my offer on the house was accepted, I'd received my mortgage offer and contracts for the purchase were signed in September, completion was delayed as the building society would not release the mortgage money until November. I remained lodging with Ted and Veronica until I could move. That was against Veronica's wishes, and I think Ted exerted some influence in maintaining the status quo for a few more weeks.

I do not know if Veronica had acknowledged to herself how Ted behaved towards me. She hadn't said anything to me even after her mother had pointed it out to her in my presence. It is possible, but unlikely, that she and Ted had together created the situation the previous year when Ted had briefly returned home during their Cornish holiday. If so, they could not have predicted I'd resign my job but remain lodging with them. My new house and job were not far enough away to be beyond the sphere of their social circle, acquaintances or influence.

On her return to Glenholme, the family home, our mother told Andrew frequently that she couldn't live on her own. Andrew wrote to me:

> 'For the immediate future I think she should stay at Glenholme either with or without a "companion", or alternatively go to a nursing home in the Sidmouth area so she can go to Glenholme easily in the daytime. I think you should tell her you are not going to look after things at Glenholme, and she is perfectly capable of doing that herself and should stay in the area. However, I do feel quite strongly that we should maintain at least some control over her financial affairs as I do not want her to get into the position of running out of money permanently as this would cause more problems, probably for all of us. There is also a significant, if not a large, risk that she could be taken for a ride financially by one of these so-called companions.'

I did not agree with Andrew that our mother was 'perfectly capable' of looking after things at Glenholme. I had noticed that Andrew was taking a much firmer line about our mother's behaviour than previously. I felt my mother would be much better in a smaller property, but as the three of us were unable to sit down together and talk about matters it seemed impossible to help her think about where she would like to live.

My mother registered with an agency that provided live-in temporary domiciliary care and arranged for a companion to come on Mondays. The pattern developed that the companion would phone me on Tuesdays. The conversations were all much the same. I would be told that my mother was not well, and that I should go and look after her and then she would be alright. My cynical summary of the position was that if the companion needed the money she would stay the week, otherwise she'd have left by Thursday. It was becoming clear to my mother that a series of temporary companions was not working, and she booked herself into a nursing home two roads away from Glenholme.

While she was there, Glenholme was burgled. Small things of value had been taken, but very little damage was done and the house had not been turned over. I was extremely grateful my mother had not been there. Soon after that my mother left Glenholme and Sidmouth for good. She took a suitcase with a few clothes and drove to Torquay, where she had a friend who was a member of The Aetherius Society. Between them they arranged for my mother to stay in a nursing home there.

Over the following few weeks, Andrew and I decided our mother meant it when she said she was never going back to the family home. The decision was made that I would deal with clearing Glenholme prior to it being put on the market, and that would coincide with the completion of the purchase of my house in Barnstaple.

Any spare time I had from work was spent at Glenholme organising the contents into a few personal items to go to my mother in Torquay, items to go into store until she bought another house, items to go to my house (including my furniture, which had been stored in my mother's house since the sale of my bungalow the previous year), items to be sold, items which were to go to Betsy, items for charity shops, and things which needed to be thrown away. Andrew had given me a list of a few items to go to him.

Had I really thought about it, I would have never been able to do the job, as I had to make a decision about every single item in the house. I was dissecting and destroying a collection of belongings that had been used and enjoyed by my parents, my brother, and my maternal grandparents, people I loved and who loved me; the paraphernalia and memories of joint lives. Also in the house were items that had belonged to my father's parents and, while I had never met them, their influence was an integral part of my family. One thing I had gained through my professional legal training was the ability to put my emotions to one side and get on with the job, and that was what I did.

By the middle of November I was living in Barnstaple. Glenholme was cleared and estate agents had been instructed to sell it.

My brother and my mother had not seen each other for ten months. After visiting her, Andrew wrote to me:

> 'Mother was quite calm but had the usual sort of complaints about being left in a mess and nobody doing enough to help her, etc. She looked very well, hair done nicely, smartly dressed and so on. I told her briefly what had been going on at Glenholme and she does genuinely appreciate everything you have done and are doing. I'm sorry I can't explain why she does not seem to be capable of conveying these feelings to you. She is quite happy about the things you have, some things being in store, some things being sold, etc.
>
> 'I think it is a load off her mind that all this has been done and it will be even better when the house is sold. She was pleased to have the particulars and the photos and how it was presented. She kept picking up the particulars and looking through them the whole time I was talking to her. I got the impression she will be showing everyone and saying what a nice house she was living in. Keeps going on about the cost of maintenance of Glenholme, so at least the sale will knock that one on the head. After I had been with Mother for a while I went downstairs leaving Mother in her room and had a chat with Philippa and Janet. They say she has improved a lot since being there and is gradually doing more things. They are trying to get her doing things like going to a self-help group, going to the theatre, etc. Apparently, she behaves completely differently most of the time compared to when either you or I are there. When she knows that one of us is coming she changes. After I phoned them at two

o'clock, Mother was pacing up and down and smoking all the time, staying at the front of the building, etc. until I arrived.

'I don't think there's anything to worry about with her and I think she is a lot happier than she makes out. There is a great deal of "playing games" when either of us is about. I could be wrong but I think she will be staying where she is for the near future, say 3–6 months. ...

'A small thing which Mother mentioned is that Philippa's boyfriend comes to visit her every weekend from Barnstaple. But I am sure you said Mother had told you that he came from Bournemouth. So it seems she is still telling us different things, so the confusion goes on!

'Confirming what I said to you, I think you have done an extremely good job clearing up Glenholme and making all the arrangements.'

Nine months later Glenholme had been sold and my mother was in Worcestershire.

8

Bolt from the Blue

IT was a pleasure to have a house of my own again, my own books on the bookshelves and to unpack and have space for all my sewing, knitting, and spinning paraphernalia. The front bedroom, overlooking the church, was my sewing room. In the middle of the room was the 6'x4' oak dining table which my mother had bought for £1 in the mid 1960s and had been my father's desk when he joined the stockbrokers in Exeter. My sewing machine lived on that table and my current projects could be left out and worked on when I had a few spare minutes. I'd spend hours there listening to the radio or classical music at weekends.

I'd finished sorting out the contents of the family home, my mother was still in Torquay and my life began to settle into a routine that was structured around my work. Three of my working days each week were fixed, but I had flexibility to choose when I did any overtime, which generally amounted to the equivalent of one day a week. That gave me the opportunity to go into the office out of opening hours, when I could do much of the longer paperwork free of interruptions from telephones. In the summer on the days I didn't have to be there, I liked to be in the office at 5.00 a.m. and leave at 9.00 a.m. when the office opened.

I remained a regular visitor to Ted and Veronica's house as we had mutual friends, but the deception, or double life, surrounding Ted and I continued. Ted had a key to my house and knew that he could come there any time he wanted to. I would give a key to my house to anyone whom I considered trustworthy and whom I believed might be experiencing domestic abuse. Whether my belief about Ted and Veronica was right I do not know, but my beliefs influenced my attitude towards Ted. Ted told me he moved into the spare bedroom when I moved out of their house. He also said things that convinced me he was liable to be subjected to extremely serious, even fatal, physical violence. I believed I could be attacked if I was in the wrong place at the wrong time. Perhaps because of childhood experiences, I'd accepted what he was saying as totally plausible. If I told anybody what he was saying it is unlikely I would have been believed, and probably he would have deny it.

Ted told me he did not like his name, Edward, being shortened to Ted. When he joined the surgery there was already a vet called Edward working there so he became Ted to avoid confusions. I decided to call him Edward when we were alone. That decision may have cemented the distinctions in the official and unofficial parts of our friendship, but then it did seem as if I had two friends. The official part of our friendship included anything that Ted did not mind Veronica knowing about, and, of course, anything involving mutual friends. Edward told me the unofficial part of our friendship gave him support and helped him to maintain family unity and support Veronica. He gave me every indication Veronica was getting on with her life, work and other interests, and their lives were becoming independent. Whether Veronica would have agreed with that I do not know. They hadn't stopped doing things together. Edward phoned me early most mornings when they had a holiday in France.

Edward was a regular visitor to my house. Sometimes, at the end of the day, if he was not 'on duty', he would look in. He had the habit of dialling my telephone number and letting it ring twice before replacing the receiver. Sometimes he'd wake me in the middle of the night for a chat when he was in the surgery before going home after finishing an emergency call. In those days I slept well and easily went to sleep afterwards.

Soon after I'd moved, Ted acquired a white and tan Jack Russell puppy that he'd rescued from a farm. Being the runt of the litter Jake would have been shot. Ted brought Jake to show me before deciding to keep him. Maybe Ted thought I'd like a puppy, but I was in no position to take on a puppy. I took Jake to dog training classes and over the years became very fond of him, but he was Ted's dog and part of Ted and Veronica's household. Jake was an intelligent dog, independently minded and terrified of sudden, loud noises.

One of Ted's administrative responsibilities was to write the duty rota for the vets in the practice. I can't remember how long it was after I moved that he started giving me his handwritten draft after a practice secretary had typed and distributed the rota. Edward acquired the habit of phoning me at 8.30 a.m. when it was his turn to relieve the overnight duty vet before the surgery opened at 9 a.m., and before he went home in the evening if he had done the evening surgery. On his 'free' or 'second duty' evenings, when Veronica was working, he'd visit. In the summer, on a 'free' evening we might take a packed supper to the coast or into the country for a walk with Jake. I had bought binoculars and had become interested in bird watching.

Walking through a wood with Edward became one of my favourite occupations. He was an expert on flora and fauna and could answer all my questions. If he saw something that caught his interest he would stop walking and take up the binoculars hanging round his neck to get a better look. I soon learnt not to ask questions when he did that but to focus my binoculars in the direction he was looking as that helped increase my observational skills. My expert companion then named the bird and pointed out its distinguishing features.

My favourite walking venues with Edward varied according to the seasons and the amount of time we each had. In winter, I particularly enjoyed watching waders feeding in the mud at low tide, or seeing large flocks of geese. In late spring, I loved being in a wood with the buds on the trees bursting open but before the leaves had developed sufficiently to hide the birds from view. We had many coastal walks between Heddon's Mouth and Woody Bay and around Porlock and Culbone.

We developed our own code words, which were either bird or flower names. We also used codes when we needed to indicate to the other that we should be in 'official' mode. The unofficial part of our relationship would have been completely unacceptable to me had I not believed I was supporting an abused husband in how he wished to manage his family situation. The support was not one-sided. Other than my brother, only Edward had some knowledge and understanding of the continuing difficulties with my mother.

Andrew and I separately visited our mother in Torquay on a regular basis. I had not given her my new address or telephone number. She was far from settled and it would not help any of us if she turned up on my doorstep. Apart from my visits to her, she had to contact me through Andrew. Andrew and I looked after her financial affairs. I did the day-to-day management. Each month after checking her monthly bank statements, I'd send her a note of how much money she had in her bank account so she was not worrying about money. Andrew and I would be more likely to spot if someone was trying to take advantage of her financially. Joy, her friend who belonged to The Aetherius Society, provided her with considerable emotional support and healing for the five months she stayed in Torquay.

My mother moved to Worcestershire as a live-in companion to a widow. I don't know how that happened; she probably had seen an advertisement in *The Lady*. My feelings about my mother at that time were very mixed. On the one hand, I was pleased she was taking some positive steps, but she seemed to have landed herself in a situation where demands were made on her that were similar to the demands she'd made at times since her widowhood. In the right circumstances, her caring and practical nature would have made her a good companion, but only if she came through her own difficulties successfully.

When she left the companion job, she moved to a vegetarian guest house in Malvern. The food there was very much to her liking and they also provided complementary health therapies. My mother's physical and emotional health improved during her stay at the guest house.

One of my mother's cousins, Rachel, lived in Malvern. Rachel, a retired school teacher, had not married and shared a house with a life long friend who was also a retired teacher. I had never met Rachel and was not aware that my mother had had contact with any of her cousins for many years. After my mother left Devon, she was in touch with Peggy, her sister-in-law. Perhaps she'd put my mother in touch with Rachel.

Andrew and I saw each other approximately every six to eight weeks. I would either go to Bournemouth or he would come to North Devon for a weekend. I was never aware Andrew rebuilt his social life, nor did I meet any of his friends when I visited Bournemouth. Of course, it could have been that he did not wish to mix family with friends. After my father died, Sally was my only friend who knew my mother. Andrew and I were in regular telephone contact, and he advised me about my car and what to say when I took it to a garage. There was one occasion when his advice could have been dangerous. On my way to Bournemouth my brakes failed at a roundabout near Bridport. Luckily, there was no traffic on the roundabout and no damage was done. I pulled into the next lay-by and thought for awhile about what to do. I tried my brakes again and as they appeared to be working I continued to Bournemouth. I recounted the incident to Andrew over a cup of coffee in his flat. After we had finished our coffee, he decided to reassure me that there was nothing wrong with my car. He was driving and I was the passenger. We weren't going fast, but were heading towards a brick wall. I was convinced we were going to crash into it. Andrew applied the brakes and we stopped with no problem. I had no further incidents with the brakes, but when I got back to North Devon I took the car to the garage for it to be checked over. I was told there was nothing wrong with the brakes, but the same problem occurred again. I took the car back to the garage as

I wasn't going to keep the car if they couldn't find and repair the fault, which they did. The brakes failed when the linings were hot. The incident on the way to Bourne-mouth happened after descending a steep Dorset hill. By the time Andrew and I had had our coffee, the brake linings were cold. The second incident was after descending a steep Devon hill.

Andrew stayed in his initial job for eighteen months. He worked for a company that specialised in motorbike insurance. He warned me to check both ways when in the middle of a pedestrian crossings in case a motorcyclist, passing the line of stationary cars, failed to stop at the crossing. The saddest part of his job was the contact with parents of young riders who had been killed or injured. He'd started studying again for his insurance exams but lost heart when he failed one set of exams. He made no further attempts at any exams. His next job had more responsibility. He was working in a motor insurance office in Basingstoke settling personal injury claims. After he'd been there a few months, we went house-hunting. There were plenty of new houses but little sense of community. Andrew didn't move to Basingstoke, but commuted by train in the summer months and stayed in digs during the week in the winter.

With my parents' house sold, Andrew back at work, and my mother beginning to give the impression she liked Malvern, it seemed the worst of the traumas following my father's death were over. It was around then I had a brief episode which was the nearest I came to suffering from depression. I had not seen Dr A for over eighteen months, and didn't go to see him, but had a telephone conversation with him. Veronica had been seeing an acupuncturist and I contacted the practice to request a home visit. Alison came to my house and stuck a number of needles in my back. Such a treatment could not change the problems I was dealing with, but could shift or unblock my energies so I was again able to think about how I dealt with my situation. I continued to see Alison from time to time until I left North Devon.

While my and my family's situations had improved over the previous twelve months, none of us was settled. I did not feel my mother could be reasonably alright until she had her own home. Andrew was keeping his head above water, but I knew he was not happy with his job. I didn't feel he was ready to make changes, and probably would not do so until our mother was more stable. We were both aware stability in our own lives helped her, and she did respect that we both had to work. My mother and I were getting on slightly better since she'd moved to Malvern. I think she was relieved the family home had been sold. She was unable to say that to me and what I had done when clearing her house was added to the list of accusations she made about me when she was distressed.

There were many plusses to my new life in Barnstaple. I was happy with my flexible working arrangements; it gave me time for other interests. Although I was still a member of the Devon Guild of Weavers, Spinners and Dyers, I had ceased attending monthly meetings in Exeter. During the time I lived in Ted and Veronica's house, Veronica had become interested in spinning, bought a spinning wheel, joined the Guild and attended meetings. Sometimes at meetings she made loud and personal comments about me to others. Two of my spinning friends separately told me they were happy to see me but they did not want to know Veronica. I stopped attending Guild meetings, not because of Veronica's comments about me, but because of the circumstances of the double life with Ted.

I had long been interested in weaving, but decided, as I no longer went to the Guild, I would not buy a loom and learn to weave. Instead, I bought a double-bed knitting machine. I had many happy hours, dropping stitches and playing with colours until eventually I mastered the machine. I enjoyed visiting Terry, a farmer's wife. She had two pre-school age children, a passion for dogs, and shared my interests in knitting and sewing. I occasionally went to the Plough Arts Centre at Torrington and The Queen's Theatre in Barnstaple. I'd go bird-watching with a small group led by a married couple who were friends of Ted and Veronica's.

I had a week's holiday in the Lake District with Sally and her mother. Sally's mother lived in a village in North Cornwall. She and I took the scenic route north, driving through the Welsh borders and avoiding motorways as much as we could. Sally joined us at the guest house near Keswick. We did some sightseeing and had a number of walks, agreeing we'd each go at our own pace and meet up afterwards. Sally's mother and I walked to the top of Skiddaw. She had no special walking gear, just her headscarf, raincoat and flat shoes and a supermarket carrier bag; a marked contrast to other walkers. Her humorous article about our assent was published in a magazine.

As I still had flexible working arrangements, I sign up for a City & Guilds Part 1 Creative Studies – Fashion course at the local college. It covered design, pattern cutting, and sewing. Attendance was one afternoon a week during term time for two years. We had practical projects that involved designing and making garments, learning about different types of fibres and fabric construction, and a project on the history of fashion. Jenny, our tutor, was enthusiastic and the classes were enjoyable. One classmate was Stephanie, who was a professional seamstress specialising in making wedding dresses. She lived with her mother, who made delicious ginger cakes, and her daughter in the same village as Terry. Our History of Fashion projects were the perfect excuse to visit Bath a number of times to shop and do research at the Fashion Museum.

The pattern of my contact with Ted and Veronica, and with Edward, changed little but my feelings for Edward did change. I cared deeply about what happened to him. Perhaps that could be termed I loved him, but it was not a romantic type of love and I didn't want to marry him, though I would have been happy to spend more time with him. Maybe Kitty's influence as my role model in my teens still affected me. I was aware that she had had a close male friend. They had their own homes and careers, went on cruises together, and were thought of as an item. Nowadays they would probably be termed 'separate-togethers'.

I accepted Ted's family circumstances were part of who he was, in the same way that my family circumstances were a part of me. Sometimes, he would talk about his duty towards Veronica because she was the mother of his children. Although by the time I met him he was not a regular churchgoer, the Christian values he had received in childhood appeared to be strong in him, and his marriage vows had meaning for him. I would never have expected him to initiate divorce proceedings, but if Veronica had wanted a divorce, I felt it would be unlikely he would have opposed it on religious or other grounds. He told me a number of times I saw him through 'rose-coloured spectacles', or that he was taking my attention away from other men I could meet. I doubt he understood my teenage resolve not to be in a relationship. Perhaps with Edward it was safe because I knew it would be unlikely to develop into a conventional relationship. Rightly or wrongly, I had satisfied myself that I was not damaging Ted and Veronica's relationship. I believed Edward when told me I helped him support Veronica. Was I being naïve? Edward acted towards me in loving, thoughtful ways and he knew how to give, take, and share pleasures. One of his sayings was, 'I'm all right if I know you are all right'. He talked to me about his children and what was going on in their lives and his concerns for them as they settled into relationships and Ted and Veronica's first grandchildren were born. He said little about the detail of his day-to-day relationship with Veronica. At times, Edward would visit and say little about anything other than the weather. When he was like that it seemed he just wanted to be held, and at such times, if I held him long enough, I would feel the tension in his body easing.

I spent a week in midsummer with Sally and her mother on holiday in the Shetlands. We flew to Lerwick, toured the islands, and took boat trips to see seals and cliffs covered with colonies of gannets and puffins. We walked across the nature reserve to the Shetlands' most northerly point. Skuas were nesting near the path. They dive-bombed us, which I found a scary experience as skuas have a four or five foot wingspan. On my return home I found Edward had been to my house and there were numerous red and green ribbon crosses up the stairs and around the house

In the spring of 1986, my mother decided that she wanted to buy a flat in Malvern. She found a second floor flat close to the park and within walking distance of the town centre. The only disadvantage I could see was that there was no lift. It had two bedrooms and the south facing sitting room had a balcony, which my mother filled with plants. Before she moved in, my mother had the kitchen and bathroom refitted, the flat decorated, and new curtains and carpets fitted. My mother had clearly turned a corner. Once she had the key after the legal formalities were completed she did not involve Andrew or me in getting the flat ready for her to move in. She had created a home for herself that epitomised all that was important to her. The glass-fronted walnut veneer corner cupboard contained some of the china she had collected over the years. Her pot lid collection was hanging on the walls in the sitting room, hall and small bedroom. In the small bedroom she kept a Z-bed folded up for use when either Andrew or I visited. One wall was taken up with a floor-to-ceiling bookcase and the rest of the room was devoted to sewing and embroidery. She had been a widow for five years and finally it seemed she had emerged to rejoin the world.

I'd lived in Barnstaple for over two years and my life was more settled than it had been since my father's death. I didn't want my legal career to remain centred on conveyancing, but I did wish to remain in private legal practice as I enjoyed the contact with clients. I wanted a job where the majority of my time was spent on probate work. I had not done any additional continuing professional training for some time, and decided to take a taxation correspondence course to update my knowledge. I did give the course adequate time and put in sufficient effort, but however hard I tried, I was not getting a proper grasp on the material I was studying. I was concerned at my failure and the implications for my ability to do my work to the professional standard I expected of myself.

One morning two weeks after my mother had moved into

her flat, I was standing at my kitchen sink under the window overlooking the garden when a thought hit me with such force it felt as if it had been shot from the heavens through the window to crash upon my head. The thought was, 'Give your notice in this morning. It is time you sorted out your own life'. One hour later I had handed my notice in. For the next two months I was busy at work and then at the beginning of December, I was unemployed.

At last I had a few weeks to think about what I wanted to do with my life. Since leaving Bristol in January 1981 when my father was ill, I had been reacting to events. Careerwise, I was where I was in 1979, spending most of my time doing conveyancing. I wanted to move from North Devon as I knew while I lived there I would not be free from the influence of Ted and Veronica or the restraints I'd placed upon myself over Edward. It was around that time I heard Veronica was planning to go abroad for a year to work. I did ask Edward whether he wished me to remain in North Devon, but he said he didn't.

I wanted to work with people as that was the part of my job I enjoyed most. I had considered training in one of the complementary health therapies. Acupuncture appealed most, but when I thought about it, I didn't want to be sticking needles in people. I had been accepted to train as a volunteer counsellor with CRUSE, the bereavement charity. I had also enrolled at the local college on a pilot course of what was to become Access Courses for adults going into further education. The course was half a day a week for three months. We looked at study skills and had opportunities for careers advice and guidance on the suitability of further education courses. I was in the second year of the part-time City & Guilds Fashion course, which I would finish in June. I obtained my City & Guilds certificate, but sewing was a hobby, not something I wanted to use to earn my living.

In the college's careers office I came across information about a Sixth Formers' Conference to be held at Loughborough University during the Easter vacation. It was about studying psychology at university. I was toying with the idea of going to university and thought the two days at Loughborough would help me decide if that was what I wanted to do. The conference included lectures on various topics that might be part of a psychology degree.

After the conference, I spent a couple of days with my mother before returning home on 1 April. When I got home there were two letters waiting for me from solicitors. One was the offer of a fulltime job in Barnstaple doing conveyancing and the other an enquiry from Jeremy about the possibility of doing some part-time work on trust files in the probate department in one of his offices near Exeter.

I'd decided after the conference that I would apply to Exeter University for a place on the psychology undergraduate course. I met the University's Admissions Officer before making a formal application to ask if they would accept me without doing some prior studying. I completed my UCAS form, the formal application for a university place, and sent it off.

Then I went to see John, who had offered me the fulltime job, and explained I'd just applied to go to university in Exeter but I didn't know if I would be going that autumn or the following year. We agreed I'd work on a temporary basis until either I wanted to move to Exeter or he found someone on a permanent basis. So, much to my surprise, I was back working fulltime, which I hadn't done for almost five years.

I had a reply from UCAS so quickly that I thought it was the acknowledgement, until I opened it to find I had been offered a place at Exeter University starting that autumn. The solicitor whom John employed in my place wanted to start the Monday after the Friday I wanted to leave.

Fortunately, the changes in my employment status did not appear to have any adverse effect on my mother. When she first moved into her flat she got into the habit of phoning both Andrew and me on Sunday mornings. Andrew and I discovered she sometimes told us different things, usually about problems she said were worrying her. We continuously monitored her circumstances and decided that before responding to anything she said to us individually we would speak with each other. That way we talked to her only about concerns she raised with the both of us. There was a danger we'd overlook something needing our attention, but it wasn't long before she stopped raising red herrings with us.

She had renewed her contact with The Aetherius Society and joined a cake decorating class. She was happy to drive to Cheltenham, Evesham, Worcester, and Chipping Camden in the Cotswolds. My mother attended a number of day workshops on embroidery run by a needlecraft shop there. There was a Wool Mill on one of her routes which specialised in mohair yarns. She knitted numerous mohair jackets and often gave me cones of mohair wool. Andrew or I visited her once a month. Sometimes we'd both visit and all enjoy walking on the Malvern Hills or visit an exhibition at the NEC in Birmingham.

I hadn't had any contact with computers since I left Bristol. By 1987 personal computers were readily available, but not yet user friendly. William, an architect, bought one for use in connection with his work. He was self-employed and didn't have the time to read the instructions and master the computer. For a few weeks, his Amstrad sat on my sewing table and I had the opportunity to learn how to use it. I don't know if anything I showed him helped him, but I was glad to have been introduced to word processing before I went to university.

I completed the training with CRUSE and was accepted as a volunteer counsellor, and attended the monthly supervision and training meetings in Barnstaple until I moved to Exeter and joined the Exeter branch of CRUSE. I made contact with The White Eagle Lodge. The local group met in Exeter, and I started going to monthly meetings.

I put my Barnstaple house on the market and contacted estate agents in Exeter. In 1987, house prices were rising, and the agents had few houses on their books that were not under offer. Stephanie came to Exeter with me on one occasion when I was looking at properties on the east of the city. She commented that if I lived on that side of the city my friends from North Devon would have a job to find me. I wanted to be within easy walking distance of the university, as my budget on a student grant would be tight and I did not know if I could replace my car. My chief priority financially was to remain a home owner, as I knew if I went into rented accommodation it might be difficult with rising house prices to get back on the housing ladder three or four years' later. I was also getting a slightly bigger mortgage than I needed to buy a house so that I would have some cash at the end of the three years at university.

I was not feeling inspired by any of the house particulars the agents sent to me. I looked at the outside of one house in the corner of a cul-de-sac, but decided not to view. Shortly afterwards the only property for which I had been sent particulars was another house in the same cul-de-sac. I decided if I didn't show interest and view some properties the agents would think I wasn't serious in wanting to buy.

I was going away for a week's holiday and decided to view the house on the Saturday morning. The owner showed me around, and, much to my surprise, I decided it was a property that would suit me well and was reasonably priced. So I offered the asking price, only to be told that it was already sold and someone would be signing the contract very soon as they were waiting for their mortgage offer to be processed.

I went into the estate agent's office to tell them I had made an offer for the property but the owner had told me it was already sold. I explained that I'd be away for a week, gave them my office phone number and repeated my offer. I got the impression he didn't believe I was a solicitor.

'Well, if I'm meant to have that house I will, you'll see,' I said as I left.

He raised his eyebrows and gave me a look that said, 'We get one like her every Saturday morning'.

I went on holiday and didn't think about the house or my offer any more until back at work and going through the accumulated messages with my secretary.

'The estate agents in Exeter want you to phone them about the house you are buying,' she said.

It was my turn to do a double take as she handed me the note.

When I phoned the agents I discovered that the other prospective purchaser had phoned them on the Wednesday of my holiday week to withdraw her offer. That was when the agents phoned my secretary. Apparently, the first prospective purchaser contacted the agents on the Thursday to say she was going ahead with her purchase after all. She was told that the vendors had accepted another offer. My house in Barnstaple had not sold but I was confident that with the rising market it would sell, so I obtained bridging finance to complete the purchase of my Exeter house about five weeks before the university term began.

I had bought a three-bedroom semi-detached house. The lounge–dining room had French windows at each end. At the dining-room end they opened into the garden, which consisted of a square of lawn surrounded by low shrubs and, on the northern boundary, three laburnum trees. At the lounge end they opened on to a west facing balcony above the garage. The carpets and curtains had been left. I acquired a bed for the Exeter house and brought sufficient belongings from Barnstaple to be comfortable until the Barnstaple house was sold.

9

University

EXETER University's Studies Skills' counsellors invited mature students who had not been studying for a while to attend a two day workshop before starting their undergraduate courses. We had talks and practice on note taking, advice on reading textbooks and journals, exercises in essay writing and a visit to the library. To my surprise I had problems writing essays and note taking. I arranged to meet a Studies Skills' counsellor, Anne Wyatt, after the beginning of term, but I was wondering what I had got myself into – two houses, a mortgage, bridging finance, no job, and doubts about whether I was capable of doing the work required at university.

The following week was Freshers' Week and my introduction to university life. The main Exeter University campus is on a hill, ten minutes walk from the centre of the city and twenty minutes on foot from my home. The campus then was one of Exeter's best kept secrets. My daily walks were through landscaped parkland and gardens with specimen trees, a variety of ornamental shrubs, lakes and streams.

The morning of my first day at university was spent sitting on the floor in a corridor in the Psychology Department outside the room of the lecturer who had to see all first year students individually. There were six or seven other mature students among the teenagers fresh from school or a gap year. It was there I met Pauline, who was a couple of years older than me and lived in Torquay. She had been studying psychology with the Open University and had come to Exeter University initially for one year under a scheme piloted by the Open University. In the afternoon, the Freshers gathered in the Great Hall for the welcoming address by the Vice Chancellor.

The morning had brought home to me that I was embarking on a new phase of my life. I no longer had a desk, telephone, secretary, filing cabinets containing my workload, or responsibilities to any clients other than my parents' friend, Mrs Harries, for whom I was attorney. She was living in the same nursing home. She died while I was at university.

Anne Wyatt worked out what I was and was not doing when reading and taking notes. We decided I'd missed some education in primary school which affected how I processed words. Anne gave me a list of vowel combinations and how they were pronounced. She advised me to get a good dictionary and to use it. She made me promise not to abandon my course without talking with her, and to contact her about any study problems I encountered. I thought a word processor would help. When my Barnstaple house sold at the end of October I bought an Amstrad computer identical to the one William had lent me that summer.

The underlying emphasis of the degree I was studying was on the scientific nature of psychology. Had my decision to study psychology been free from the pressures in my personal life, it is likely that I would have looked at other psychology degree courses and would not have chosen one with such a scientific approach. I cannot now recall the detail of my undergraduate studies. I enjoyed the lectures by Ian Gordon and Dave Earle on perception. I did not enjoy reading about the research experiments carried out on animals in connection with perception and conditioning. I found Stephen Lea's and Denver Daniels's topics of animal behaviour and observational studies interesting. I still think of Stephen when I see blackbirds on a lawn extracting worms. His lectures convinced me that working no more than twenty hours per week was all that was needed to provide the necessities of life. Dick Eiser lectured on attitudes. For me, understanding attitudes and how they are formed and used is key to gaining a deeper understanding of complex situations and interactions between people.

Friends from North Devon visited me when they were in Exeter. Edward was a frequent visitor at my house in Exeter. He was known as Edward and not Ted on the rare occasions when he had contact with anyone in my circle in Exeter. I was more comfortable about my relationship with Edward, as I had convinced myself Ted was no longer in a conventional married relationship with Veronica. What remained was his 'duty to the mother of his children' and his wish 'to maintain family unity', as he put it. If Ted had not been responsible in his attitudes towards Veronica and his family I would not have wanted to know him.

Edward and I had easier telephone contact while Veronica was abroad. After she'd been away for six months, I felt Edward was more relaxed in himself. I became aware of a subtle change in him about two months before Veronica was due to return home. It felt as if some of the old tension in him was returning. He never discussed it directly with me, but the impression I had was that for Veronica, absence had made the heart grow fonder, but whether of him or her life in England, or both, I did not know. Perhaps, for Ted, absence had made him appreciate having his own space. My absence from North Devon had also created more space for him.

Edward and I found new favourite places for walking when he and Jake came to visit. In winter we'd frequently go to the beach at Exmouth, where dogs were allowed, or along the Exe estuary to go bird-watching. We also liked the Otter estuary and would extend walks along the coastal path towards Sidmouth. Other times we'd visit Sidmouth and walk inland along the ridge overlooking the valley where I had spent my childhood, and through the woods and the paths at the top of the golf course up the road from the convent. Once or twice on a summer's evening we'd go up there to listen to nightjars. Closer to Exeter we would go to the woods adjoining Killerton House, a National Trust property. Edward wouldn't go into Exeter city centre with me as he thought it was likely he would meet someone he knew. When anyone was approaching while on one of our rural or coastal walks and we were holding hands, he would let go of my hand and assume his 'uncle' persona.

In complete contrast to my degree studies, I attended a weekly White Eagle absent healing group in Exeter. The group was lead by Ann, a widow in her sixties. Another regular member of the group was Eileen, about twenty-five years older than me. According to White Eagle's teachings,

> 'Spiritual healing awakens and strengthens the inner light – the Christ self – which gradually takes control, bringing increased mental and emotional harmony, restoring and recharging the diseased body. Spiritual healing firstly restores the soul, and the physical healing follows.

> 'Absent healing is given by groups, each consisting of six healers under the leadership of one who is a member of the White Eagle Star Brotherhood and specially trained in the projection of healing power by thought and prayer. The healing groups meet weekly and each gives individual treatment to between fifteen and twenty patients. The soul of the patient is alerted and linked to the healing centre by calling of the full name, which sets up a powerful vibration in the invisible ether. Healing rays of light and colour according to White Eagle's prescription are then poured onto that soul through the thought and prayer of the sitters in the group'.[1]

I attended the monthly supervision and training meetings of the Exeter branch of CRUSE. The local organiser of the branch received the requests for counselling, and allocated each referral to an appropriate volunteer counsellor, who then arranged to meet the bereaved person. Each counsellor has a supervisor, who was an experienced member of CRUSE.

Generally, the training was done by senior branch members. I can recall one session which was run by a guest speaker. It was a role-play exercise where the scenario was the death of a young child. We were allocated different roles within the family; I role-played a surviving sibling. After the role-play we had a discussion about the different needs of the family members when grieving, and the special considerations when a child is bereaved. All regarding the training evening was handled correctly but I recall experiencing a reaction afterwards that was out of proportion to what had happened in that training session.

During the first university summer vacation I had to do a book review assignment. We had been given a list of eighty titles from which to choose one to review. The book I chose was *The Wound and the Doctor: Healing, Technology and Power in Modern Medicine* by Glin Bennett.

'Traditional Indian Medicine' was the heading for the last four pages of the chapter entitled 'Harmony and Balance in the Human System'. The author wrote:

> 'Early Indian medicine, which developed into the Ayurvedic system, had a recognisable humoral structure a good five hundred to a thousand years before Greek medicine; and there is good evidence of its spread westwards to ancient Greece'.[2]

In the notes to that chapter Bennett wrote:

> 'Also I have felt that the underlying ideas – particularly about the whole – in the Indian medical systems occur also in Chinese thinking, and I have chosen to concentrate on the Chinese. Nevertheless, the Indian systems deserve much closer study by Western scholars, who can deal with the primary sources, than they have hitherto received'.[3]

I knew a little about Chinese medicine as I had had acupuncture. Before completing the assignment, I looked at a book on complementary therapies to see if I could find anything about Ayurveda, and then gave it no further thought.

A few weeks later, Felicity, a yoga teacher who lived in London whom I'd met through The White Eagle Lodge, phoned me. We were discussing possible dates when we could meet.

'I think I'm on a course that weekend. Just a minute, I'll check the programme,' she said, putting the receiver down.

'It's here somewhere. . . umm . . . Ayurveda. Oh, here's the one I'm going on,' she said, reading the programme aloud to herself as she picked the receiver up.

'What did you say just then?' I asked.

She started to read details of the yoga course to me.

'No, before that,' I said.

'Ayurveda,' she said.

The four-day introduction to Ayurveda was to be held at a residential yoga centre run by The Yoga for Health Foundation charity. The centre occupied a large house, Ickwell Bury, in a peaceful rural setting near Biggleswade in Bedfordshire. Howard Kent, the founder of the charity, believed that yoga was for all, including anyone with a chronic illness or disability. The charity was known for its therapeutic work, especially with those who had multiple sclerosis. The cost of the Ayurveda course was reasonable and I decided a short break before starting the second year at university was a good idea.

Each morning before breakfast there was an optional yoga class. As the Yoga hall was used throughout the day for regular classes, the Ayurveda course was held in the centre's sitting room, a large room with easy chairs and a window seat filling the bay window, which was where I sat. The introduction to Ayurveda was given by Dr Vasant Lad, a native of Pune in India, and a practitioner and Professor of Ayurvedic Medicine. He spent part of his time in America, and in 1984 founded the Ayurvedic Institute in Albuquerque. The course was Dr Lad's first teaching engagement in England.

Dr Lad introduced us, in an eloquent and humorous manner, to the principles of Ayurveda, which has the same philosophical roots as yoga in the Vedas of India. Although Ayurveda was new to me, I felt I was being reminded of something familiar, as it had many resonances with my parents' interests in Eastern philosophies and naturopathy.

At the end of the first session Dr Lad had to cross the sitting room to the door. As he did that he stopped to speak with a lady in a wheelchair, squatting down to be at her level and speaking with tenderness and understanding. When he rose, he turned and was facing the bay window where I was sitting. Our eyes met. Nothing was said as he left the room, but I had the feeling I had met Dr Lad somewhere before.

After the course and shortly before leaving, I was going up the wide staircase at Ickwell Bury as Dr Lad was coming down. We stopped on the half landing. I thanked him for an enjoyable course and he asked me what I did.

'I am just about to start the second year of a three-year psychology degree,' I said.

'That is good. Finish your degree. There is plenty of time,' he said.

The amount and nature of reading and writing in the second year challenged me. I found most of the degree topics interesting and that carried me through on many occasions. The module I had most difficulty with was physiology. By Christmas I was close to giving up. There were too many words I could neither read nor write. Between Christmas and New Year I learnt a handful of keywords by segmenting them into syllables, then copying them over and over, and saying them out loud repeatedly to get their pronunciation until, after three days and many tears, I got a breakthrough. A further frustration was doing that amount of work just to enable me to read the textbooks and I still wasn't confident enough to be able to discuss the topic. I was tired of making the effort and felt I was close to running out of personal resources. I'd wanted to do the Brain and Behaviour Module in the third year, but decided I'd jeopardise my degree if I attempted it.

The most handicapping aspect of the deficiencies in my literacy skills was my feelings. The deficiencies were invisible so I didn't accept there was a real problem and it wasn't something I'd invented. My level of performance was inconsistent, with some days being worse than others. When reading on a bad day all the effort was on recognising the words and there was little comprehension of the text. I'd managed to get through it, but had learnt little. At those times it was best to give up and try later. More usually it was a smaller percentage of words that were not easy to recognise. It seemed the letters transposed themselves or the words didn't break down into the correct syllables so that bits of one syllable would be attached to another. As my vocabulary was limited there were words I'd recognise but, either did not know, or was not confident of knowing, their meanings. I could skip such words if the broad sense of the text could be obtained. That strategy failed when keywords were skipped or I was failing to cope with enough words, as happened when studying physiology. I did resort to the dictionary as Anne Wyatt had advised, but the interruption in reading and the assimilation of new meanings into the text was a slow process.

Sometimes I would make a mistake in the subject matter by misinterpreting a word early in a text. It was possible to misread a word a number of times before seeing that the printed word was not the word I took it to be. The false information absorbed had to be corrected when the realisation dawned that it was my own interpretation that was wrong rather than having the reference for an irrelevant and odd text. In reading the material I also had to deal with my frustration at having made yet another stupid mistake. I found it hard to evaluate texts I'd had difficulty with because I was never sure if it was me or the text.

The problems with essay writing centred on the choice of words. Sometimes I knew there was a word for what I wanted to say, but could not bring up the word or get an approximation so I could look it up in the dictionary. I had to rephrase what I wanted to say to words I could write down. If not confident about a word's meaning, I would be hesitant about using it, or would stop to check the word's meaning. The difficulty in clothing my thoughts in words affected the flow of my essays. A frequent criticism was my jerky style.

Spelling was another of my weaknesses. I could usually get the first syllable, but often the rest was a jumble with a reasonable approximation to the correct letters. Sometimes I had no idea how to spell a word or where to begin, and that could happen with short or common words as well.

The choice of words, spelling, transpositions of letters in

words I knew how to spell, or writing a totally different word to the one I had intended, meant my written work was very messy and I hated being so untidy. The word processor helped, and Edward read my essays before I handed them in.

Note taking had its problems too when I wasn't able to write down the word I wanted or only an approximation of it. If I concentrated too much on my notes I was missing the next points in the lecture. I could decipher my notes immediately afterwards but they had to be rewritten to be use later. If a word was spelt I'd hear a jumble of letters that had to be repeated slowly if I had to write it down.

I was inefficient using indexes because of problems with words and transposing numbers. So I'd often find myself on the wrong page. Time would be spent not finding the required information and backtracking to the index to start again. The microfiche in the library was my pet hate. If I knew the book was in the library I persisted. I once spent fifteen minutes looking up 'Gregory'. The frustration and annoyance with myself was enormous. I would not bring myself to ask for help because I felt stupid not being able to do something so simple. That was no reflection on the library staff, because they were always helpful when I did ask them anything.

During the three years I was at university, my mother's and brother's lives were settled, apart from Andrew not really enjoying his work, though he did do it competently. The three of us rented a cottage for a week's holiday in the Yorkshire Dales.

Andrew and I went on holiday together in Pembrokeshire, renting a bungalow in St David's. I'd taken my spinning wheel, dye pot, and some fleece, which I dyed before Andrew was awake. He complained about the smell from the dyeing when he came for his late breakfast, but after that we were out for the rest of the day. We decided our next holiday should be in France. Neither of us had been abroad since going to Ireland with our father in our teens.

When I saw Andrew at Christmas 1988, I asked him if he would like to have a holiday in America. I wanted to look at

The Ayurvedic Institute in Albuquerque. I'd started thinking I might like to go there for a while after finishing my degree. As I didn't like going to London for the day, it did seem ludicrous I was thinking of staying in an American city for a few months, and I wouldn't even go to America for a holiday without my big brother. Andrew spent a while thinking about my request before telling me we'd go, but I'd have to agree to his conditions. He stipulated I'd have to make all the arrangements, we'd fly direct as he didn't want to deal with changing planes, we could go to Albuquerque during the first week and after that I would have to do whatever he wanted to do.

All the arrangements were in place for Andrew and me to spend two weeks in America in April. I could sit in on classes at the Institute for three days. We were flying to and from Denver and the hire car was booked, but no other arrangements were made. Andrew drove our mother and me to Gatwick Airport as she wanted to see us off.

At the departure gate we said our goodbyes and then she said to us, 'There will be nobody in the country now that belongs to me.'

She then turned and walked away. I watched her go until she was lost in the crowd. On one level she appeared a lone, vulnerable figure, yet before we had taken off she would be driving on busy motorways on her way back to Malvern.

Andrew and I picked up a rental car at Denver Airport and spent a couple of nights in Denver before heading south to Albuquerque. We hadn't experienced such a wide, dry landscape before, a complete contrast from lush, green Devon. A sand storm was blowing as we approached Albuquerque on Interstate 25.

'Well, you wanted to come here', Andrew commented.

We found the Ayurvedic Institute. I went in to say 'Hello', or should that have been 'Hi', and to checked the arrangements for attending classes. Dr Lad was teaching between 6 and 9 p.m. that and the following two evenings. The Institute was smaller than I had expected. On the ground floor were the administration and reception areas where I met Charles, the Institute's administrator, and Teresa, with whom I had spoken on the phone. Dr Lad's consultation room was at the front of the building and at the rear was the herb department. On the lower floor were two pancha karma treatment rooms and the classroom.

Andrew and I went to take a look at Albuquerque – Route 66, Old Town and downtown around the Convention Centre – and get something to eat before he left me at the Institute for the evening class. I was not well the next day. Andrew explored more of Albuquerque before taking me to the Institute in the evening. On the morning of our third day in Albuquerque we drove up Sandia Crest, the 10,678 feet high summit of the Sandia Mountain, which rises above the city's eastern boundary, to appreciate the panoramic views. It is a wilderness area popular for hiking, biking and, in the winter, skiing, but the weekday morning we were there we had it to ourselves. In the evening I attended class again at the Institute.

I had had my visit to Albuquerque and, until we returned to Denver, I had agreed to do whatever Andrew wanted.

'What's next?' I asked.

Andrew smiled.

'The Grand Canyon', he said.

We left Albuquerque heading west on Interstate 40 towards Arizona. At Gallup we drove north to visit Canyon de Chelly. I was awed by the vastness of the landscape, and the power of nature and water to carve rock. We spent a night in Winslow. The next morning it was the Grand Canyon. We visited the Grand Canyon IMAX Theatre to have the big screen experience of going into the canyon.

We'd planned to spend our last day in Denver as we had an evening flight. Our final night in America was in Colorado Springs. The next morning Andrew wasn't feeling well and thought we ought to go direct to the airport to return the rental car. We did that and checked our bags in as early as we could. Andrew then said he was feeling ill and wanted to lie down. The person at the check-in desk summoned someone whose proper title and role I do not know, but she appeared to be employed by the airport in connection with passenger welfare. She told us the only place Andrew could lie down was a bed in one of the men's restrooms. She took us across the terminal and disappeared inside the restroom with Andrew. I settled myself on a seat on the opposite side of the concourse. When she emerged from the restroom she told me she would come back from time to time to check we were alright. When she did, she'd stop at the entrance to the men's restroom and bellowed, 'Woman entering, woman entering.' She came to collect us when it was time to be at the boarding gate.

We had been allocated seats immediately in front of the movie screen, with Andrew having an aisle seat. Once he had strapped himself in, he shut his eyes and I did not see him speak or move until after breakfast had been served and collected, and we were approaching Gatwick airport. I had seen people in meditation being very still and had heard of yogis meditating for hours, but I had no idea my brother, whether sick or well, could be in, or imitate, such a state. One or two passengers asked me if he was alright, and each time I replied in the affirmative. He did look peaceful with no signs of any distress, and I wasn't going to be the one to disturb him unnecessarily.

When he woke up he appeared fine, and made no comment to any of my enquiries about how he felt. He dismissed all my concerns about going home on his own. At the top of the steps to the train station at Gatwick, he gave me a quick hug and disappeared down the steps before I could say anything. Two days later he was back at work and I was back at university preparing for the end of year exams, all of which I passed.

The first half of the summer vacation was spent at home or doing legal locum work. Edward and I continued seeing each other on a regular basis. Usually he would come to Exeter and we would go to the coast or walk elsewhere in East Devon. Sometimes I would meet him and Jake at Tiverton for a walk along the canal towpath. Once or twice we had met on campsites in Savernake Forest or near Chepstow above the river Wye, before or after he had spent a few days walking Offa's Dyke, a linear earthwork and a hundred and seventy mile trail roughly following the Welsh-English border.

My visit to the Ayurvedic Institute had left me with mixed feelings. I'd been glad to have seen Dr Lad teaching again, and that confirmed I had met an exceptional person. It was possible to think of Dr Lad as an Indian guru and to indulge oneself on a 'guru trip'. I knew I did not want a guru trip to India, America, or anywhere else. I had had the opportunity to see the Institute, its location, and to talk with some of the students. I could see it might be possible for me to spend a few months in Albuquerque following graduation from the psychology degree, but I could not see how I would use the experiences gained in my life in England. I was no clearer about how to earn my living. I still did legal locum work occasionally, mainly time-consuming drafting or research work but I had no direct contact with clients. The literacy problems I was having at university were convincing me I would not be returning to a legal career. Something was drawing me to complementary medicine, and the obvious choice would still have been acupuncture, but I did not relate to the Chinese system in the way I was finding I related to Ayurveda. Dr Lad was coming to England again at the end of August. I decided to attend his seminar to have another opportunity to meet him. I hoped to clarify why I was even considering going to Albuquerque.

I enjoyed listening to Dr Lad again talking on introductory Ayurveda, which I was becoming more familiar with as I had his book, *Ayurveda The Science of Self-Healing: A Practical Guide*. At the seminar I met Dr Ann Roden, a registered medical practitioner. Over lunch she was talking about the organisation of the seminar, or rather the lack of organisation.

'Yes, I'd do it better', I commented casually.

I had been given the organisers' telephone number when I was in Albuquerque. When I phoned I was told they knew nothing about an Ayurveda seminar.

After the seminar I concluded any time spent with Dr Lad would be time well spent, but spending time in Albuquerque in the year following my degree could not be justified on any logical grounds connected with finding what I should be doing to earn a living. Apart from those I had met at the two Ayurveda seminars I'd attended in England, I didn't know anyone who knew what Ayurveda was. I hoped I'd find a job I wanted to do after discussions with the university's careers' adviser. I'd have been content to work in a medium-sized firm's probate department but my failure with the taxation course raised such big doubts in me I did not consider it as a serious option.

A few weeks after the seminar with Dr Lad, I received a letter from Ann enquiring whether I would be interested in being involved in organising a seminar the following year for Dr Lad. She wrote that she and her friend, Peter, had enough contacts to make it feasible.

My mother wanted a holiday in Yorkshire and to visit some of her old haunts. We booked a two-bedroom flat close to the river in York for a week in September. Andrew came by train for a long weekend. On the Sunday, we went to Doncaster, and my mother took Andrew and me for the first time to see the house where she was born. We visited Edna's grave in the local churchyard. Then we went to the village where my mother had lived until she was called up during the Second World War, and where my grandparents and uncle had farmed until they moved to a farm near Gainsborough when Andrew and I were children. We spent Monday in York, and visited the Jorvik Viking Centre before Andrew went home.

My mother and I had planned to spend the remaining four days in York and perhaps go to Scarborough. The morning after Andrew left my mother did not want to go out. I thought that if I went out for an hour I might, on my return, be able to persuade her to come out with me. But she still did not want to go anywhere and was not in a mood to be persuaded. Over the next couple of days I walked the city walls and then returned to tell her about it and see if she would come with me but she wouldn't. I acquired a leaflet on York's Snickleways, a maze of hidden alleyways, and followed the route around York. Again, I could not persuade my mother to come with me. I went to York Minster but, yet again, my mother was not interested. It seemed my mother was slipping into 'flipmode' and I was not getting through to her. Her mood deteriorated further and it seemed she was likely to be violent. I continued my short sightseeing walks around York as I did not know what to do to help her. When I returned from yet another walk and was sitting at the table having a snack, she want to beat me up.

'Okay, you can beat me up', I said.

For some reason all fear had left me for that moment. My mother crumpled, didn't touch me, and was quiet for the remainder of our stay. She told everyone, including Andrew and me, she'd enjoyed her week and hoped to go to Yorkshire again. It was only with hindsight I understood the true poignancy for my mother of the visit to the farm where she was born.

In October, the third and final year of my degree course began. I spent much time in the careers office but was not finding any answers about what to do next. The thought of going to Albuquerque kept recurring. I discussed the possibility from time to time with Andrew, and he cannot be faulted for the trouble he took to ensure I looked at it from every conceivable angle. He was not putting any pressure on me one way or the other, and I recognised elements of our father in him and how my father had reacted when I had told him I was not going to the College of Law to study for my Part II law exams. Andrew and I knew going to Albuquerque would not be a sensible financial decision, as I would use the money I had put aside when I started university. The decision could be put off and maybe, somehow, everything would become clearer during the following months.

During the Michaelmas and Lent terms I had six modules and a project to complete. In the child development module we had a seminar about abuse. The lecturer was describing the details of a research project where the researchers had decided to assess the level of abuse according to the size of bruises visible on the child's body. Part way through the seminar I was feeling so angry, but I did not trust myself to speak. Nothing was being said about psychological abuse, and I did not feel the size of bruises was the only valid measurement of child abuse. I felt angry for some time after the seminar, and my feelings were out of proportion to what had been said in the seminar room.

While I was at university, Andrew and I had visited our mother on a regular basis. After the Lent term, Andrew told me he did not expect me to visit her until my finals were over unless I wanted to. My exams revision timetable included yoga and relaxation. I had stopped using a word processor as soon as my continuous assessment work was finished. In the final exams I was able to let tidiness go out of the window, as Anne Wyatt had told the Psychology Department about the problems I had. I don't remember the detail of the exam weeks, just that at the end of them I was exhausted. I had had seven three-hour exams to sit; one for each module and a general paper. I had a stroke of luck in the general paper as a topic I'd revised well for the perception paper came up. I had anticipated the general paper would be my worst paper; it turned out to be my best.

There was a three week wait before we got our degree results. During the wait I had ten consecutive days of Ayurvedic foot pressure massage *Chavutti Thirumal,*. The therapist massages the client, who is lying on the floor, with his foot, while balancing and supporting himself with the aid of a rope suspended from the ceiling; thus the client receives long sweeping strokes. A greater amount of oil is used in Ayurvedic massage than, for example, in aromatherapy. Duncan Hulin, a yoga therapist and teacher had studied in India with Dr B. P. Pillai at his Institute of Yogic Culture in Kerala, South India, and conducted his massage practice from his home fifteen miles from where I lived. I visited each morning and spent the rest of the day relaxing; for me it was the perfect antidote after the exams.

Results day dawned and with some trepidation I went to the Psychology Department and was delighted with my results; I'd achieved a 2:1 degree. Pauline had transferred from the Open University to Exeter at the end of the first year and graduated with us. An abiding memory of that day was the exuberance of Steph, classified as a mature student because she was just over twenty-one when we were Freshers, on achieving a first class degree.

I would not have attempted the degree had I known the extent of the literacy problems I'd encounter, but determineation and my interest in the subject had carried me through. Despite the hard work I did not regret doing the degree, and was pleased I had done a psychology degree that had an emphasis on its scientific nature. I'd enjoyed the opportunity to think about consciousness, the selective nature of sensory information and its manipulation, the central role of attitudes in connection with human interactions, and what it is to be a human being. Since graduating, I adapted the title of Thomas Nagel's paper, 'What is it like to be a bat?', to 'What is it like to be a particular human being?' I find that a useful reminder to myself that I can never know what another person's accumulated experiences are like for them.

The week our exam results were announced I had a telephone call from Betsy to tell me that her brother, Bert, had died suddenly. My mother had had no contact with Betsy or Bert since leaving Sidmouth. My mother contacted Betsy and their friendship resumed. They had a couple of holidays together and Betsy visited my mother in Malvern.

Earlier in the year, Ann Roden, her husband Ron, Peter and I had approached Dr Lad to ask if he would give another Ayurveda seminar in England. He agreed, and the four of us put some money in the kitty to fund the initial arrangements. Ann and Peter would make the contacts and I would find the venue and do the administration. Roger Hill, an acupuncturist and co-director of the Complementary Medicine Department at Exeter University, suggested the Quaker Hotel and Conference Centre, Old Jordans, near Beaconsfield in Buckinghamshire for the venue. The atmosphere there was perfect and they were experienced in catering for vegetarians. They generously agreed we could book just the conference facilities and they would deal with the accommodation individually with the delegates. The seminar was to be in September.

I had decided that if everything worked out I would go to Albuquerque that autumn. Soon after finishing at Exeter University, I had a few days' retreat at The White Eagle Lodge's centre at New Lands in Hampshire. That gave me an opportunity away from home to reflect on my decision to go to Albuquerque before making all the necessary arrangements. I had a peaceful stay and no new doubts came to my mind about going to Albuquerque. One evening, while waiting to go into dinner, a colourful hot-air balloon floated past the window. As I had not seen a hot-air balloon in England before, it was something I commented on. There is an international, hot-air balloon fiesta in Albuquerque in the autumn; perhaps the Hampshire hot-air balloon was a positive omen.

Back at home, I contacted a letting agent who advised me on letting my house. I was told I would not be able to let it unless I got an automatic washing machine – my twin tub was not acceptable – and my oak dining table was removed from the bedroom I'd been using as my sewing and study room over the previous three years. He advised on the rent I should expect to receive, and I said I'd be in touch once the house was ready for viewing. The agent phoned me before I'd had a chance to rearrange the furniture as he had an applicant who wanted to view. The applicant offered the rent I required and didn't want to move in until towards the end of September.

Letting my house set the pattern; everything I did to prepare for going to Albuquerque happened easily. I made short visits to Malvern over the summer to see my mother. We went shopping together in Worcester and Stratford. She'd read Dr Lad's book, *Ayurveda, The Science of Self-Healing*, and gave me every indication she was pleased I was going to Albuquerque for a few months. I'd received my visa and my flights were booked. Arrangements were in hand for my books and personal belonging to go into store whilst I was abroad.

The Ayurveda Seminar with Dr Lad in England was fully booked. The delegates, apart from one or two, worked either as complementary medicine therapists or within the allopathic system of healthcare. Dr Lad inspired them, and the success of the seminar laid the foundations for future visits by him and the formation of a number of friendships.

I stayed with Ann, the leader of the absent healing group for the week after vacating my house before I flew to America. Steph had invited Andrew and me to stay overnight with her and her parents so I'd be close to Gatwick airport. The next morning Steph and Andrew accompanied me to the airport and ensured I was on the flight to America.

10

Wide Horizons

THERE was no going back. I was on the plane to America. I had an aisle seat in the middle of the plane, sitting next to a toddler and her parents from Australia doing a round the-world trip. They were on their way to California. As we all settled in for the long flight they gave their daughter an 'Old MacDonald had a Farm' sticker book. She and I entertained each other with cows, pigs, sheep and horses until she fell asleep. I then closed my eyes, and allowed big tears to roll down my cheeks.

I had arranged to be met at Albuquerque Airport and taken to a house near the university owned by Torri, who shared it with six or seven students. It was late when I arrived. I was shown into a meditation room in the basement where I was given a mattress on the floor. I was just glad to have arrived in Albuquerque and wanted some sleep. Only Torri was in when I went up to the kitchen the next morning. She showed me the empty shelf in the double door fridge reserved for my use. I was still expecting to be offered something to eat and drink.

After a while she said, 'I'll take you to get some breakfast.'

We drove to a Mexican eating house near the university. The menu was in Spanish and I didn't recognise anything on it. I ordered some coffee and something off the menu which I would eat whatever it was. I was so hungry.

I was the second student from the Institute to lodge with Torri. I met Patricia later that day. Over the following days she shared her meals with me and ensured I had some food in the fridge. I moved into a small bedroom, and the jetlag was receding. JW was the next Ayurvedic student to arrive. He drove me the eight miles to the Institute. I was beginning to think I had made a serious mistake in not allowing for a car in my budget. I would be dependent on always needing lifts back to my digs after evening classes. Apart from that, I was not happy at Torri's house. I felt Torri would have preferred a 'spiritual lame-duck', whose inner development she could influence. I hadn't found my feet in Albuquerque, but I was not a 'spiritual lame-duck' and would not be happy around her influence.

At the Institute it was suggested I look at an apartment complex about a mile away. When I'd been planning my visit to Albuquerque I had considered renting my own apartment, but rejected the idea as I thought it might isolate me and I didn't want to have to deal with utility companies or perhaps a difficult landlord. But after my experiences with Torri I was having second thoughts.

The complex had a number of two or three storey apartment blocks arranged in the middle of a fenced compound with parking around the perimeter fences. The apartment blocks were randomly arranged and reached by paths curving through grassed areas with sprinklers and landscaping that had yet to mature. It would be a pleasant and convenient place to live. It was on a direct bus route to the Institute and not too far to walk in an evening after buses had ceased running for the day. As all utilities were included in the rent I wouldn't get any unexpected bills, nor I would feel isolated as the Institute's administrator and receptionist lived there. My reason for being in Albuquerque was to spend time at the Institute. So I convinced myself renting an apartment where the essentials were within walking distance was a sensible idea. Apartment H17 became my home while I was in Albuquerque.

H17 was on the second storey, carpeted but not furnished. The front door opened into the living room which had a sliding door to the balcony, and was separated from the kitchen area by a breakfast bar. The walk-in closet off the bedroom was about the same size as one of my bedrooms at home. JW and others helped me get a mattress and bedding, two small armchairs, a coffee table, a couple of pans and a few pieces of cutlery and crockery from a thrift store. I discovered yard sales and acquired a few more odds and ends for H17. I had all I needed to be comfortable and cook my meals. Adjacent to the back entrance of the complex was a farmers' market shop. Abertsons Supermarket was opposite the Institute and there were other shops within walking distance.

Once the phone was connected I phoned my mother who had gone into 'flipmode'. She was not interested in anything I had to tell her, was distressed that nobody cared about her problems and how she couldn't cope, and blamed me for going away and leaving her. Nor was she able to tell me what she had been doing. A few days after I had flown to America she'd had a week's holiday in St Ives with Betsy. Andrew had said they'd enjoyed the holiday, as her postcard from Cornwall confirmed. I'd sent Andrew a postcard soon after I'd arrived in Albuquerque so he'd know I had landed safely. I said I kept having moments of homesickness, but basically I was okay. I had not telephoned him as my voice would have been a giveaway and I'd have been bound to cry on hearing him. I was so unhappy during the first ten days in Albuquerque I'd have been on the next plane home if I hadn't let my house. With no house and no job in England, there seemed little point in returning. H17 made all the difference and I was meeting other people who had come from the East or West coasts, or had interrupted settled lives because something had inspired them to find out more about Ayurveda and spend some time listening to Dr Vasant Lad.

There had been changes at the Ayurvedic Institute since I'd visited with Andrew eighteen months earlier. The classroom was bigger and was on the same level as the reception area. Shoes were not worn in the carpeted classroom, but left on racks outside the door. There was a large blackboard on the wall above the twelve-inch high dais, covered with an oriental rug, on which Dr Lad sat cross-legged when teaching. Many of the students would sit cross-legged on cushions in front of Dr Lad and those who preferred chairs sat behind them. There were always flowers and plants in the classroom. On the wall at the back of the classroom were notice boards, a number of anatomical charts and a diagram of the chakras. A glass fronted wall cupboard contained herb samples.

Three framed and garlanded pictures of Hindu gods hung on the walls. On a small table covered with a red and gold cloth was a statue of Lord Ganesh, and hanging on the wall above was a painting by Dr Lad of Lord Ganesh. Ganesh is the elephant-headed god, the first Lord of the Gods and the remover of obstacles.

One of the pictures was of Dhanvantri, the God of Healing and Ayurveda. Dr Lad explained:

> 'Dhanvantri is an incarnation of Lord Vishnu, who is the protector, the sustainer of life. The whole world was suffering from disease, as now. Disease begins in attachment and fear, which both breed anger. The disease process begins in the mind, in their consciousness. Everyone was looking to some remedy, some cure, to remove the disease and to live long.
>
> 'Since the beginning of the world there have been two streams – the stream of clarity, called devas, and the stream of confusion, called demons. The demons are your negative thinking – anger, hate, envy, jealousy, judgement, criticism. The devas are awareness, love, compassion, care, forgiveness, the God aspect in you.
>
> 'The devas and the demons decided to churn the ocean of consciousness. They brought a big meru (mountain), which is nothing but the spinal-cord, and a Cobra, which is Kundalini Shakti. The ocean is your daily operating consciousness.
>
> 'So devas and demons, positive and negative energies, churned the ocean and on the thirteenth day Lord Vishnu came up from the bottom of the ocean in human form as Lord Dhanvantri, but with four hands. In his hands were a conch, a wheel, a leech, and a pot of amrit kalash.
>
> 'If you blow the conch it creates a sound – om – and sound is

used for healing. The conch is a symbol of mantra (sound). The wheel is light, the circle of light, a very short wavelength which cuts the darkness and removes the attachment. The leech is a bloodsucker, but its saliva contains an anti-coagulant substance that purifies the blood, and can even heal gangrenous tissue.

'Amrit kalash means the nectar, the holy sacred vessel of nectar that removes the disease, that gives you longevity, bliss, joy, contentment, happiness. Lord Dhanvantri brought back a vessel of Ambrosia for this planet to cure all the mental, the physical and the spiritual suffering of mankind.

'What is the meaning of Dhanvantri? One meaning of "Dhana" is wealth. "Antar" means internal. So Dhanvantri means "the God who gives the inner wealth". And what is inner wealth? Health is the wealth, good health – physical, mental and spiritual. When the three aspects of human life are perfectly healthy, that is the wealth. So Dhanvantri is the lord of wealth, of health.

'The second meaning of "Dhana" is a bow. An inner bow with an arrow killed the disease, the suffering. So Dhanvantri is the Lord who heals suffering. There is no healing without killing. You have to kill bad elements, the bad habit, bad diet and toxins through right attitude, right intention, right awareness, right thinking, right diet, right lifestyle and the right kind of clear relationships'.[1]

Dr Lad started his teaching sessions with a melodious chant in Sanskrit. He taught in the traditional manner through the use of Sanskrit sutras. Many hundreds of years ago in India, Ayurveda was an oral tradition transmitted through generations from teacher to student. The body of the Ayurvedic knowledge was recorded in poetic verses or sutras. A sutra acted as an aide-mémoire, which did not contain full information and needed interpretation from a wise teacher or guru. The chanting at the beginning of the class, in addition to drawing the attention and energies of those present to focus on the class, attuned the learning process to the accumulated wisdom of Ayurveda on subtle levels.

That method of learning was a contrast to the Western learning methods I had been using at university. My experiences of Western education had been a 'stuffing' of information into my head, filling it with facts that I would need to answer exam questions. Guru means 'to lead out from'. I experienced the Eastern style of teaching to be a leading out from the head into unlimited universal knowledge that was cohesive and comprehensive. The tools to access such universal knowledge were a disciplined and open rational mind working in tandem with a sensitive and intuitive mind. The individual and their personal development couldn't be separated from the acquisition of knowledge.

Dr Lad was well versed in allopathic medicine and he blended the Eastern and Western models of health and disease, treatments and healings in such a way that an understanding grew of wholeness and the interleaving levels of a human being, each person's uniqueness, connectedness with community, and dependence on the bounty of nature and of the Earth for existence and survival. Ayurveda is indeed the science of life.

Dr Lad's teachings ranged from the Absolute to the minutiae of an individual's daily existence and how, for example, to deal with indigestion. For me, holding all this together was a growing appreciation of recognising patterns and relationships, which according to context, could be analysed using the Ayurvedic way of thinking. Also emerging for me were the beginnings of knowing *the* universal energy is unconditional love and that human evolution, as well as individual growth, involves an awareness and manifestation of such energy. Physical, mental, and emotional *dis*-ease disrupts the manifestation, but can be used by an individual as a tool for growth in awareness.

The group in the classroom consisted of a core group, most of whom, like myself, were newly arrived in Albuquerque. We had chosen to spend time listening to Dr Lad's teachings and gain an understanding of Ayurveda through the structured presentation offered by the Institute. Those visiting the Institute for treatments took the opportunity to sit in on the classes. Some present resided in Albuquerque and had ongoing, periodic attendances at the Institute. The core group possessed a wide range of life experiences and skills, and accepted there was a 'spiritual' dimension to life.

Dr Lad is Hindu and in a very natural way I learnt more about the practices and Gods in Hinduism. There was no pressure at all to embrace Hinduism. In fact Dr Lad was very clear about people staying with what was familiar and meaningful to them. I heard him talk about Christ in a more profound way than I had heard any Christian talk. What I picked up as important is the expression of love that is the true message of all religions, the human need for something sacred in life, and a safe means of going beyond oneself and resting in the sacred.

The classes prior to Christmas laid the foundations of Ayurveda's basic principles and its concepts of health and disease, learning about the body and mind from an Ayurvedic perspective, many new Sanskrit words, grasping concepts for which there are no words in the West, and learning to classify our experiences according to the doshas – vata, pitta, and kapha.[2] Put simply, they are vital energies.

> 'The three doshas are responsible for all physiological and psychological processes in [the] body and mind. They are dynamic forces that determine growth and decay. [All] physical characteristics, mental capacities, and emotional tendencies can be described in terms of the three doshas. ... The doshas ... cannot be detected with our senses, but their qualities can'.[3]

Dr Lad started with an outline of philosophies which are part of India's culture before giving us a fuller introduction to Sankhya's philosophy of manifestation. He explained that all creation is a dance between two energies: Purusha, which does not have any attributes and is 'unmanifested, formless, passive, beyond attributes, beyond cause and effect, space and time',[4] and Prakruti, which is 'the creative force of action, the source of form, manifestation, attrib-utes and nature'.[5] Prakruti is the primordial energy of the cosmos from which everything physical originates. That includes objects, matter, and energy that we can observe and measure, but thoughts and subtle energies are also regarded as part of the physical world. Purusha witnesses the evolving creation.

Sankhya's philosophy of creation gives a theoretical account of how primordial energy manifests through cosmic intelligence into the world we experience. Understanding the attributes of the five elements (ether, air, fire, water, earth) and of the three doshas provides a means of analysing an individual's constitution and the factors affecting their health and well-being.

A concept I first came across when learning about Sankhya's philosophy was ahamkara.

> 'It is a concept that is not fully formed in the West. Sometimes, the word "ego" is equated to ahamkara, but this is misleading, since ahamkara embraces much more. In essence, it is that part of "me" that knows which parts of universal creation are "me". It is my unique vibration to which all physical parts of "me" resonate. "I" am not separate from any part of creation, but "I" have an identity that differentiates and defines the boundaries of "me". All parts of creation have ahamkara, not only human beings'.[6]

The concept of ahamkara aided my thinking as I learnt more about Ayurveda's concepts of the disease process, immunity, and digestion. Ahamkara is my sense of 'I-ness'. An apple has an ahamkara: its apple-ness. So, for example, by eating an apple, the apple loses its ahamkara. Its physical structure, along with its associated qualities (including, for example, sweet or sour) gets absorbed into me through the digestive process. Generally, the effect of eating one apple would not have a noticeable beneficial or detrimental effect on my wellbeing, but the accumulated qualities in my food, life experiences, thoughts, and relationships form dynamic interactions that affect my wellbeing according to how I assimilate or respond to them. My ability to assimilate or respond will vary according to my constitution, my current balance of health, and the qualities in foods and experiences I encounter.

In contrast to Western science, which deals primarily with quantities that can be observed and measured (though this seems to be changing), Ayurveda deals with qualities, context, relationships and subtle energies. The initial key to understanding and using Ayurveda in one's daily life is to learn which qualities are associated with each of the three doshas.

Qualities come in pairs, being each end of a continuum. Three principal pairs are hot–cold, light–heavy and dry–oily, though every quality can be associated with one or more doshas. Among the qualities associated with vata are cold, light, and dry; with pitta, hot, light, and oily, and with kapha, cold, heavy, and oily. That may seem a strange starting point to learn about a complex system that understands the human body, is a comprehensive medical system, and is capable of being used by just about anybody to assist in managing their health and wellbeing in daily life. But consider how two familiar symbols, 0 and 1, form the basis of the binary system and play a crucial role in computer science and technology; the alphabet's twenty-six characters can be arranged in infinite ways to capture and convey concrete and abstract meanings. Every system takes time to learn, understand, and gain competence in, and it's like that with Ayurveda, whether using it for self-help or when training to be a practitioner.

By November there was snow on the top of the mountains above Albuquerque and I enjoyed a ride with JW to Sandia Crest. It was only a light covering of snow and there would have to be more before skiers would be up there. At Thanksgiving I went with fellow students, Lois and Sarah, to Bandelier, an area north of Albuquerque and west of Sante Fe. It contains the remains of cliffside dwellings and sites occupied by the Pueblo people between 1050 and 1550 AD. There was a paved path for visitors to follow and view some of the partially reconstructed ruins. Wooden ladders allowed visitors to climb into the ceremonial kiva. I enjoyed being away from the city. At dusk we joined our fellow students, Patty, Wynn and Bhakti, for a Thanksgiving supper around their campfire before returning to Albuquerque.

There were no classes at the Institute over Christmas and New Year. Jim and Jeanine invited me to join them and other friends for lunch on Christmas Day, and I indulged in pumpkin pie instead of Christmas pudding. On the following day, I visited Yosuna and stayed overnight in Santa Fe. I had a front seat on the Greyhound bus, which gave me a good view of the wide snow-covered landscape alongside Interstate 25. In the evening, Yosuna took me to a spa to experience a hot tub under the stars in the snow.

The next morning she was working, and I looked around Santa Fe with Veronica. Veronica was visiting an American friend she had met when working overseas. It was coincidence we both happened to be in Santa Fe that morning. I did find it strange that of all the people I knew in England it was Veronica who was in New Mexico, and for those few hours I returned to the pretence I thought and hoped was coming to an end. Edward and I had been corresponding regularly during the three months I had been in America. He had moved out of the family home into his own one-bedroom end-terrace cottage on one of the main roads through the market town.

Andrew had spent Christmas and New Year with our mother. He sent me a postcard to say he had had a reasonable Christmas, and they had visited Ludlow and Worcester. He had walked six miles along the canal in spite of the high winds. Andrew and I had exchanged letters on a regular basis and sent each other postcards. He sent me a number of postcards of Basingstoke and its high-rise office blocks. On the postcard of Basingstoke he sent me in the April he wrote, 'Hope this grim p/c of Basingstoke does not put you off wanting to return to UK. Promise this will be the last one from this location.'

The tempo of the classes increased in the new year. Our core group, which included a nurse and complementary therapists, was joined by four people who had allopathic medical qualifications, including Dr Swami Shankardev Saraswati, medical doctor, yoga therapist, and direct disciple of Swami Satyananda Saraswati.

During the Fall we had become familiar with how Ayurveda views a healthy body and mind, the roles and functions of the energies governing physical and psychological processes, vata, pitta and kapha and their sub-types, the Ayurvedic classification of the body's seven tissue types, septa dhatus, and their transformation sequence from plasma and lymphatic tissue to ojas:

> 'A subtle substance on the border between mind and body, it maintains life and is closely related to immunity. The West has no concept of ojas; it literally means vitality or bodily strength.'[7]

Ayurveda puts a strong emphasis on the importance of good digestion for maintaining health. We were learning to understand the digestive process from the Ayurvedic perspective, which also includes proper digestion of our emotions and life experiences. We learnt about the theory of the disease process and how imbalances in the dynamic functioning of vata, pitta, and kapha are seen as the root cause of all illnesses. We were taught how the accumulated effects of diet, daily experiences, relationships, and external factors such as climate and environment, affect doshic balance and thus health.

The disease process is described in six stages. Imbalances and symptoms in the first three stages of the disease process are easier to deal with. In the latter three stages the excess doshic energy is adversely affecting tissue metabolism, healthy tissues and normal functions within the body, as well as creating, or failing to expel, toxins.

In the West, there is a tendency to regard the signs and symptoms of the first stages of the disease process as trivial, but Ayurveda sees the early stages as the time to take steps to avoid serious illnesses developing. Ayurveda lifestyle principles give individuals ways they can maintain a healthy doshic balance and thus have good health, as well as reversing the small imbalances experienced by everyone from time to time. Ayurveda's lifestyle principles are excellent preventative measures.

From January to Easter, we learnt how Ayurveda breaks the vicious circle of doshic imbalances, poor digestion and ama found in many who are not well. We were taught about Ayurveda's treatments to pacify the doshas and restore a patient's natural balance of doshas, before rejuvenating weakened tissues. The principal treatments used in Ayurveda are herbs, panchakarma and shirodhara, but many other treatments now available as complementary therapies have been used within

Ayurveda for millennia. We all had the opportunity to receive panchakarma at the Institute. Panchakarma is a means of purification,

> 'which is unique to Ayurveda, which enables the body to release excess doshas and toxins from its cells, gather them in the gastrointestinal tract, and expel them. Panchakarma means five actions. These are therapeutic vomiting to remove excess kapha, therapeutic purgation to remove excess pitta, therapeutic enema to remove excess vata, nasal administration in cases of diseases of the head and neck, and bloodletting in the case of blood disorders.
>
> 'The body has to be properly prepared for a number of days. This involves deep, generous oil massage followed by steam treatment. The steam helps the oil to penetrate the skin as well as releasing surface toxins. Herbs may be used with the oil or steam. When the oil has penetrated deeply and the body is fully prepared, the appropriate "action" is taken.'[8]

I decided I'd like to experience panchakarma. I had an imbalance of the vata dosha. Panchakarma would be beneficial. All panchakarma programmes have to be individually tailored. I had a consultation with Dr Lad and he determined the detail of the programme which would be carried out by the trained therapists in the Panchakarma Department.

Before starting the programme I needed to prepare my body by simplifying my diet, restricting myself to kitcheri, drinking herbal teas, and increasing my intake of ghee. I was going to receive a number of consecutive days of treatment at the Institute. Each day I had two hours of abhyanga, a two-person synchronised oil massage with luscious amounts of warm herbal oils. The oiling was followed by swedana, sweating therapy, where my body, but not my head, was in a steam cabinet. I also experienced shirodhara. Warm oil was continually poured on my forehead, which was positioned so the oil ran over the top of my head through my hair and into the collecting bowl. I was monitored each day to check there were no unexpected adverse reactions; there were bound to be some reactions as my body was going through a cleansing process. I experienced a deep psychological understanding and release relating to some of the challenging times in my life. Again, that was to be expected, and I was in a very supportive and nurturing environment. The 'action' to reduce vata imbalance was a therapeutic enema, which I self-administered at H17.

After the panchakarma treatment, I gradually returned to a normal diet. Panchakarma depletes agni, the digestive fire. If my body's ability to digest food well was not restored, I'd lose the benefits gained by receiving panchakarma.

There were regular weekend seminars at the Ayurvedic Institute with Dr Lad or guest speakers. The guest speakers at the seminars I attended included Usha Lad, Dr David Frawley, Vyaas Houston, Donald VanHowten and Hart de Fouw.

The cookery seminar was lead by Usha Lad, Dr Lad's wife. She demonstrated how to make kitcheri and chapattis. Those interested in Ayurveda generally enjoyed cooking, and wished to choose foods that are doshically beneficial for them and which the body will digest. Kitcheri, a dish made of rice, split yellow mung beans, spices and vegetables, if cooked properly, is nutritious, delicious and digestible. It was eaten by many at the Institute. The use of different spices and vegetables determines the doshic qualities of kitcheri. Another favourite was lassi, a blend of yoghurt, water, and spices, which also aids digestion. Usha made a large pot of kitchari, which the group ate for lunch after we had made our own chapattis.

My introduction to Sanskrit was an intense twenty-two hour weekend seminar with Vyaas Houston of the American Sanskrit Institute. Vyaas's weekend was called Sanskrit Immersion, and he aimed in the two days to teach us to pronounce and read the Devanagari alphabet. Languages definitely are not a strong point of mine, and I had no expectation of learning much Sanskrit during the weekend. But it was no ordinary introduction to a new language. Vyaas's love of the Sanskrit language and his teaching methods meant his claim could become a reality if the student kept his or her mind 'on the point'.

Vyaas's teaching methods were based on the theory and

practice of yoga, which include detachment. Such a method of learning was severely hampered when the mind raised self-doubt and the question, 'Am I getting it right?'

Sanskrit is no ordinary language. Vyaas wrote in his article *Sanskrit and the Technology Age*:

> 'In ancient India the intention to discover truth was so consuming that in the process, they discovered perhaps the most perfect tool for fulfilling such a search that the world has ever known – the Sanskrit language. ... NASA, the most advanced research centre in the world for cutting-edge technology, has discovered that Sanskrit, the world's oldest spiritual language, is the only unambiguous spoken language on the planet'.[9]

It is possible to experience the sounds of syllables forming in the mouth as well as the breath bringing them forth. We were introduced to the alphabet through a series of diagrams and colour-coded charts demonstrating the five basic mouth positions and means of producing each sound with the correct amount of energy and breath. I was surprised I'd learnt the alphabet in a weekend and gained a foundation that helped me appreciate the importance of the Sanskrit language for a true understanding of Ayurveda.

After the weekend, I reinforced my learning of the alphabet by chanting it using Vyaas' method while waiting for buses as I was usually on my own. Though once or twice a week, while waiting to go to the Institute, I chatted with an American lady who knew more about the British Royal Family than I did.

Donald VanHowten's weekend seminar was a very practical, hands-on experience, where he explained the method of bodywork he had developed to release life impressions that are stored and become solidified in the connective tissues of our bodies. As he wrote in his book, *Ayurveda and Life Impressions Bodywork*:

> 'We carry in our minds and bodies all the events of our personal histories. Some of this history is still relevant to our present-day lives, but some of it is quite outdated, which leaves us stuck both in our beliefs and our membranes. We then function and behave

according to an old self-image based on who we used to be.'[10]

VanHowten's Life Impressions Bodywork methods are such that they can be used by practitioners with their patients, between trusting friends, or for self-help. During the weekend we only had a taste of VanHowten's work, but it provided further integration of the mind–body connection and the practical application of the Ayurvedic principles that we had been studying.

Hart de Fouw's visit to the Institute gave us the opportunity to attend his seminars and have a personal consultation with him. Hart's specialities were Jyotish (Vedic Astrology) and Hasta Smudrika Shastra (a Vedic form of hand analysis). I wasn't going to attend Hart's seminars; I thought I'd concentrate on Ayurveda, Sanskrit, and western anatomy and physiology. I had not booked myself a consultation. I respect astrology, but only in the right hands. My western chart had been done by Eileen, who had been trained in astrology through The White Eagle Lodge, so any consultation with Eileen would be in the context of the ethos of The White Eagle Lodge.

Hart's reputation preceded him, so I changed my mind and booked one of the last consultations available. Hart was another teacher who had studied in the Vedic oral tradition from teacher to student over a long period of time, and had a vocation to teach in the West in a manner appropriate for a modern culture but without losing or diminishing the essence of the universal wisdom of the Vedic sciences.

I had heard Dr Lad refer to Jyotish from time to time when teaching Ayurveda. Hart's introduction to Jyotish helped me gain a wider understanding of the integration of the different disciplines in Vedic sciences. The hand analysis, which should not be confused with western palmistry, was more accessible to me than Jyotish.

During my time at the Ayurvedic Institute I was gaining a picture of the holographic nature of the human mind and body, and discovering there were depths and connections that I did not find in western anatomy, physiology, or psychology books. One of Dr Lad's sayings is, 'Your biology is your biography'.

The skill is knowing how to read the living book and use the information for health, well-being and good relationships.

At my consultation with Hart he used both Jyotish and Hasta Smudrika Shastra. He started by giving a broad overview from my chart and about my hand type. I was told I had complex motivational strategies to my life compared to the majority, and therefore my life was significantly unusual or different. But that probably applied to many at the Institute. He told me Ayurveda was the current interest for me and there were other unusual interests to come. From my hand type, he told me communicating was a requirement for me to be happy in life, but my hand also indicated adaptability, intuition, sensitivity, and impressionability. Apparently, adaptability was my strongest talent – I could make do under any circumstances, and is my strongest weakness – if I did every assertiveness training course going I'd only get to a level of eighty per cent of where most people start. He indicated a marking on my hand, a hypothenia bar, which can indicate exposure to abuse, especially emotional abuse, a sensitive physiology, and a tendency to be misdiagnosed by allopathic doctors. He told me a little about the position of Saturn in my chart which indicated my dislike of authorities and large institutions. The positioning makes for a good citizen but one who has a conflict in conforming and being something of a rebel.

Hart gave me an overview of my life with no distinction between what had already transpired and what was to come. He started the overview by saying that, '... your family circumstances in your youth were so unfriendly, so unsupportive, that you learnt a strategy whereby you constantly had radar out, so to speak, to intuit what was about to transpire as a matter of survival. I think you did that so often in your childhood that you resorted to that strategy in your adult life. As a result of resorting to that strategy in adult life you are, perhaps, in overdrive and constantly anticipating what other people do, how they will react, etc. It became so much part of you ...'

He probably already knew from the brief chat we had that I

was in the throes of wanting a new career and that I had not yet seen what that was to be. He was very clear that writing and communication and disseminating information were strong in my hand and in my chart.

Towards the end of the consultation, I asked one or two questions. In connection with my mother, Hart indicated that 'three and a half to four years down the road there would be an opportunity to be reconciled and start to find the people we are'. He said it would be best if I had a compassionate acceptance of her even if pushed to the limit. My last question was about Andrew. Hart gave me a rather vague reply which I put down to there being no time left to discuss it properly.

I was pleased I had had the consultation with Hart. I found his description of my experiences in childhood about having my radar out uncanny. It had been like. A phrase I used, though I don't know when I started using it, was 'always being on red alert'. No one had indicated to me before in such a matter-of-fact way that there had been some challenges.

The last of the weekend seminars was to have been with Dr Robert Svoboda. Although we knew he was in Albuquerque the seminar was cancelled. A group of students invited him to have lunch with us. I told him about Dr Lad's seminar in England the previous year and that another was being planned. As I had not heard him teach in Albuquerque, I asked if he might come to London sometime to give a seminar.

The classes at the Institute finished at the end of April. I had an oral exam with Dr Lad. I was amongst those who successfully completed the Institute's Ayurvedic Studies Program Level I.

Earlier in the year the tenants of my house in England said they intended vacating at the end of June. My mother had given me some money which enabled me to stay longer in Albuquerque and also allowed me to do the additional seminars. I'd extended my visa and could stay in America until August, but I was planning on going back to England sometime in June. Andrew was encouraging me to have a holiday whilst still in America. What I'd have liked was for him to join me for a couple of weeks in California, but I was not able to persuade him.

Bhakti invited me to go with her to San Francisco for four days. She was going to the Whole Life Expo to assist her friend, Gaya, whose business was exhibiting there. We stayed with Gaya's friend at Walnut Creek. Soon after our arrival I was left with Gaya's friend's mother and son in the kitchen while Gaya and Bhakti went on an errand. I was generously fed with the most delicious mangos I'd ever tasted. As soon as I had finished one bowl of sliced mango it was refilled. I suddenly realised how un-British I was being. The grandmother of the house recognised my embarrassment, but as we had no common language we smiled and laughed and she gave me more mango.

The next day I looked around the Expo, and then became a tourist and went on a sightseeing bus tour of San Francisco. The following day Bhakti and Gaya were working, so I took a bus trip over Golden Gate Bridge to Muir Woods and Sausalito. On the Monday, with the Expo over, we went to the coast north of San Francisco. I enjoyed seeing the sea again and had a brief, cold paddle at Stinson Beach, just to be able to say that I had been in the Pacific Ocean.

I was surprised how much I missed the English spring, which for me starts in January when the first snowdrops and aconites appear, followed by daffodils, hyacinths, and tulips, and the fattening of leaf buds on trees and the appearance of small, soft green leaves which fully clothe the trees during May. Spring appeared more swiftly in Albuquerque. I was out with Liz, a class mate, and called on her parents. I delighted in their front garden, which was different from most as there was a colourful display of bulbs. Liz's mother picked me a bunch of spring flowers.

In May, the Sandia Peak Aerial Tramway celebrated its twenty-fifth anniversary by having 1966 prices. A group of us took the two-and-a-half mile ride to the top of the mountain to see the sunset. It was a spectacular ride over canyons and inaccessible terrain with panoramic views over New Mexico. At the top we had a walk, watched the sunset, and saw the lights of Albuquerque appear 5,000 feet below. We then went to the bar at the restaurant at the top of the mountain for beers and hot chocolate.

On my birthday, I took a picnic lunch to the university campus, which had lawns, trees, shade, and lakes with small fountains and ducks. The evening was spent at Wynn and Patty's house. They'd invited me and other friends to dinner. Instead of a birthday cake, we had individual servings of shortbread, strawberries and whipped cream, each with a lighted candle. For me, it was not only a memorable birthday, but a loving conclusion to my months in Albuquerque.

The time had come for me to vacate H17. My tenants vacated three weeks earlier than expected, so my house would be empty when I returned to England. I shipped two boxes of books and notes home. The contents of H17 were collected by the grandson of the lady at the bus stop, who was moving into his first apartment. Wynn and Will took me to airport, where I said a tearful goodbye to them and Albuquerque.

The flight from Albuquerque to Houston was delayed. On the plane was a party of hunters returning after their week's hunting trip in New Mexico. Hearing their conversations brought home to me that I had been cocooned in an environment where there were shared values of respect for nature and an understanding of the oneness of life, and had listened to teachings that expanded my thinking about human potential and the power of selfless love. The flight was turbulent due to thunderstorms, and arrived at Houston very shortly before my flight to England was due to depart. I was whisked across the airport on one of the terminal's buggies and was among the very last to board the flight to London Gatwick.

11

Shaft of Sunlight

ANDREW was at Gatwick Airport. We drove to my house in Exeter. The first thing Andrew did when we arrived was to inspect the house.

'All's fine. In fact it looks better than when you lived here,' he added.

I was pleased the tenants had left the house so clean and tidy. Once I'd retrieved my personal belongings from storage the house was my home again. My first weeks back in England were spent catching up with friends. Pauline was working as an occupational psychologist. I gave brief explanations about Ayurveda when asked what I'd done in America. Only one person had heard of Ayurveda; she'd seen Deepak Chopra on television talking about his book, *Quantum Healing*. Often I'd have to explain I'd been studying one of Asia's healing systems not a Native American Indian one. I resumed bereavement counselling with CRUSE.

Edward had booked us a holiday cottage for a week in Wales. I'd have loved to have gone but, in arranging the surprise for me, he'd overlooked my mother's seventieth birthday. He had also overlooked the fact that I couldn't disappear for a week so soon after returning to England without raising suspicions among our and Veronica's mutual friends. I gathered he still had to manage maintenance of family unity and needed the 'official' and 'unofficial' way of conducting our relationship to continue even though he'd lived on his own for eight months.

Andrew and I had planned to stay with our mother for a few days and take her to Stratford-upon-Avon for lunch on her birthday. The day before her birthday Andrew had taken the train to Malvern and I had driven from Exeter. My mother seemed alright when I arrived but soon went into 'flipmode'. Her mood deteriorated and agitation increased during the evening. By the time she went to bed the atmosphere in her flat echoed something I'd not experienced since the period following my father's death. At breakfast the next morning Andrew told me he was going home. I knew there was little I could do to salvage anything of a birthday for my mother, and if I stayed her agitation and distress would increase. I knew of no way of helping her and could only hope in a week or so she would talk to us again on the phone as if nothing had happened. After breakfast Andrew drove me to Bath. We bought sandwiches for a picnic in the sunshine in a park before Andrew took a train to Bournemouth and I drove home.

Andrew said very little to me about how our mother had been while I'd been in Albuquerque. I never did get the full story, but I gathered he'd had a difficult time with her, especially at the beginning. I was having concerns about Andrew's general health. He did not look well, had often had headaches and was drinking water frequently. He wasn't working, and I didn't find out when he'd stopped. Perhaps it was when he sent me that last postcard from Basingstoke. I was surprised how little he'd used my car; after deducting the mileage to and from Gatwick, it had hardly been anywhere. Whenever I mentioned anything about his health, or asked him to see a doctor or a complementary health practitioner, he would always tell me, 'There is nothing anyone can tell me that I don't already know.'

My time in Albuquerque had changed me, but little had changed in the lives or circumstances of those close to me, and it was time for me to face up to earning a living. I worked intermittently and part-time for a solicitor, and would have been happy to return to probate work, but I wanted to use the knowledge gain in Albuquerque. I continued with locum work and began training as a massage therapist. I intended to offer Ayurvedic Lifestyle Guidance which would include massage and other energetic therapies. I signed up for a business start-up scheme offered by the government for those wishing to be self-employed.

Stewart Mitchell was a naturopathic practitioner trained by the Kingston School of Naturopathy in Edinburgh. He founded the School of Complementary Health in Exeter. He was well versed in the same Nature Cure principles my mother loved. Stewart offered courses that fitted with my way of thinking and vision for how I'd like to have developed my work. For the practical work on the massage course, we worked in pairs, massaging and being massaged. Sheila, a teacher, and I were massage buddies for the duration of the course, and by the time we had both passed our exams had become friends.

The start-up scheme gave an overview of legal issues relating to running one's own business, preparing business plans to take to a bank, and advice about taxation, maintaining records and accounting systems. There were also two or three sessions about our individual suitability to be self-employed. I remember filling in various questionnaires and coming out with low scores which showed I was not suited to be self-employed, but I had a high score on determination. The low scores were due to not having a settled, stable and supportive family situation, and wishing to be an Ayurvedic lifestyle practitioner and a masseuse. Undeterred, I opened my business bank account and became self-employed.

Dr Lad came to London in September 1991. Ann and Peter had organised six days of seminars. The first three days were an introductory seminar about Ayurveda held at Regent's College in London. Then two days for those with some knowledge of Ayurveda were arranged at Old Jordans, the Quaker Hotel and Conference Centre. It was attended by complementary health practitioners who engaged in discussions on pulse diagnosis, and on the second day the relationship between agni (the digestive fire) and ama (the production of toxins in the body), and how low agni and ama can be a cause of disease. For the sixth day Dr Lad was back in London for a seminar where he demonstrated and discussed Ayurvedic methods of clinical examination and assessment.

I loved seeing him again and being able to listen to him teaching. Of course, much of what he was telling us was familiar to me, but I had learnt that by listening with a fresh ear to even introductory lectures I had new insights or made deeper connections with the vast teachings of Ayurveda.

While I had been in America, Ann and Peter had arranged regular meetings at Old Jordans for the Ayurveda Seminar Group. The autumn meetings included a herb-tasting of herbs and videos of pancha-karma treatments which I'd brought from Albuquerque.

In Autumn 1991, I had sent a questionnaire to those who had attended Dr Lad's seminars. I wanted to know if there was any interest and support for a newsletter and the setting up of an informal network of people interested in Ayurveda to exchange information and share together in learning about Ayurveda. There was a positive response to the questionnaire. Those responding indicated that they wanted information about seminars and courses, practitioners, books and tapes, availability of herbs, Ayurveda in India, case studies and research. Some were interested in being networked with others.

In January 1992, I produced the first issue of *Ayurveda News* – seven sheets of A4 stapled in the top corner. Angela Hope-Murray wrote a detailed account of the third seminar with Dr Lad the previous September, and a delegate at the second seminar wrote a report on that event.

All Dr Lad's seminars had been well attended, and participants hoped he'd return the following year. The seminars had been a financial success. I felt that Dr Lad should receive a percentage of the profit in addition to the modest fee that had been agreed. Ann and Peter disagreed with me. We had had no discussions about what we would do with any profit made from the seminars in 1990 or 1991. The surplus from the 1990 seminar financed the 1991 seminars after which the surplus was larger. Some of the money was used to finance the three-day seminar with Dr Robert Svoboda the following April at Old Jordans. There were discussions between Ann, Peter and myself over a few months, but I was not happy with what they were saying. I was committed to finish arranging Dr Svoboda's visit, and decided I would not be working with Ann and Peter after that. In early 1992 I told Dr Lad I could not be involved in organising his next visit to England.

A few weeks later, I received a phone call from Dr Lad. He asked me if I would arrange his next visit to England in September. I told him I'd not be able to organise anything in London. By the end of the conversation I'd said I might be able to organise a seminar in Exeter. I'd received the phone call in the early hours of the morning because of the time differences. My phone was downstairs and the central heating had switched off hours earlier. I was so cold after we'd finished speaking I had to have a hot bath to get warm.

I discussed various possibilities for a venue with Edward, who'd always encouraged me over my work. I checked out three or four venues and did some rough costings. In the end I decided it would be feasible, as Dr Lad would stay at my house and the only major financial commitment would be the hire of rooms. In September there'd be plenty of accommodation in and around Exeter, so delegates could make their own arrangements. I'd have preferred the seminar to be residential as the delegates gain much by being able to socialise easily in the evenings, but I could include in the programme an optional evening meal at an Indian restaurant.

Edward and I spent quite a while discussing ideas for a trading name under which to organise the seminars. One of Edward's suggestions was 'Ayurvedic Living', which was the name I went for. I booked a lecture hall on the St Luke's Campus at Exeter University for three days of seminars, a room at the Postgraduate Centre on the University's Streatham

Campus for the clinical assessment day with therapists, and a room in Reed Hall on the campus for individual consultations with Dr Lad.

The university's booking office suggested I should talk to their press office so they had information about the event. The person I met in the press office quickly realised how limited my experience was. She spent half an hour explaining about press releases, telling me how to write them and where to send them. She offered to look over my draft press release. She taught me things that proved invaluable, and without which Ayurvedic Living would not have grown as it did.

I heard Dr Svoboda teach for the first time at his three-day seminar in England the year after meeting him for lunch in Albuquerque. The programme was covering two topic; first Ayurveda's approach to food and digestion and the effects of food and medicines on the body and mind; and second, the disease process, disease management, a survey of a variety of diseases recognised in Ayurveda, and a correlation between Ayurveda and modern medicine to show how the two systems differ and complement one another. It was a treat. He was an excellent speaker, using humour and anecdotes, and soon had the audience participating and responding to his questions and making the Ayurveda concepts relevant to our everyday lives. And the depth and wisdom of the ancient teachings was infused through it all.

My absence in Albuquerque had set my mother back. Six months after her birthday she was beginning to be more settled. Andrew continued to look after the day-to-day management of her affairs. He or I visited her every month. She'd phone both of us on Sunday mornings. Her moods varied, but as far as I could tell she was going out quite often and spending time doing the things that interested her. Neither Andrew nor I felt any undue concern.

I'd planned to stay in Malvern with her for a few days in the middle of May. She'd told me she'd arranged an appointment with her medical herbalist and wanted me to go with her. I'd always been reluctant to accompany my mother to see complementary health therapists because of experiences my father had when they lived in Sidmouth. My mother saw the therapist once or twice, and then at the appointment she went to with my father she'd try to persuade the therapist her problems were due to my father's behaviour. My mother did have physical complaints a medical herbalist could help with. As she was seeing a responsible practitioner, I agreed to go with her.

I'd left Exeter to drive to Malvern. I was on the motorway forty miles from Exeter when I started crying. I couldn't stop crying. I left the motorway at the next junction and stopped in a lay-by. The crying just continued. I sat for forty minutes, still crying. I decided I'd better go home and not visit my mother that day. Things weren't much better when I got home. In the end I decided I should see a doctor.

Although I hadn't seen Dr A for six years I still thought of him as my doctor, simply because I had not needed to see a doctor nor had I registered with one in Exeter. It was easier to phone Dr A's surgery for an appointment and drive to North Devon. The surgery no longer had my notes. Initially Dr A didn't remember me. I said things to him about my family and crying on the motorway. He suggested I saw a counsellor in his surgery.

The following week I met the counsellor in a south facing room on the first floor of the surgery on a sunny morning. She was seated with her back to the window.

'Can you move your chair over so I can see your face?' I asked.
'No, it's fine here.'
'Could we swap places then?' I asked, thinking she'd assumeed I'd referred to her non-white ethnic background.

We changed seats. Once she'd understood, we rearranged the furniture and she explained about person-centred counselling, asked me a few questions about my mother and my feelings about her. Then she started talking about mother-daughter relationships and telling me what I should be doing. I had no confidence in her and I cancelled the next appointment. Edward told me later the counsellor was a friend of Veronica's.

I was able to review for myself the realities of the emotions I was dealing with. They related to my concerns about the three people I loved. I was worried about Andrew's health and the fact he wasn't working. Since childhood he had suffered from car sickness. It hadn't been a problem as an adult if he was driving. So when he visited me, we used my car but he drove. But he was refusing to drive my car. On one occasion when we'd been to the coast he was sick on the return journey. He was using trains and gave no impression he was thinking of replacing his stolen car.

The problems with my mother were continuing and from time to time I would not be able to cope. I would like to have been able to discuss the situation with somebody who could accept I loved my mother and did not want to cut myself off from her, and who would support me when she was at her most difficult.

I was also realising Edward's situation with Veronica had not changed even though he had his own front door. It was easier to speak to him by phone and he came to Exeter to visit me frequently. He continued to tell me about managing the situation with Veronica and the need to maintain family unity. He rarely made definite plans with me because he was always waiting to see what Veronica and his children would be doing. That hadn't bothered me as I always had plenty to do and could be flexible as I wasn't tied to set working hours.

For a few weeks after the 'motorway breakdown' I experienced a hypersensitivity to touch on part of my back and left-hand side. During that time Sheila asked me if I would 'be the body' at an extra tutorial session she had arranged with Stewart Mitchell, as she had missed some massage classes. I agreed, but only on condition that she did not touch the left side of my back.

Bookings were coming in for Dr Lad's seminars in September. Edward had agreed we'd both go to meet Dr Lad at Heathrow, and he'd look after Dr Lad during his visit to Exeter. They'd stay at my house and Edward would take Dr Lad to and from the venues and bring him back to my house each day for lunch. As I was thinking the detail through I realised I needed help with the catering at my house. Elizabeth Greer, a professional caterer, was recommended as in addition to her culinary skills she 'cooked with love'.

My mother had booked a consultation with Dr Lad and was coming to the first seminar. I was hoping Andrew would come and meet Dr Lad, but he told me he would come to Dr Lad's next seminar.

The second issue of *Ayurveda News* had grown to twenty pages, with an extract from one of Dr David Frawley's books and contributions from subscribers, including a report by Anne Green, a Medical Herbalist, on the seminar with Dr Svoboda in which she concluded,

> 'As presented to us by Dr Svoboda, Ayurveda is not something exotic, elitist and elusive, but accessible and appropriate to our personal paths. I look forward to Dr Svoboda's booster shot of easily simulated Ayurveda. His teaching is compelling evidence that nothing is lost in translation and much is gained.'

By mid-September all was ready for Dr Lad's visit. The hundred and eighty mile journey from Heathrow after a flight from India was a mistake. Dr Lad was very tired and not well by the time he got to Exeter, but he went ahead with the consultations the following day. I was pleased my mother met Dr Lad and had a consultation with him. She told him she was lonely, there had been traumatic events in her life, and that she loved Nature Cure. The notes Dr Lad made after taking her pulses and examining her were the only comprehensive information I ever had about her physical condition. He noted also that she was experiencing deep-seated grief and sadness.

The next morning I was setting up the registration table and bookstall before delegates arrived. The seminar was well attended; there were many familiar faces as well as new ones. My mother was sitting in the front row with Betsy when Edward and Dr Lad arrived just before the start time. They'd been to the local radio station, where Dr Lad had been interviewed about Ayurveda. Dr Lad opened the session with a Sanskrit chant and another interesting seminar was under way.

At the morning break I noticed my mother was showing the initial signs of distress, and might make a scene at the lunch break. The medical herbalist she was consulting was at the seminar and I asked her to speak with my mother when the second session ended. Sadly, my mother was not alright and, after a prolonged talk with the medical herbalist in the car park, left with Betsy and did not return. The seminars were a success, but from Dr Lad's point of view, Exeter wasn't a good location because of the extra travelling.

Only Andrew went to our mother's for Christmas 1992. He spent a weekend with me in January. My car was giving me some problems and I no longer liked using it for longer journeys. He had a long conversation with me about the pros and cons of changing my car, and gave me detailed advice about choosing a new car. He told me our mother wanted to buy me a better car, but I was not willing to accept such a big gift. We visited Betsy and all went to Sidmouth for lunch.

After Dr Lad's visit I'd contacted the editor of *Yoga and Health* magazine to ask if she would like to publish any of Dr Lad's articles. She was interested and also asked if I would write an article about Ayurvedic lifestyle principles. I had already had a short article published in *Resurgence* and one alongside two of Dr Lad's books in *Cygnus Review*. I submitted an article, 'The little things in life', which was published in April 1993 in *Yoga and Health*. Later in 1993, my four-part series of articles called 'Ayurveda: the science of qualities' was published.

Dr Svoboda was coming to give another seminar at Old Jordans at the beginning of April and had been invited to speak at an event organised by the National Institute of Medical Herbalists at the University of East Anglia.

Having run a bookstall at Dr Lad's seminar, I was putting together a small mail order business to sell Ayurveda books and tapes. I had completed the massage training and had arranged one bedroom in my house as a treatment room. It would take two or three years to establish a client base, but the groundwork had been done.

Dr Lad was coming to England again in September, but the workshops had to be in London and I had to find a venue. In February, I went to London for the day to look at a university lecture room, one other venue, and the Quaker International Centre near Tottenham Court Road. As soon as I walked into the Quaker International Centre I knew the atmosphere was just right. They were happy to let me book the lecture room and let the delegates book their own accommodation. The only slight problem was the L-shaped lecture room. I decided it was big enough if the Speaker and flipchart stand were in the corner of the L.

I phoned Andrew to tell him about my visit to London and finding a venue. He said he'd meet Dr Lad when he was in London. Since I'd come back from Albuquerque, Andrew had always been helpful and encouraging about anything to do with my work, but he had been adamant he would not do anything for me that he thought I might come to rely upon.

One night early in March I had a dream about Andrew, but I couldn't remember the detail when I awoke. It was as if I had been cocooned in all that my brother meant to me and the essence of who he was; his intelligence, his common sense, his sense of humour, his care and love for us. It was too early in the morning to phone him and by the time I'd was dressed and had started on the practicalities of the day I thought he would just think me silly and sentimental.

When my mother phoned me the following Sunday, she told me Andrew was not answering his phone. I told her he'd probably gone out for the day. She phoned me that evening as she still hadn't spoken with him. She was beginning to get agitated and started telling me how I didn't care about my brother and that I wasn't doing anything about him not working. I told her he was old enough to go out for the day if he wanted to without having to tell his mother and sister.

My mother phoned me on the following two days as she still hadn't been able to contact Andrew. She told me I should do something about it. She had reached the point where I couldn't cope with her. I told her not to phone me again and if Andrew wanted to go away for a few days he should not have to deal with us getting upset about it. As things had not been too easy between my mother and me again I did think he might just be 'taking a break from us', but I did post a note to him asking him to let our mother know he was alright.

As I reflected on the situation I realised since our father had died Andrew and I had always known how to contact each other. I started to become concerned. First I had his phone number checked to make sure there wasn't a fault on his line, but it was fine. Then I asked Sally if she would go by Andrew's flat after dark to let me know if there were any lights on. She did that and there were lights on. I was slightly reassured, but by the weekend I had started contacting my friends to give them each other's telephone numbers and I said I didn't want to be on my own when I was told anything bad.

Sally phoned on the Monday to say she wasn't certain she had been looking at the right flat. By then I had decided to leave it to the end of the week and if I hadn't heard from him I would take the spare key and go into his flat. When I told Sally that she suggested I send the key to her and she would go to his flat. I posted the key the next morning. The following morning I was convinced I would know that Andrew was either a missing person or was dead.

It was Edward's birthday and he was having lunch with Veronica. In the morning I went into town to get a copy of a photograph of Andrew in case I needed it later. By 6.30 p.m. no one had contacted me. I sat massaging Rescue Remedy Cream into my face. At seven o'clock the front doorbell rang. It was Barbara and Jack. They took me into the sitting room, sat me down, and told me Sally had phoned them. She had gone, with the police, to Andrew's flat and had found his body.

I screamed.

I was told the coroner had been informed and there would be a post-mortem the next day. The only other recollection I have of that evening was of Ted (not Edward) coming, looking shocked and shaking hands with me.

I know somebody stayed in the house overnight but I can't remember who. In the morning there were phone calls as my friends worked out who was going to be with me. They were amazing, and worked out a rota so I was not left on my own.

Someone arranged for me to see my doctor. I had registered with Dr B's practice and had seen the practice nurse, but had not met Dr B. The person who stayed overnight took me to Barbara and Jack's house until someone came to take me to see Dr B. I was sitting in their kitchen when Dr A phoned, asking to speak to me. I don't know why he'd phoned, as I had not seen him for some months and he was no longer my doctor; presumably he was phoning because Ted had contacted him. Dr B gave me some sleeping tablets and made another appointment for me to see him.

I contacted Angela and she and Anne took over the arrangements for Dr Svoboda's visit. All the planning was done, and they had to look after him and the delegates and deal with whatever cropped up at the seminars.

Since I'd been told of Andrew's death I'd wondered whether my failure to go to his flat had contributed to it. After the post mortem the coroner's office left a message on my answerphone. Andrew had died of totally natural causes. He had had a stroke, and even if a medical team had been present they could have done nothing to save him. The message also said the state of his heart and coronary arteries was so bad he could have had a severe heart attack at any time.

No one had contacted my mother. Ted was putting pressure on me to do so. Alison slept overnight on my sofa, and Ted was coming in the morning to take me to Andrew's flat. Before Ted arrived I'd asked Alison to explain to him that I had to have all the information before my mother was informed and I doubted I was capable of telling her.

Ted and I drove to Bournemouth, stopping at Dorchester to buy flowers. It was the day I had intended to go to Andrew's flat if I had not heard from him. There are occasions in life when one's friends do something for which it is impossible to express adequate gratitude. In the previous two days Sally had saved me from a situation I would have been unable to deal with and which would probably have broken me. Not only had she gone to the flat and found my brother's body, she'd dealt with the formalities with the coroner and registered the death. She had been back to the flat and removed half the carpet from the study where Andrew collapsed at least two weeks earlier, and had cleaned the room and used plenty of disinfectant. Other than that, and his post having been placed in the sitting room, the flat was undisturbed. Breakfast was laid up in the kitchen as he had left it. All the curtains in the flat, apart from the ones in the study, had been drawn. Judging by the unopened letters, he had died in the middle of the week prior to the Sunday when my mother first phoned me saying he was not answering his phone, which was on the desk beside him.

Before my mother was told I needed to know whether he had left a will or whether she, as next of kin, was the person responsible for dealing with matters. Andrew's personal papers were in the most immaculate order I had ever seen anybody's, and on top of the box of his papers was his will. He had appointed me sole executor and beneficiary. The papers relating to my mother's financial affairs were in another box, all neatly filed. I took the two boxes with me and also half a dozen of his vinyl albums which I selected randomly.

The next day, Saturday, Pauline came to stay with me for the weekend. Sally went to see my mother in Malvern and stayed overnight. She had arranged with the police for them to visit my mother and tell her what had happened. The police visited shortly before Sally was due to arrive. In their own ways, my mother and Sally looked after each other that weekend. While Sally had been taking care of things for me she had also been dealing with the suicide of one of her clients. She was pretty tired.

As Andrew's executor, I was responsible for making the funeral arrangements. Apart from our father's funeral I had never discussed funerals with Andrew and had no idea what form he would have wished his funeral service to take, and there was the dilemma that I was incapable of talking with my mother. One thing I was clear about was that it was her son who had died, and she should have every opportunity to say where she wanted the funeral to take place and what kind of service it should be. It was one of the things I hoped could be decided over the weekend with Sally's and Pauline's help.

On Sunday morning I became agitated that Andrew's body was still at the mortuary in Bournemouth, but by the time Sally left Malvern that afternoon it had been decided that Andrew's funeral would take place at Exeter Crematorium, and that my mother, his mother, was not well enough to attend.

On Monday I contacted a funeral director in Exmouth and Stuart, a member of The White Eagle Lodge, who would lead the funeral service. I asked for the service to be recorded so that my mother would be able to hear the service at a later date if she wished. I also requested that Stuart speak with my mother and ensure that she chose one of the pieces of music. She chose *Amazing Grace*. The other music consisted of two tracks from the records I'd taken from his flat.

In reply to my letter telling Peggy Andrew had died, she wrote, 'I shall always remember him for his love of 'life' and his quiet understanding'. Eric was too seriously affected by Parkinson's disease to be told Andrew had died.

Ted took me to visit the Chapel of Rest. He told me Veronica wanted to come to the funeral. He knew I didn't want that, but said it would be difficult for him if she didn't. Pauline and Steph supported me at the funeral, and I'll always remember the look of surprise Steph gave me as the last piece of music, The Rolling Stones' *Dance Little Sister, Dance,* started.

Early on the grey morning of my fortieth birthday, Edward drove me to Sidmouth. We walked to the top of the hill where I had scattered my father's ashes almost twelve years previously. I scattered Andrew's ashes under the same beech tree. As I finished scattering the ashes, a shaft of sunlight broke briefly through the clouds and tree canopy, falling on his ashes.

The recording of Andrew's funeral was not clear enough to give to my mother. I sent her a transcript (See Appendix 5) which I hoped would give her some comfort. It was a source of strength for me.

12

Out of the Ashes

DURING the months following Andrew's death my priority was to keep myself afloat. I was incapable of speaking with my mother. The situation for both of us was worse than in the months following my father's death. I was beginning to understand the enormity of what Andrew had done for me and my mother by keeping the seriousness of his illness to himself. For the first three months I maintained contact with my mother through Stuart, as she would talk with him and he would talk with me. I listened incessantly to The Rolling Stones' 'Dance Little Sister' until it ceased to be The Rolling Stones and became my brother telling me not to give up.

Initially I saw Dr B weekly. I took the sleeping tablets he prescribed for four nights only. On the fourth night I'd woken up shortly after falling asleep. Something was troubling me and I had to make a phone call. My phone was in the little bedroom which had become my office. Having dealt with what was on my mind I collapsed on the landing a few inches from the top of the stairs. I decided my mind was stronger than tablets. It wasn't worth risking injury to myself.

The week after Andrew's funeral I went to see John, the solicitor I'd worked for in Barnstaple before I went to university.

I'd decided to administer Andrew's estate myself, but until I was better and able to talk with my mother, John would look after her financial affairs. I was remaining as her attorney. John understood my mother and I cared about each other, but should any differences arise involving her finances she would talk to him and I could rely upon him to give her independent advice. When Stuart went to India that summer to work for a children's charity, John became the link between me and my mother. She'd often phone him around 5.30 p.m. John went well beyond any professional duty, and I experienced a very practical application of his Christian values in the care he showed towards my mother and me. John's attitude and actions were probably crucial in preventing a complete breakdown for one or both of us.

Two weeks after Andrew's funeral, I had a hospital outpatient appointment prior to a wisdom tooth being extracted. When the doctor was checking through routine questions and asked me whether any of my close family had been affected by cardiovascular disease, I became too upset to answer or be calmed down. I was sent home to be recalled three months later. On the second visit, the doctor was Indian and his grandmother knew about Ayurveda.

Pauline and I spent two days in Bournemouth sorting through Andrew's belongings. Lying on top in the top drawer of his bedside cabinet was the poem 'Promise Yourself' (See p157) which I had sent him ten years earlier. He had left it for me.

I think it is rare not to learn something about the person who has died when going through their personal belongings. Andrew had few books, so I was surprised to find books and detailed insurance folders on anatomy, physiology, and medical conditions. Until I saw these I had not realised the level of his medical knowledge, even though he had told me gruesome stories about road traffic accidents. He'd had authority to negotiate and settle large personal injury and fatality claims. I knew he had dealt with claims where drivers had died of heart attacks at the wheel. Andrew was right when he had said about his health, 'Nobody can tell me anything I do not already know.' There was nothing in his flat indicating who his doctor was or that he was on, or had been on, any medication.

In June I bought myself a camera, and went to the local college of art a couple of hours a week to learn about black and white photography and developing film. I met new people and had to go out each week to take photographs so I had a film to develop.

Following Andrew's death I was not in a fit state to do any one-to-one work. I ceased doing counselling and massage, intending to resume both when I was well. I did not do any legal work after Andrew's death. His death had taken the pressure off me financially. If I hadn't increased my income by the end of that year, I wouldn't have been able to pay my mortgage and would have to have sold my house.

I thought I was capable of continuing the work with Ayurvedic Living. I knew how to organise Dr Lad's London seminars in September. The venue had been found and booked but I still had to arrange a suitable venue for lunches. The next issue of *Ayurveda News* had to be produced, and I could continue developing the mail order sale of books. That was what happened over the following months, with much support from my friends.

Andrew's flat remained furnished until it was sold. His television and video recorder had been brought to my house. I had not had a television for some years, and had never owned a video recorder and did not know how to use one. I had the instruction book and thought I ought to find out. I set it to record a documentary about Indian restaurants in England. Later I checked the programme had been recorded. I was not watching it, just listening to it in the background as I did something else. One of the restaurateurs caught my attention because he was talking about food and consciousness. I played it back. Ramesh Patel, the owner of the Mandeer Restaurant in London was speaking. As the commentator introduced Ramesh the camera panned over the street and restaurant names. I found my map of

London and discovered The Mandeer was within walking distance of the Quaker International Centre, the venue for Dr Lad's seminars.

We lunched each day of the seminars at the Mandeer, which didn't open on Sundays, but Ramesh opened that Sunday especially for Dr Lad. Unusually, the chair next to Dr Lad was unoccupied. Part way through the meal I had a strong feeling of my brother's presence. To me, the empty chair was Andrew's and as promised he'd come to London when Dr Lad was there. What would have been more appropriate than for him to join us for lunch?

Patty and Wynn had invited me to stay with them in Albuquerque to help me get my life back into perspective. I had initially been reluctant to do that, but Patty persuaded me. I was going in the middle of October for a month. The arrangements for Dr Svoboda's visit in the spring had been made. Jack had agreed to deal with mail and any bookings while I was away.

At the beginning of October I was contacted by a publisher, who had seen the articles in *Yoga & Health* magazine. I was asked if I'd write a book on Ayurveda according to the outline they'd prepared, which resembled Dr Lad's book *Ayurveda: The Science of Self-Healing*. I told them that I was not qualified to write a book on Ayurvedic medicine, but would consider a book on Ayurvedic lifestyle principles, and that I was about to go to America for a month.

I'd been toying with the idea that after Andrew's flat was sold, I could add a room onto the side of my house which would be dedicated to my one-to-one work. Shortly before I left for America I had a site meeting with a planning officer. I also asked him about enclosing the balcony at the front of the house. He explained planning permission would be required and I need the adjoining owner's consent to alter the balcony.

I went to Albuquerque via California and stayed with Bhakti for a few days. I have an abiding memory of the large glasses of freshly squeezed orange juice she made for me. We visited the Monterey Sea Aquarium and drove further south to Big Sur.

Patty and Wynn had moved to a new house on the edge of the city, not far from the Institute and close to the open space at the foothills of the Sandia Mountains. Their daughter was crawling and just learning to stand up. Wynn and Patty opened their home to me. I was able to relax and hang out with Patty and her daughter. She and I spent much time on the floor playing with her toys, books, and keyboard. I met up with classmates from 1991 who were still in Albuquerque, sat in on some classes at the Institute and enjoyed delicious meals and potlucks with friends old and new. I had another consultation with Hart deFouw. I learnt more about what my Jyotish chart indicated regarding the influence of my brother on my life.

Patty and Wynn suggested I extend my stay and I spent Christmas with them, returning to England in mid January. Patty had been like a sister to me and had been quite right about me needing to have a change of scene to gain some perspective.

During my extended stay in Albuquerque, two authors asked if I'd like to read the manuscripts they had just completed, and I was invited to sit in on an editorial meeting for one of Dr Lad's books at The Ayurvedic Press. I had not seen a manuscript before and knew nothing about the process and work involved in turning a manuscript into a book. There's more to a book than writing it. The publishers in England contacted me while I was in Albuquerque, but I wanted to defer thoughts about writing a book until I was home.

I arrived home on a Saturday in the middle of January. I was surprised to find a 'For Sale' sign outside the semi-detached house adjoining mine. Gavin was going through a career change and had let his house in the autumn, but had had problems with his tenants and had decided to sell instead.

On the Monday, John, my solicitor, phoned me as the previous Friday he'd accepted an offer on Andrew's flat. The offer was £500 less than the figure I'd instructed him to accept without consulting me. John had accepted the offer as it was a cash purchase and the purchaser had left instructions with his solicitor to go ahead in his absence abroad if the offer was accepted.

The thought started going through my head that I could buy Gavin's house when Andrew's flat was sold. Simultaneously with such a thought was one telling me it was a crazy idea to buy the house next door. The thought of buying persisted along with reasons why it wasn't totally crazy.

'I do need some extra space for my work.'

'Yes, but not a whole house.'

'It would be a good investment.'

'Yes, but the money could be invested in stocks and shares and provide some extra income.'

'I could regard it as my pension policy. I haven't yet made any provisions, and pension policies don't provide income until you retire.'

'Yes, but houses incur expenditure and need maintaining.'

'Well, that really will kick-start me into doing something then, won't it.'

And so the argument with myself went on, but the idea of buying the house was getting the upper hand in the argument. I decided I would do nothing at all until I knew contracts were exchanged and the sale of Andrew's flat was definite.

In the meantime, I wanted to buy a new car. Andrew had provided the money, but for the first time I had to go and sort everything out myself. I wanted a white estate car with power steering. It seemed the decision was made for me as Ford dealers had a special offer on estate cars and the dealer in Barnstaple had a white one, which I took for a test drive and bought.

Contracts were exchanged on Andrew's flat two weeks after I'd come home from America. I didn't visit the flat again and arranged for the furniture to be collected and stored. Buying the house next door was beginning to seem like an opportunity I should not overlook. I didn't want to disclose to Gavin or my neighbours that I was interested in it until I had really made up my mind. I told a white lie, saying a friend was interested, so I could borrow the key and look around inside. I knew it was a mirror image of my house, but I needed to know that it 'felt' right and I could only do that by viewing. I think Gavin was quite surprised when I made an offer, and after some negotiation we agreed on a price.

The survey of the new house had shown that the leylandii hedge roots were about to push the boundary wall over, the willow tree in the back garden was too close to the neighbour's drains, and the patio was covering the air vents and needed relaying at a slightly lower level. I talked with master builder and plumber, Maurice Jones, about an internal link between the two houses to make one house. The following year the dividing wall between the two balconies was demolished and a sunroom created across the front of the property over the garages. The back bedroom of the new part of the house was turned into the room for my one-to-one work. I never resumed doing bodywork. I used the room for individual consultations on Ayurvedic lifestyle guidance.

The publishers contacted me soon after I returned home from America. I was feeling cautious about agreeing to write a book having had a tiny insight into the publishing world and seen two manuscripts. As the publishers paid my expenses, I saw no harm in going to see them. I hadn't given the matter much thought, apart from knowing that I was not going to write a book on Ayurvedic medicine. It hadn't dawned on me I was, in effect, going for an interview, so I was surprised when three people questioned me vigorously for almost two hours about Ayurveda before one suggested we went for lunch and talked about an advance. I was even more surprised on the train home that I'd agreed to write a book. With hindsight I was glad I'd been so naïve. They needed to know I had enough knowledge to write a book, and the process had demonstrated to me that the experiences during the previous ten months hadn't wiped out that knowledge. In the following weeks an outline of the contents was discussed and agreed and contracts signed. All I had to do was deliver a manuscript by July 4th. Independence Day had a new meaning for me.

Before any adaptation to the two houses was done, I'd put a desk and computer in a front bedroom of the new one. Each morning I went next door to work, going 'home' for lunch.

Thus, I got into a good writing discipline and the book began to take on its own life. At times I experienced the joy of writing that came when I was so totally engrossed in what I was doing it seemed the words were being given to me.

Dr Svoboda had asked me if I could arrange somewhere for him to spend a quiet week writing before his workshops at Old Jordans in April. I suggested the house next door. I gave him a key to both front doors as meals would be in my other house. I'd made a start on my Ayurveda lifestyle book. Dr Svoboda read the initial chapters, questioned me about them and gave me helpful advice about writing books while I was driving to Dartmoor, where we walked, and over tea at The Cider Press at Dartington.

Since then, having tea there evokes memories of Dr Svoboda's voice quizzing me, 'And why have you said that?'

The manuscript was delivered on time. Turning it into a book was a collaboration between the editor, the art editor and the illustrator. I was involved throughout. It was a learning curve for me, but the editor knew I was a first-time author and guided me through. There were some disagreements, which arose because the logic of Ayurvedic thinking can initially challenge the Western mind, but all was ironed out.

In the previous months I'd experienced the crushing pain of grief, the sudden welling up of tears, a series of physical ailments, odd transient pains and a loss of confidence; all normal experiences following bereavement. For my health's sake it was a blessing to have been approached to write a book which tapped into my passion for Ayurveda. I would have to discipline myself to ensure I'd be happy to put my name on the manuscript. As I was working from home I could take breaks when I needed to and keep to a regular daily routine.

I regarded the new part of my house as 'Andrew's house'. Many visitors commented on its peaceful atmosphere. I found it healing to sit quietly in that part of my house. I embroidered a cross-stitch sampler with a border of roses and rosebuds to enclose the words of *Promise Yourself*.

PROMISE YOUSELF

- to be so strong that nothing can disturb your peace of mind;
- to talk health, happiness and prosperity to every person you meet;
- to make all your friends feel that there is something in them ;
- to look at the sunny side of everything and make your optimism come true;
- to think only of the best, to work only for the best and to expect only the best;
- to be just as enthusiastic about the success of others as you are about your own;
- to forget the mistakes of the past and press on to the greater achievements of the future;
- to wear a cheerful countenance at all times and give every living creature you meet a smile;
- to give so much time to the improvement of yourself that you have no time to criticise others;
- to be too large for worry, too noble for anger, too strong for fear and too happy to permit the presence of trouble;
- to think well of yourself and to proclaim this fact to the world, not in loud words but in great deeds;
- to live in the faith that the whole world is on your side so long as you are true to the best that is in you.

Anon

The first talk I gave on Ayurvedic lifestyle principles was in a converted barn in mid-Devon. I had been invited by Duncan Hulin of The Devon School of Yoga to speak to trainee yoga teachers. I had also been asked to give a talk on Ayurveda at Exeter University to complementary health studies students. I was so nervous about that talk my knuckles were probably white as I gripped my notes, hoping no one would interrupt me or ask questions. I'd yet to learn I'd enjoy giving talks and workshops once I realised I didn't have to know everything and could say, 'I don't know, but I'll see if I can find out.' I also discovered when talking about the doshas it was better to ask the questioner questions that would encourage the group to ask questions of themselves as that would help them develop their ability to think in the Ayurvedic way.

The venue for Dr Lad's August 1994 visit was Ickwell Bury, the centre of the Yoga for Health Foundation in Bedfordshire. Workshops with both Dr Lad and Dr Svoboda were reunions of friends amongst the regular core of delegates and the making of new friendships as the popularity of the workshops grew. *Yoga & Health* magazine had included an article by Dr Lad about incompatible food combinations in Ayurveda, and had mentioned his forthcoming visit.

In organising the workshops, I was beginning to encounter the problems of catering for those interested only in Ayurveda's self-help aspects, as well as for those who worked in allopathic and complementary healthcare who would have appreciate more in depth information. At that time it was not financially feasible for me to arrange further seminars, and nor were the physicans' visits to England long enough to allow that.

Fifteen months after Andrew's death, my life appeared more settled and the work I'd been doing was taking shape. I still had not had any direct contact with my mother. She'd indicated she wanted to move back to Devon and live near Exeter. I was not against her doing that, but I was not then strong enough in myself to deal with her or help her without support for myself. Ideally, I'd have liked someone to treat us like a family and work with both of us. I asked Dr B if he would help me obtain support, and whether his practice would accept my mother as a patient if she moved to Exeter. Dr B was against the latter suggestion and did not appear willing or able to offer any help to support me in having contact with my mother. I spoke to a complementary therapist who was also trained in psychological matters, but again to no avail. I was failing to convey that I wanted help for myself and that I was not asking for help for my mother or to get her to communicate better with me.

I couldn't explain my circumstances clearly to anyone. I knew what had happened in the years following my father's death and I was still distressed about it, and everything had been compounded by Andrew's death. I was beginning to understand that my requests for help were being heard through the filter of whatever prejudices or preconceived ideas were held by those from whom I was seeking help. There appeared to be such a deep belief that because I became upset when dealing with my mother, I should have no contact with her. Nobody was asking whether I cared about my mother, whether I loved her, whether I wanted to help her. Walking away was not a solution for me. I would still be affected adversely, but in a different way. It might have been convenient for my healthcare practitioners to remove my mother from the equation, so to speak, but they would be asking me to conform to their wishes, not my own.

I suggested my mother postponed her move to Devon until she had found a suitable flat or bungalow to make the move as smooth as possible. I'm not sure how much house hunting she did, but her move to Devon was not well planned. She'd arranged for everything in her flat to be picked up and stored by the removal company in Devon, which still had some of her belongings from when her Sidmouth house had been sold. Her houseplants ended up in the firm's office until I collected them. One of the removal men drove her car to Devon and she moved into a nursing/care home that catered for vegetarians. My mother was dreadfully unhappy. She was befriended by a long-term resident of the home. I went to see the GP she had been registered with.

He was not a man who was willing to listen to me and I was quickly dismissed after he said, 'What do you expect if she lives in a place like that?' He wouldn't explain what he meant.

After a while, I started thinking my mother was living in a home that was run by some kind of cult, for want of a better phrase. The woman, who had befriended her, although of retirement age, appeared to have some connection with the management.

By the autumn shortly before I went to Albuquerque for three weeks to stay with Patty and Wynn, my mother had started talking about wanting to buy a flat in Exmouth. I contacted estate agents to start the process of looking at flats. My mother's knees were affected by rheumatism and arthritis, and walking had become painful for her. She refused to consider a ground floor flat, so I restricted the search to blocks of flats which had a lift.

At the beginning of 1995, my mother decided to have an extended stay at Tyringham Clinic in Buckinghamshire, a naturopathy clinic. A friend of Edward's drove her there in her car.

My mother had few of her personal belongings with her. I wanted to deal with the numerous cardboard boxes that had been placed in store with no indication as to their contents. I had the walls and floor of the garage of my new house treated so the garage was clean and dust free. I visited the store to assess the situation and to give instructions as to what was to be brought to my house. On the top of the first box I asked to be opened was my brother's teddy bear, much loved and played with in the 1950s but long since abandoned by him. I picked it up and, holding it like a long lost friend, continued giving instructions until I became self-conscious. Then I sat teddy on the front passenger seat of my car. We didn't open all the boxes. I would need to go through them at home. When I unpacked the boxes I discovered the removal men literally had picked up everything from my mother's Malvern flat, even the contents of wastepaper baskets.

My mother's stay at the Tyringham Clinic was shorter than I had expected. I received a phone call saying she was distressed and wanted to come back to Devon. I arranged for her to go to a nursing home on the outskirts of Exmouth. After my mother's death, in the box of family photographs, I found a photo with the words 'Xmas 1948' written on the back. It was a picture of the front of the nursing home when it had been a hotel. I wondered whether my parents had spent Christmas there the year before they married.

Dr Svoboda visited England in February, during the time my mother was at the Tyringham Clinic. In addition to the workshops, Dr Svoboda offered a limited number of individual consultations. His workshops took place at the Quaker International Centre in London. Dr Svoboda paid a second visit to England in December, and spent three days teaching at Ickwell Bury and two days at The Sivananda Yoga Vedanta Centre in Putney, London. Dr Lad's workshops were again held at Ickwell Bury. Individual consultations with Dr Lad were not available, but a few people had detailed assessments as they had volunteered to be case studies in the clinical assessment workshop. Hart deFouw also visited London that year and gave Jyotish consultations.

Ayurvedic Living was turned into a limited company, with Dr Svoboda and me as directors. I was employing a bookkeeper one day a week to keep the accounts and the paperwork in order. The advice I had been given in 1992 about press releases was paying off. Since then I had regularly mailed women's and health magazines and some national papers. A number were mentioning the workshops or giving Ayurvedic Living as a contact for more information about Ayurveda.

In the course of organising workshops I received calls from many seeking a private consultation with one of the Ayurvedic physicians. Often these were from people with a serious, long-standing, chronic condition or who had been given a terminal diagnosis and had also been told there was nothing further allopathic medicine could do to help them. Some had seen complementary health practitioners, but could find no one who could help them. Sometimes we'd talk for an hour or more, and often the conversation would turn towards their spiritual values and the meaning for them of their illness. Just occasionally I would receive a note from someone, long after I could recall who they were, telling me our conversation had helped them.

Part of the reason for turning Ayurvedic Living into a limited company was to make a clear distinction between the work I did in arranging workshops for Dr Lad and Dr Svoboda and my personal work. The publication in 1995 of *The Book of Ayurveda: A Guide to Personal Well-Being* resulted in me receiving more requests to give introductory talks. There were encouraging reviews of the book in magazines. I started offering one and two day 'Ayurveda: Qualities and Lifestyle' introductory workshops. The handouts were derived from tables and charts in the book. The Ayurvedic Press had given permission for Dr Lad's Food Chart to be reproduced in the book. I turned it into a double-sided A3 handout, which I hoped would be used by participants after the workshop as easy reference as they adjusted their diets to one more suitable for their individual constitutions and imbalances. Many people were drawn to finding out about Ayurveda because of its teachings on food and digestion. They were pleased to discover for themselves the improvements to their health when they made the right small changes in their diet and habits.

During the breaks in workshop sessions, individuals would ask me questions they didn't wish to raise in the group. Many such chats related to digestive and bowel problems. I started noticing people who had been widowed or bereaved asked questions about experiences which I recognised as a normal part of the grief process. When I was talking with somebody who was bereaved, I often had a strong feeling of the presence of Andrew, as if he was standing behind my left shoulder. I found that as I listened to the person, thoughts were forming in my head of something I should say. The thoughts were not necessarily a logical response to what had been said to me and I did not voice them. As such experiences continued, I prefaced the thoughts with a comment, 'While you've been talking, these thoughts have come into my head but I don't know if they are relevant or helpful for you.' Usually, the comments were well received, and more than once I was thanked at a later date for what I said,. But by then I could not remember what had been said. Maybe I had been given an opportunity to put into words something they wanted to hear at that time.

Edward and Jake continued to be frequent visitors to my house. Jake usually travelled curled up on his rug on the passenger seat. Without any prompting Jake would wake up and bark when they were two streets away from my house. We went on many walks along the beaches and coastal paths of East Devon, the woods around Exeter, and sometimes on Dartmoor. Edward had remained interested and involved in my work since Dr Lad's visit to Exeter. He did most of the proofreading with me on *Ayurveda News*. He read the first drafts of the manuscript of the book, as well as other things I wrote.

Something changed with Edward, which I think might have been due to Veronica forming a brief friendship with another man. Edward became more open among my circle of friends about our relationship. My close friends, Sally, Pauline and Eileen, and some connected with my work, were aware that Edward and I were more than just friends. So I doubt Pauline was surprised at what I told her prior to an event at The Plough in Torrington to which Edward had invited us both. I was pleased to have finally ended all pretence with my friends. Edward was still not being open with Veronica or among his circle of friends.

I rarely visited Edward in North Devon. He had moved from his one-bedroom cottage to a two-bedroom cottage with a garden after he'd received a legacy from a relative's widow whom he had visited regularly. When he was thinking about moving, we had discussions about whether he might move closer to Exeter. There seemed little merit unless he moved to Exeter, which he didn't want to do. He found a cottage in a village in North Devon six or seven miles from his home, which he seriously considered buying. When we talked about it, we discussed his commitment to taking care of Veronica, and I pointed out that he would have to use his car for all visits, rather than having the convenience of being able to walk to her house.

Sometimes, when Veronica was out of town, he would invite me to stay overnight, but he required my presence not to be noticed by his neighbours. At times it bordered on farce as he wouldn't let me enter or leave his home with him. When he asked me to leave first I'd walk out of town in the direction we would be going and he would come along and pick me up as if I was a hitchhiker. Once when he left first, a group of his neighbours gathered outside his front door, chatting for what seemed like hours, preventing me from leaving unnoticed.

Edward was retired and the pattern of his life was dominated by worries about and visits to and from his children and grandchildren. He'd talk to me about them and how he managed Veronica's moods, as he led me to believe she could be quite emotional and perhaps difficult at times. One son had moved to France. Edward visited once or twice a year. If he was taking the ferry from Poole, he'd meet Sally for a meal before sailing. He was in the habit of visiting me before returning home. Sometimes I felt he was having a debriefing session before reporting to Veronica. To me, it was just part of our relationship. I accepted how he wished to manage his family. That was how it was, though at times I felt frustrated he'd neither talk with Veronica nor his children. I wondered if the children, who were adults with families of their own and knew their parents lived in separate houses, would have objected to their father having a discreet woman friend. I thought Veronica would be naïve if she thought I was just another one in the group of people he visited on a regular basis in his role of 'caring uncle'.

The nursing home where my mother was, appeared to be providing a good quality of care, but I think my mother was too much of a challenge for them. Again, the doctors would not speak with me, but she was good at upsetting them.

My mother had arranged for a complementary therapist to visit her at the home. The therapist concurred with my mother that she wasn't being well treated by either the home or me, and undermined our efforts to get her settled. The therapist was not willing to discuss my mother with me, even though my mother told me she wished the therapist and me to talk together.

Peggy wrote to me during the summer to tell me Eric, my uncle, had died. He'd been diagnosed with Parkinson's disease fifteen years earlier. Apart from brief spells in nursing homes, Peggy had cared for him. In the latter years he had been unable to walk or talk, but she told me he had been generally content provided his routine was not upset.

13

Resonance

IN the autumn, my mother secured herself two rooms in sheltered accommodation provided by a small local charity. The residents got their own breakfast and evening snack but were provided with a cooked meal in the dining room at lunchtimes. The day before my mother was due to move, some of her personal belongings came out of storage and I spent the day unpacking boxes, arranging furniture and making the rooms ready. Before lunchtime the smell of meat cooking pervaded both rooms. I knew my mother would not tolerate that and crisis would be looming. My mother moved in on Friday the 13th. I decided not to be available until the initial dust had settled.

I'd arranged to meet Edward and Jake on the Saturday to go walking on Exmoor. Edward was late picking me up from a cul-de-sac on the edge of the industrial estate where I was leaving my car, and he looked exactly as he did when he came to my house on the day Andrew's body had been found. I knew something shocking had happened.

He told me he'd looked in on a close friend on his way to meet me. While he was there a police officer had arrived to tell the friend his son had been killed in a car accident. Edward asked me to take Jake for a walk. He'd be back after he had seen Veronica. When he returned it was clear I needed to make myself scarce. As I drove home the problems with my mother started weighing in on me. By Sunday I couldn't stop crying, and I was missing Andrew with the intensity I'd experienced two and a half years earlier when he'd died.

Over the following two weeks it became clear the crisis with my mother was serious. She had alienated the residents, the trustees and the care staff. Some agency care staff knew my mother from the nursing home and the trustees were upset that they'd not been properly informed before giving my mother a tenancy agreement. It transpired the usual trustee who dealt with admissions had been in hospital when my mother applied for the accommodation. Her application had been dealt with by a trustee with little experience in selecting potential residents. She was being blamed by the other trustees for causing the problem by having approved my mother's application. She introduced my mother to Mr Danby, her solicitor, as my mother said she wanted to buy a flat. Of course, all involved were aware that my mother's problems would be solved if only her daughter would help.

By the end of the month I had seen Dr B, as I was not coping with the situation and was doing a lot of crying. Dr B referred me to the mental health services, and I soon had an appointment with Community Psychiatric Nurse A. I think he was only doing an initial assessment to make sure it was safe to put me on the six-month waiting list to see a clinical psychologist.

Having been referred to a psychologist, I realised it would be an opportunity to see if I could learn anything more about the times I had difficulties understanding what was going on around me. I asked for a hearing test. I didn't think I had a hearing problem, but it needed eliminating. Following a test in the doctor's surgery I was referred to the audiology department at the hospital. They did various tests over three months. I was informed I had a congenital hearing loss, nothing could be done about it, hearing aids wouldn't help me, and over the years I had developed good coping strategies, but I was referred to a consultant.

The temporary admission trustee helped my mother look at

flats, and Mr Danby acted as if he was convinced he had to protect his new client from her daughter. I was not convinced he was acting totally independently and in the best interests of my mother. I was surprised he didn't have a conversation with John, being the solicitor who was conversant with my mother's affairs. I'd have expected that as normal practice between solicitors. I doubted Mr Danby would have assisted my mother to find alternative accommodation if she hadn't had the money to buy a flat. When a flat was found which my mother was going to buy, I made it very clear to her and Mr Danby that I would not be involved with her care or visiting her if she went ahead and bought a flat, unless suitable care arrangements had been made before she moved in. Before Christmas she withdrew from the sale, and soon afterwards the trustees served her with formal notice to quit.

A new massage therapist, Jan, came on the scene at around that time. She had a very practical approach and was a constant positive factor in the situation which unfolded. From the beginning she understood the nature of the problems between my mother and me.

Edward had been affected by the sudden death of his friend's son. He spoke often about his friend and his friend's wife, his concerns about them, and the health problems they had since their son died. Edward did not speak much about himself, but I had a feeling he was thinking, 'There but for the grace of God go I.' He became more protective about his family, being there for his children and grandchildren and preserving family unity. There was a subtle change in our relationship around that time, which I wasn't aware of for over a year when I had less free time and was less flexible in making arrangements with him.

By the beginning of 1996, my working hours were occupied by Ayurvedic Living and my own work in connection with talks, workshops and individual sessions discussing Ayurvedic lifestyle principles. I enjoyed the variety of working with people and working on my own, working at and away from home, and of being in constant contact with interesting people who shared my interest in Ayurveda and health. I was working with Liz

Greer developing cookery workshops. Her bubbly, practical personality made working with her fun. I found her approach to food and its preparation inspiring, and wanted to offer a workshop with practical guidance on the preparation of a simple, but delicious meal based around kitcheri. Seminars were being planned with Dr Lad in the summer and with Dr Svoboda in the autumn.

Problems regarding my mother's care continued throughout 1996. My mother had changed GP again. I'm not sure if Jan influenced the choice as his surgery was in the neighbouring town. He referred my mother to a community psychiatric nurse, Ruth and to a social worker. I don't think my mother was cooperating with anybody other than Mr Danby, as he was again helping her buy a flat. I had been excluded from the decisions regarding my mother. Her medical, social care and legal advisers had known her for less than three months.

In the middle of February I went to Albuquerque for three weeks to stay with Patty and catch up with my other friends there. When I returned home, Ruth contacted me. She was a nurse with wide experience of working with the elderly and adopted a sensible approach. Ruth told me the doctor had arranged a case conference at the beginning of April to which I'd been invited. If I went my mother would use it as an opportunity to make a personal attack on me so as to avoid the issues and advice being given by the professionals. Instead, I wrote a four-page report and sent copies to her GP, social worker, Ruth, and Mr Danby. I concluded by saying I had deposited all her securities in a bank until I was satisfied that her advisers were fully aware of her background and circumstances, and were giving fully informed advice. I said I would only release the securities to her if her doctor confirmed to me in writing that she had full mental capacity to manage her financial affairs and make informed choices about her living arrangements. I pointed out the date she was required to quit her flatlet was not a magic date by which rushed decisions had to be made, her furniture could be returned to store, and she could go into some form of temporary accommodation while longer term arrangements were made. I became increasingly concerned about the deterioration in my mother's physical and mental health, and the increased distress she was displaying.

Ruth replied to my report. She told me she was visiting my mother regularly, trying to point her in the right direction and was keeping an eye on her weight loss. She concluded her letter by saying, 'It is sometimes not easy when people are supposed to be given choices as outlined in government information. What the clients choose is not always what I might view as the best way forward. I try to give the best advice I can at the time, considering the various circumstances'.

While I had been in America, my name had come to the top of the waiting list to see a clinical psychologist. Clinical Psychologist B thought it would be beneficial for me to look at my childhood issues. I knew discussing my childhood with a clinical psychologist would be counter-productive and I did not want psychotherapy. What I wanted was help in dealing with the situation that was ongoing between me and my mother. I agreed to see a cognitive clinical psychologist and was put back on the waiting list. Clinical Psychologist B advised counselling would be damaging for me, but also said if I needed assistance before I could see the cognitive psychologist, I should ask for counselling.

After the case conference my mother's GP had arranged, Mr Danby informed me my mother had not been dissuaded from buying a flat, but he said the situation would be monitored. He said he was taking a power of attorney for my mother to sign which would appoint him as her sole attorney. Once that was signed I'd have no authority in connection with my mother's financial affairs. The doctor confirmed my mother's mental capacity was alright and her securities passed to Mr Danby.

Mr Danby had arranged for the new flat to be decorated and new carpets laid prior to my mother moving in, but no arrangements had been made for her care. At the end of April, my mother moved into a first floor flat in a block with no lift. As predicted, I started receiving phone calls about her.

It was a tough decision to stick to my guns and say I wouldn't visit her in the flat. I had been clear before she bought the flat and I knew there was nothing practical I could do without the unreserved backing of her medical and legal advisers.

At the beginning of July, I wrote her a long letter, in which I was frank with her about how I saw her situation and made suggestions about how it could be ameliorated, and I was honest with her about my circumstances. I said in the letter,

> 'There is a further difficulty that most people have in understanding our problem. That is the paradox that we cannot get on with each other but that neither has ill will towards the other, and there is probably much more goodwill than those outside the situation realise. Basically we are gridlocked and need some external assistance to relieve the situation. My opinion is that you are not aware of most of your unpleasant and unreasonable behaviour, and thus cannot understand why people, but especially I, respond to you as we do. I think this is as a result of extremely sad and hurtful experiences you had many years ago. I would prefer to act towards you in a loving and caring way, but I do not have the resources within myself to do what you ask, and the accumulation of events over many, many years has taken its toll on me. My priority is my health and establishing my life and work in a sustainable way.

I also wrote:

> 'My personal view is that part of your problem, that a doctor should take into account when considering your overall care, is that you have a phobia about doctors, which makes it very difficult for you to elicit and accept the help you would like, and your manner makes it very difficult for your carers to meet your needs.'

I suggested she showed my letter to her doctor and solicitor, and ask for help in finding a means whereby we had contact. I'd given Ruth my doctor's name and Dr B permission to speak with my mother's doctor. Dr B had a copy of the letter to my mother. The doctors never made contact.

My mother wrote to me thanking me for my lovely long letter. She told me the decorator was doing her shopping.

Then she recounted some of the experiences she had had with the first nursing home. By the time she got to the Tyringham Clinic she had lost two stone and was anaemic. She hadn't realised she had lost so much weight. That was the reason why she rang me and asked me to book her into a nursing home in Exmouth. She wrote other things about her time in the nursing home and the sheltered accommodation. She was not having an adequate diet at either establishment and did not understand her financial position. She wrote, 'At [the nursing home] I had such stress that my mind began to give me trouble which I thought was serious.' At the end of the letter she wrote, 'The thing I miss most is you and I am very sorry if I upset you. All I would like is that you would visit me because I have been working very hard to keep going.'

I'd missed some of the problems when she was in the nursing homes, but they would have been spotted had her GPs established reasonable communications with me.

I received her letter a few days before her seventy-fifth birthday. I had already asked Liz to make my mother a cake, which was beautifully decorated with fruits. I left the cake at Ruth's office requesting she took it to my mother. Ruth did so on the afternoon of my mother's birthday. My mother invited her to stay for a cup of tea and a piece of cake. Ruth talked with my mother and suggested she went into a home for a couple of weeks for respite care. Jan had given my mother details of a residential hotel a short distance from my mother's flat.

The residential hotel had a room vacant for two weeks. My mother agreed to go for respite care. I visited her as soon as she was there. Towards the end of the two weeks she asked if she could stay, but they didn't have a vacancy then and my mother returned to her flat. Ruth confirmed a care agency was visiting morning and afternoon and had been asked to let Ruth know if my mother cancelled the arrangement. Six weeks later my mother moved to the residential hotel.

My first appointment with the cognitive clinical psychologist was two days after the summer workshops with Dr Lad.

Clinical Psychologist C was pleasant and friendly. He appeared to have notes from Clinical Psychologist B. He explained the cognitive model to me and how I needed to change my patterns of thinking and behaviour. He asked me to buy and read *The Feeling Good Handbook* by David D. Burns, start doing what it said, and at my next appointment we'd see how I was getting on understanding the principles of cognitive behaviour therapy. He said I shouldn't have any further contact with my mother.

I bought the book and read it. At the end of June I'd been to the audiology department at the hospital and knew I had a hearing impairment. As far as I was concerned the hearing loss explained the difficulties I had sometimes relating to people. By the time of my next appointment with Clinical Psychologist C, I was applying what *The Feeling Good Handbook* was advising. I had started asking people to repeat what they'd said if I thought I hadn't heard them correctly.

At my next appointment with Clinical Psychologist C I told him I was not going to cut myself off from my mother. I explained she wasn't well, was moving into residential care, she hadn't any other family and I wanted to stay in touch with her. He didn't give me the impression he approved of my decision, but he didn't repeat his advice that I shouldn't see her. He was pleased with the progress he thought I was making using the cognitive therapy, and made another appointment for me to see him.

Prior to that appointment I saw the consultant otolaryngologist. He told me my hearing loss affected vowels, was probably congenital and would explain the educational difficulties I'd had. He confirmed hearing aids wouldn't help. I was referred for another hearing test six months later to ensure I didn't have a progressive hearing loss. I was satisfied the problems of not understanding what was going on around me were due to hearing loss and nothing else.

The residential hotel my mother moved into in September was owned and run by a husband and wife team, Adrian and Sylvia. Most of my contact was with Adrian, whom I will forever bless for the care and practical support he gave my mother and me. During the weeks my mother had returned to her flat, Adrian had taken her to see the naturopath doctor she had seen when staying in the first nursing home. I sent Ruth information about Nature Cure to pass to my mother's GP.

When I saw her GP I raised the issue of my mother having a phobia about doctors.

'If she had a phobia about spiders you would be able to cope with that. Please don't take it personally because her phobia is about doctors,' I said.

To his credit, he and one of his partners spent sufficient time with her and gained her confidence, so much so that she requested operations on her knees.

At the end of October I had a letter from Mr Danby. I think he was beginning to understand his client a bit better, though I wasn't happy about his attitude, and he did not appear to be working towards my mother's wishes for me to be involved in looking after her financial affairs again. Mr Danby wrote to me:

> 'I believe that Adrian has always been very kind and patient with your mother, but there have been occasions when Sylvia and your mother have not seen eye to eye! At present your mother says she has no intention of staying at the residential hotel permanently, but I take this with a pinch of salt. Your mother has indicated that she does not wish to consider a sale of the flat at present, and I have accepted that a decision on this can be left until the spring,'

I replied to Mr Danby's letter three weeks after receiving it. I wrote to him:

> 'When I see my mother she asks me a number of questions about her affairs and also indicates that she wishes me to be involved. I have explained to her that unless she gives instructions to you to discuss her affairs with me you are unable to do so. As you have mentioned some information about her affairs in your letter to me, I presume that she has indicated something of her wishes to you. I would be glad if you would please let me know exactly what her instructions are regarding my involvement. I am aware that she is capable of saying one thing to me and giving you

different instructions. This I regard as part of her condition, but I suspect from some of the comments in your letter you are becoming more aware of the difficulties.

'In view of her health situation I feel that the position regarding her wishes on her doctor communicating with me should also be clarified. I appreciate that when he entered the situation earlier this year, things were already a long way out of hand. He did write to me on 19th March saying that "It is obviously very difficult for me to break my confidentiality with her". This I totally respect. If you feel it is appropriate I would be glad if you would please take my mother's instructions as to whether her doctor can disclose and discuss her medical situation with me. If her instructions are in the affirmative, could you please arrange for her doctor to be informed of her wishes and also for me to have confirmation that he will not be prevented by confidentiality from communicating with me.

'From my discussions with Ruth and Adrian, I gather it is felt that it is in my mother's best interests that she remains in touch with me. I presume that all her advisers are now aware that her problems have a long, difficult and painful history. I feel that my family knowledge should be taken into account in dealing with her problems. Provided my health permits it, I intend maintaining regular contact with her. It is easier if I am fully acquainted with her affairs so I can sieve the relevant from the repetition when I see her.'

At the end of November, I wrote to Adrian. I said:

'Mr Danby did write to me following his visit last week to Mother. I was not happy with his letter and had discussed with Ruth whether his approach is the best way of handling Mother. Ruth does agree with me that Mother is in the best place she can be, and I would like to see her stay with you and become more settled. Ruth also confirmed that no one is now likely to help Mother back into her flat. Mr Danby's letter seems to indicate that he is only just becoming aware of Mother's problems and feels I need protecting from them. I feel both Mother and I need protecting from advisers (both health and fiscal) who have in the past taken their fees, and, without fully consulting with all involved in her care nor acquainting themselves with all the facts, have adversely influenced her circumstances. Such advisers rarely stay to see the consequences of their actions.

'From my conversations with Ruth and with Mother last week there are a couple of optimistic signs that she is being more accepting. Andrew and I found it usually took 4–6 months of repeatedly telling her some piece of advice before she would accept it. Mother did suggest last week that the arrangements for her finances be restored to how they were earlier this year, when I was attorney, backed up by professional advisers who had known the family for a while. I discussed this with Ruth and she indicated that such an arrangement would not be detrimental to Mother. Her financial affairs are not difficult to manage and I have written to Mother to say that I am not willing to be attorney jointly with Mr Danby, but am willing to be sole attorney if that is what she wishes.

'I enclose a copy of the letter I have sent to Mother for your information. I do not think it is advisable to let her know I have sent a copy to you, but I am concerned that she is presently telling different bits of information to different people to confuse the situation and I would rather you know what I have said to her.'

Mr Danby told me my mother wanted him to contact Peggy. When Peggy received Mr Danby's letter she wrote to me to ask how I wanted her to reply. Peggy told me a little about how, some months after my brother's death, my mother had been repeatedly suggesting she went to live with Peggy and Eric. Peggy had withheld that information from me at the time with the best of motives, but it underlined for me the tragedy that my GP and my mother's GP never spoke to each other.

In her letter Peggy told me my mother and her siblings had been sexually abused over a period of time as children by people who worked for my grandfather. My mother had been very young when the abuse started. That information helped me make sense of much of my mother's distressed behaviour and confirmed suspicions I already had. Peggy replied to Mr Danby in a way that ensured he did not write to her again.

Three times my mother instructed Mr Danby she wanted to

revoke the power of attorney in his favour and make me her attorney again. When Mr Danby told me the new document was signed and I could collect it together with my mother's securities from his office, I was not willing to do so without him telling me how he'd managed my mother's affairs in the preceding months. He was not co-operative about that, and in the end agreed I could borrow his file over the Christmas and New Year break.

I was given the keys to my mother's flat and visited it for the first time two days before Christmas. Although the front door was locked, the delivery hatch was not and was big enough for me to go through into the flat had I so wished. I discovered the heating was off but the mains water stopcock was turned on. I found it emotional seeing my mother's personal belongings arranged in a similar manner as they had been in her Malvern flat. The new carpets were an identical colour to those in her previous flat. She had had an unsuccessful attempt to hang on to some independence. I felt it was an attempt that might have succeeded if our respective doctors had cooperated and I had been given support to oversee appropriate care arrangements for her.

I gave Adrian a key to the flat. He turned the water off and set the heating to come on to prevent frost damage. When I returned Mr Danby's file in the New Year, his office confirmed he had failed to arrange insurance cover for the contents of the flat and my mother's personal possessions.

Diary Dates for 1997 in *Ayurveda News* reflected the changes in my working life and the growth of interest in Ayurveda in the UK, to which the regular seminars and workshops given by Dr Lad and Dr Svoboda had contributed. Their visits that year were held at nationally recognised yoga centres that trained yoga teachers and therapists. Dr Svoboda's April visit was organised by The Sivananda Yoga Vedanta Centre in London. Dr Lad gave an evening talk there in July prior to his workshops at Ickwell Bury, which I organised. There were three informal London discussion days at the Mandeer Restaurant; details of Hart deFouw's visits to London and Bath organised by Paul

Harvey; a weekend organised by Dr Ann Roden; and my lifestyle workshops in Devon and Scotland. Hart was staying with me in Exeter in June and offering individual Jyotish consultations. That year I had also been invited to give workshops for yoga groups in London, the Midlands, Dorset and Devon.

Dr Mauroof Athique, an Ayurvedic physician who had graduated in Sri Lanka and been resident in England for a number of years, had taken the first steps to form The College of Ayurveda. Some of the regular participants in Dr Lad's and Dr Svoboda's workshops were among the first students of The College. The College's degree course in Ayurveda was validated and run at Middlesex University. Ayurvedic physicians in the UK formed professional organisations. A decade later, some had amalgamated into the body known as The Ayurvedic Practitioners' Association to represent Ayurvedic practitioners in the UK. The Association has been involved in negotiations with British and European legislators to ensure Ayurveda is recognised as a healing system in its own right.

Life was hectic before I went to America in spring 1997. Maurice, my builder, would be converting two bedrooms into one and having the new carpets laid while I was away. In January my mother decided she wanted her flat sold and it had to be cleared of her furniture and personal possessions. No items were going into store. My mother had many pieces of furniture I liked and was pleased I was keeping our favourite pieces. By the beg-inning of March I had seen the usual removal firm, and an auctioneer about selling my mother's collection of china and some furniture. Estate agents had been instructed. John, the solicitor, was instructed to deal with anything regarding the sale in my absence. We'd re-established the arrangements that had been in place before Mr Danby's intervention for John to deal with any emergency regarding my mother while I was abroad. Edward came on a few occasions when I was going through the contents of my mother's flat. I did not have much free time and it was one way we saw a bit of each other.

I'd finished the sessions with Clinical Psychologist C before

Christmas and had a final session with him to conclude the referral. He said he was impressed by how hard I had worked in getting my life together in the previous nine months and developing good ways of coping. He didn't seem to be aware of the changes that had happened regarding my mother's care and that it was those changes that were making the difference to me. I understood how the hearing impairment affected me, and when it mattered I knew how to clarify my understanding. The psychologist was someone who was easy to talk, to and having an hour's conversation with an intelligent person was supportive. However, he was pleased to think I had made excellent use of cognitive therapy concepts. He didn't close his file then, but left 'a session in the bank', as he put it, which meant I could contact him without having to be referred by my GP.

The second audiogram was identical to the test performed the previous autumn, and the consultant otolaryngologist confirmed my hearing loss was likely to have been congenital.

At the beginning of March I spent two weeks in Albuquerque, staying with Wynn, Patty and their family. During my stay I visited California to fulfil a speaking engagement at The Natural Products Expo trade show held at the Anaheim Convention Centre. I had not experienced an exhibition of that size before. After returning to England, I received the audience's feedback. It was the first such feedback I'd had. My performance had been satisfactory. I was invited to the East Coast Expo in September, but I had other work commitments then and Dr Svoboda was visiting Exeter.

In March, the twelfth foreign edition of *The Book of Ayurveda: A Guide to Personal Well-Being* was published in Japan. It was four years since Andrew's funeral. Opportunities had been given to me to write a book about Ayurveda which had gone to a number of nations. One of my friends told me she had seen it on a bookstand at Singapore Airport.

14

No Diagnoses

THE still waters I thought I'd arrived at with a settled routine and work I enjoyed did not stay calm for long. My absence in America unsettled my mother. She wanted to move to Torquay and had been visited by a woman who ran a care home there. My mother had also contacted one of the retired Nature Cure doctors, by then in his nineties, whom she'd consulted thirty years previously. She had fallen out with Sylvia over food and was losing weight again. I asked a medical herbalist to visit my mother monthly to advise about diet, supplements and herbal medicines. Jan continued regular massage therapy sessions which my mother enjoyed and which benefited her legs.

Initially, the change in my relationship with Edward was subtle but came to the fore when I was considering an invitation to give a weekend workshop in Scotland. I told Edward I was not happy driving that far on my own and asked him if he would like to come with me, visit his relatives, who lived thirty miles from where I'd be working and then spend a few days walking with me in Scotland. He agreed to that plan but did not mention it then to his relatives. When he did, it was not convenient for him to stay. He told me he was going to France, but should be back a day or so before my workshop and we could still drive to Scotland together. Edward had back problems and pain increased when he was sitting in a car, so it wouldn't be sensible to drive from mid France to Scotland.

For the first time since I had known Edward I felt he was not being open with me. I made arrangements to fly to Scotland. We'd exchanged letters in April. I don't have a copy of my letter to him. In his reply he wrote he had read and re-read my letter a good many times to try and absorb it all. He said I had demonstrated that I was every bit as much the person of perception, sensitivity and thoughtfulness he'd always thought me to be. He continued,

> 'Please never doubt that I realise you are growing and embarking on serious business and that you are continuing in faith even when the way ahead is not always clear, showing courage I suspect you didn't know you had – though without courage you would scarcely have achieved everything you have come through from childhood onwards, For all this and more I admire you tremendously.'

Edward went to France at the beginning of June. I would be fully committed with work for five weeks on his return, so I suggested it would be better if we each did what we had to do and met up at the beginning of August.

I enjoyed the workshop in Scotland and was pleased to meet a lady who had subscribed to all the issues of *Ayurveda News* since its launch.

In the middle of July I was at home preparing and packing the items for Dr Lad's visit. I had carried a couple of boxes of books down the steps to the garage under my house. I was back in the house when I experienced an excruciating pain in my back and abdomen. That was followed by vomiting and diarrhoea, and I was doubled up on the floor. I managed to call an ambulance and it wasn't long before I heard the comforting sound of its siren approaching my house. I was observed in casualty for a few hours and the pain subsided. They weren't sure what had happened to me and told me it could recur. They thought it was best if I went home, and if it happened again during the night I was to phone and would be admitted to hospital. The night passed peacefully. In the morning I was alright but I wasn't well enough to drive to the Sivananda Yoga Vedanta Centre in London at the end of the week so I went by taxi. The Sivananda Centre looked after Dr Lad and me and drove us to the Yoga for Health Foundation in Bedfordshire the day before Dr Lad's workshops there. We had a brief sightseeing visit in London on the way. I was very tired while staying at Ickwell Bury and missed much of Dr Lad's workshops as I was resting in my room while he was speaking.

The situation with my mother was deteriorating again. Despite everybody's best efforts she was not eating properly and was complaining about the food. She was still losing weight. Her GP suggested she spent a few days in the cottage hospital for observations. My mother agreed, and I was told she would probably be admitted the following week.

On the Monday of that week Liz Greer and I went to a meeting with publishers to discuss a book proposal we'd put together about food. I was driving and on the way home when we were south of Bristol there appeared to be a smudge on my glasses. I stopped to clean them. It wasn't on my glasses, but something was affecting my left eye slightly, but it wasn't bad enough to affect my vision for driving. The next day my eye was the same.

My mother was admitted to the cottage hospital that day, and when I saw her she was being a difficult patient, but it was not clear what was upsetting her. I had been prepared, but not told directly, that Adrian and Sylvia probably would not want her to return when she was discharged.

The following day my vision was affected. I saw a locum GP as Dr B was away. After examining my eyes and my eyesight he handed me a note and told me to go home, pack a bag, report to casualty and expect to be admitted to hospital.

When I got home I phoned the cottage hospital to tell them they wouldn't be seeing me for a few days as I was likely to be admitted to hospital. I phoned Edward and cancelled meeting him the following evening; we hadn't seen each other for two months. At casualty I was transferred to the eye unit. By then, the vision in my left eye had deteriorated to the point where I could just about count how many fingers the doctor was holding up in front of my nose. I had no pain, but a dull ache behind my eyes. It was not necessary for me to be admitted. I was told to have a quiet, restful weekend and return to the eye unit the following Monday for further tests.

Edward visited me the next day. I felt we had lost our former ease of communication, relaxed manner with each other, and closeness. In the fifteen years Edward and I had known each other, many difficult situations had happened in both our families, but the closeness I felt with him had not been affected. I didn't know if I'd hurt him when I'd asked him not to phone me or write to me when he went to France in June. Maybe I hadn't conveyed to him the feeling I had that he was no longer being open with me.

Edward had a very strong, and at times stubborn, will. When there was something he didn't want to do or tell me, I'd learnt that unless it really mattered to me it was best to accept he was not going to change his mind. We were fairly evenly matched in our abilities to take a strong stand over matters of principle. If our relationship had changed, or was naturally coming to its conclusion, I didn't want him to continue visiting simply because I had a health problem. I phoned him on Saturday morning and told him I thought it was better we stopped seeing see each other.

He phoned me later that morning to tell me he'd spoken with Veronica and was coming to spend the weekend with me. By the time he arrived on Saturday afternoon, the sight in my left eye was almost gone. What was happening to me? I was scared. I was telling myself I valued my sight more than my relationship with Edward.

Despite the advice given to me by the eye unit, Edward thought it would be better if I went out. We drove to a wood a few miles from my house for a walk. It was not a good idea. I was convincing myself it was the last time I'd see a wood. My left eye wasn't seeing it and it appeared to me that the vision in my right eye was also deteriorating. If I wore my glasses to help my right eye I got severe headaches, and had ceased wearing them. By the evening I was quite distressed and Edward took me to casualty. The duty doctor in the eye unit was kind to me, but told me to go home and come back on Monday morning as arranged. Edward went home on Sunday.

I spent Monday at the eye unit having tests and experts peering into my eyes. An urgent brain scan was arranged. There was something about my left eye that interested one doctor, but was not part of the problem. He asked if I would agree to have it photographed for use with medical students. I had no objection and that was done as well. At lunchtime, a volunteer from the WRVS took me to the cafeteria. Although I had some vision in my right eye, I had lost my binocular vision and could not co-ordinate my hands accurately, so I was just as likely to knock a glass over as pick it up.

At the end of the day I was given a phone number to call to get the result of the brain scan and an appointment to return to the eye unit the following Monday. When I phoned about the brain scan, I was told it was clear. That was the best news I could hear. At my next appointment the consultant told me I had optic neuritis in my left eye, and over a period of months the sight should return to normal or near normal. He said I could be treated with steroids, which would speed up the return of the sight, but he only recommended using steroids when the sight was lost in both eyes. I was given a follow-up appointment for two weeks later.

When my mother was due to be discharged from the cottage hospital, she returned to Adrian and Sylvia's residential hotel. Adrian had been visiting my mother after he heard about my sight problems. Her hospital stay had produced no information about any new medical problems. She realised I was unable to help her and appeared to be more settled and accepting of where she was living.

The optic neuritis was not giving me any pain. The problems I experienced due to it were the inability to drive, not seeing faces clearly, reading had become difficult and the loss of binocular vision made me clumsy. When pouring hot water out of the kettle, I deliberately placed my other hand behind my back to ensure I didn't scald myself inadvertently. Perhaps, if I had not been self-employed, the doctor would have signed me off until my sight was fully restored. I wanted to continue with life as normally as possible. I took the train to Exmouth when visiting my mother. I went by train to Barnstaple and discovered, when walking to the town centre, how hard it is to negotiate a busy road junction with impaired sight.

I was due to present an Ayurveda Workshop at a three-day residential yoga seminar in Dorset. Friends took me there and Edward had agreed to meet me afterwards. I found it strange teaching when I wasn't getting feedback from the audience's faces, as all I saw were blurred outlines. On the first afternoon I was presenting details of Ayurveda's theory of health and disease. Usually there were few comments from audiences as I presented the information they'd use when they started applying it to their own constitution, diet and lifestyle. I was pleased the audience had grasped essentials and were using the information constructively throughout the rest of the workshop.

Edward met me at the end of the workshop. Then, and for the following few weeks, he was more attentive, loving and caring towards me than he had been at any time in our relationship. I didn't put his reaction down to my sight loss, which we knew was temporary.

The first Saturday of September was Princess Diana's funeral. I'd cancelled the discussion day in London and travelled by train to Putney for the Sunday meeting at the Sivananda Yoga Vedanta Centre. I usually used the Underground to travel in London having taken a train to London's Paddington station. That Saturday I used the Exeter-Waterloo line so I could change trains and go direct to Putney. I'd arranged with the disability services for rail users to be met when I changed trains and put on one to Putney, but no one met me. A fellow passenger assisted me onto the platform where I stood somewhat disorientated and unable to read any signs. I asked for help until I was standing on a different platform and hoped the train I boarded was going to Putney. It was. The following weekend Edward drove me to the Midlands. I had other talks and work-shops planned but cancelled them without causing financial loss or inconvenience to anyone.

The consultant at the eye unit was satisfied nothing further had developed. He reassured me my sight would return and didn't need to see me again. Three weeks later I had a routine appointment with my GP. He said he had discussed my brain scan with the consultant at the eye unit. I was surprised as I'd been told my brain scan was clear. My GP told me something had shown up on the scan they wouldn't normally tell patients about, but as I had no relatives he thought I ought to know. He reassured me it was nothing to worry about, but there were abnormalities which sometimes were found on the scans of people who later developed multiple sclerosis. He said it didn't mean I would develop MS, and if I did it wouldn't be for ten or fifteen years. It would just mean I would get old before my time. He reiterated the scan was not showing I had MS, but something that could turn into MS.

I decided I needed a holiday, and went to Ickwell Bury for a week of rest and yoga classes. When I got home there was a message from my mother's GP asking to see me. He explained he didn't think my mother would live for more than six months. I didn't understand. The only diagnoses she had were rheumatism and arthritis, neither of which I thought could be fatal. My mother's health had deteriorated in the previous couple of months and she was losing weight, but I didn't understand why he'd said she was dying. Later, one of the care assistants let slip that my mother had refused tests for cancer.

It seemed that my eyesight was slowly improving, but what the two GPs had told me influenced my decision not to take on any work commitments that would take me away from home for the following six to twelve months. I wished to be there as much I could for my mother, and I wanted to give myself plenty of time for the grief process that would not only be for her, but for my family.

Two weeks later my mother went into a phase the care assistants called 'being with the fairies'. She knew me and where she was, but much of her time was spent with jumbled thoughts, which were often distressing her. I found if I listened carefully, I could relate some of them to events which had happened in her life. I had an impression of those dreams where the previous day's events were relived, and the brain was reviewing or reinterpreting events. I tried to listen to what she was saying as if I was a counsellor and let her feel she was being heard.

She started wondering why Andrew didn't visit. It seemed she couldn't remember he'd died, or perhaps some part of her was 'in' a stage of her life before he had died. Initially when she asked about Andrew, I tried to explain gently he had died, but I found it was better to speak about a shared memory of him.

I think she was frequently difficult with some of care assistants, but I must have said something to Adrian about what I thought she might be experiencing. Some of the things my mother said had intelligible elements with which a care assistant could empathise, even though it was not often possible to understand the detail or relevance of what my mother was saying. One day, a care assistant told me that the previous night my mother had thought she was in labour.

'It was so real to her. She is too frail for all that pushing,' the care assistant added.

I found it difficult when my mother asked about Andrew. I kept my tears for when I got home. Then I indulged in copious tears as I missed him so much. His death had been harder for my mother than my father's, and her life since then hadn't been free from misery and pain. I asked Clinical Psychologist C for support during the last months of my mother's life. He agreed to see me.

Something was troubling Edward, but he wouldn't talk about it. I didn't know whether it was to do with me and the inevitable changes in my circumstances after my mother had died and my self-imposed responsibilities to her had ended, or whether it was connected with Veronica, his children, or something else. I was concerned about him and his unwillingness to speak to me or, it seemed, to anybody about what was troubling him. He did agree to speak with Pauline who tried to facilitate some communication between Edward and me, but to no avail.

I can only speculate. Was he conflicted about continuing our relationship or leaving me free, or at least to feel free, to form new relationships when I started the next phase of my life? He appeared conscious of the age difference between us. He was five years younger than my father and I was five years older than his eldest child. At times I'd had the impression he felt he didn't deserve to be loved by me. Or maybe it was simply that he had reached the age when he no longer had the energy or wish to lead a double life, and the unofficial one needed to end. He had lived in his own house for seven years, and, from what he told me, Veronica was getting on with her life. I no longer felt I was supporting someone in the way I had when I lived to Barnstaple. I was finding it difficult he wouldn't end the pretence about me with his family. Was he afraid of Veronica's reactions, or did he feel his children couldn't cope with being confronted openly with the situation and that it would affect his relationships with them? What irritated me about the pretence with his family was the number of times he curtailed something we were doing in order to return home in case one of his children phoned. Why didn't he give them my phone number? I asked him if he would talk with Veronica.

By December, my sight had improved and I was able to drive again. Before the optic neuritis happened I'd been embroidering a border of daffodils on a cross stitch sampler. I could see to do cross stitch but my colour vision had changed. The four shades of yellow threads for the daffodils all looked the same. I continued the sampler, selecting the threads by number. When my colour vision returned the daffodils looked fine.

Two weeks before Christmas I met Edward at one of our usual walking places. He seemed quite miserable but was not telling me why. We didn't walk. He sat in my car and we ate our sandwiches before driving off in different directions. A few days later he and Veronica were away for three weeks visiting family.

I visited my mother on Christmas afternoon with Betsy. I'd taken my wicker shopping basket filled with a variety of Christmas fare and little gifts, which we unwrapped after a cup of tea and piece of Christmas cake. My mother had come out of the phase of 'being with the fairies'. She was pleased to see us and enjoyed chatting with Betsy.

My mother talked briefly and peacefully about my younger sister. That was the first and only time I'd heard my mother talk about her without being distressed or violent. It wasn't appropriate to ask my many questions then, and there was never another opportunity.

On the first Saturday of 1998, around lunchtime my phone rang. My mother had had a fall and was being taken to casualty in Exeter. She was in the X-ray department when I arrived and I had to wait while the X-rays were finished before I could see her.

When she saw me she declared, 'I have just been to my funeral. It was a lovely funeral. And I've seen Andrew.'

I took her hand and held it as she was taken on a trolley back to casualty. Apart from what she had just said to me she seemed very clear about where she was, what was happening to her, and what had to be done. She had broken her hip and would need a hip replacement. We were told the operation would be done the following morning, and she would stay in the Exeter hospital for a while before being transferred to the cottage hospital. She signed the consent forms and was transferred to a ward.

Before I left casualty I was told my mother was not expected to survive the operation, but they had to do it as she could not be nursed without it.

I spent Sunday morning at home on my own, thinking about my mother and trying to pray for her. The thought that they were killing my mother kept coming into my head. If she did not survive the operation the hospital would be phoning me; otherwise I was to phone the hospital in the middle of the afternoon to find out how she was. When I phoned, my mother was back on the ward. When I visited she was well medicated and did not seem to be aware I was there. Over the next few days she was uncooperative and distressed, and had a fear and hatred of anyone in a uniform, which made nursing her difficult. From some of the things she said, part of her was 'in' Wrexham during the war. I did not know what had happened to her in Wrexham, but Wrexham had been mentioned from time to time when she was distressed and violent in my childhood.

A nurse told me my mother was to have invasive tests for cancer the next day. My mother hadn't consented, but a doctor was so concerned about her obvious weight loss he had arranged the tests. I told the nurse my mother had previously refused such tests, and as she was not in a state to be able to give consent herself I, as her next of kin, did not agree the tests should be carried out. Whatever the tests could have revealed, it was clear my mother was not strong enough for treatment, and there were still doubts as to whether she was going to survive to the end of the week. No tests were carried out, and at the end of the week she was to be transferred to the cottage hospital.

It was January, and there was a shortage of hospital beds. She left the Exeter hospital but couldn't be admitted as planned to Budleigh Salterton hospital. I didn't know where she was. In the evening Sidmouth Hospital phoned to say she was there. The next afternoon she was transferred to Budleigh Salterton.

On my arrival at the hospital I was expecting to have to complete the admission formalities with one of the nurses. All the nurses on duty were locum nurses and none knew my mother. To my surprise, my mother had been able to give the nurse all the information required on admission, and I was amused that my mother's interests were noted as 'Ecology'. I suspect she had told them she loved Nature Cure.

My mother was pleased to see me and was co-operating with the nurses. She was in the cottage hospital for three weeks, during which time she showed none of the previous distress. I admired her courage and tenacity as she became more mobile and able to walk around the ward and the day room with a walking frame. The hospital told me that on discharge she would have to go to a nursing home and not residential care.

The weekend my mother was transferred to Budleigh Salterton

hospital, Edward came to stay with me. He sat in the hospital car park while I visited her. My mother knew of my friendship with Edward, but had been critical of him. I don't think her criticism was about him personally, but would have applied to anyone with whom I had a close friendship.

During the weekend Edward told me he had not spoken with Veronica about us and that he was afraid to do so. I felt he didn't wish to disturb the status quo, and if he had wanted to talk with her it should have been possible to arrange to do so through an organisation like Relate. Maybe what to me was a small adjustment was a much bigger step for him in his relationships with his family. I was emotionally exhausted and told Edward I couldn't continue seeing him. He didn't say anything, but had tears in his eyes.

Unusually, Veronica phoned me and asked to speak to Ted. She wanted him to give her lodger, who was in Exeter, a lift back to North Devon. It was ironic that she'd done what I had been requesting Edward to arrange.

Adrian contacted me when my mother was due to be discharged from the cottage hospital to say she could return to her room at the residential hotel and be nursed there. I was grateful and deeply touched as it was the first time somebody had wanted my mother to stay. My mother needed a special mattress which was only provided on the NHS to those diagnosed with cancer. I must have got angry and spoken with Adrian to the effect that she should be given one of the special mattresses, and asked him to go ahead, get one and send me the bill. I don't know what he did, but she had the mattress the next day and I wasn't sent a bill.

On my first visit after my mother had returned to the residential hotel I met Alice in the hall. Alice was in her teens and over the previous year, had been one of my mother's regular care assistants and, I think, my mother's favourite. My mother said she preferred Alice to give her her bath.

'Your mother isn't the dragon she used to be,' said Alice.

I laughed, and said, 'Thank you for not telling me when she

was a dragon.'

It was true. The emotional distress and pain of a lifetime had left my mother. She was the person my father had fallen in love with and married almost fifty years earlier, and the loving mother my brother and I knew was always there, somewhere there, under the distress which had at times engulfed her.

Over the following six weeks my mother's physical health deteriorated. She was fading away in front of me and had much physical pain in addition to the site of the hip operation, which was not healing. I spent time sitting with my mother or reading to her. One morning I was reading her a story about a man and a donkey. I thought she had shut her eyes, but when I looked up at the mirror on the wall at the end of her bed our eyes met in the reflection. She smiled when I turned to her.

'I was enjoying looking at your face', she said.

As she got weaker sometimes I'd sit beside her and sing very softly.

During the last weeks of her life I was experiencing tiredness bordering on fatigue. My mother was concerned about my health. She worried how I'd manage on my own. On one occasion she commented she was glad Edward would be looking after me. I didn't tell her my relationship with Edward had finished. Sometimes I took the train to visit her, other times Eileen took me, and on one occasion Adrian picked me up from Exeter and took me home after I had seen my mother.

My mother had expressed a wish to see the sea. Adrian said he'd take us both to the seafront a couple of mornings later. That morning he phoned me before I left home and told me there had been a change in my mother and asked me to see him before I went to my mother's room.

He told me my mother's breathing had changed during the night. He didn't expect her to live more than a day or two. He very gently asked me if I'd thought about funeral directors and explained that when somebody died with them he preferred the funeral directors came to remove the body to the chapel of rest in the evening, after the residents had gone to bed. We put in place the necessary arrangements. He asked me whether I wished to be phoned during the night if my mother died, or in the morning. As my answer machine often received phone calls from America during the night, I asked him not to phone me until the morning.

When I saw my mother she was on a morphine drip, but she knew me and was peaceful. For over two weeks I telephoned each morning to see how my mother was, expecting to be told she had died during the night.

Early one morning before I phoned, my telephone rang. It was Veronica, who told me Ted had told her about our relationship. I was taken aback, as I had been expecting the call to be from Adrian about my mother. Veronica didn't tell me what Ted had said. Why was she phoning me so early in the day? Was it anger? Had Ted talked with her because he wanted to see me again? I assumed Edward would be in touch with me and told Veronica we should all be kind with each other.

I wasn't with my mother when she died. Her funeral took place at Exeter Crematorium five years to the hour after my brother's funeral service there. The service was taken by Gilbert, a vicar who had retired to Exeter and whom I knew through friends who lived in and close to his parish in North Devon, and also through his wife, who had done research at Exeter University when I'd been studying there. I asked for my father and my brother, as well as my mother, to be remembered in the service. At my request, only Eileen and I attended the service, which included 'Amazing Grace', 'The Lord is my Shepherd' and ended with The Spinners' version of 'Lord of the Dance'.

On the seventeenth anniversary of my father's death, I scattered my mother's ashes between my father's and my brother's ashes under the beech tree near Sidmouth.

I sent Alice some gift vouchers to thank her for the care she had given my mother. On the card she sent to me, she wrote, 'Your mother was a remarkable person who taught me to never give up. I will always remember her for this. It was a pleasure to have known her.'

Finding an understanding about my mother was a process of putting the pieces together until it all made sense to me. I will never know how close to the reality of her life my picture is.

Perhaps the 'flipmodes' started after the death of my sister. I do not know if she was still-born or died shortly after birth, nor do I know if the pregnancy went to full term, nor how seriously ill my mother was. Was her life at risk? Did the death of my sister reignite the loss she felt when her sister died? Did physical and psychological traumas connected with my sister re-expose my mother to the distress of her childhood abuse? Or was I the trigger causing resonances with her childhood as I grew? All these questions will remain unanswered.

I found an acceptable explanation for the violence towards me when I saw Jan Sutton's 'The Cycle of Self-Injury' on the Internet.[1] The model describes six stages of the cycle, starting with a build-up of trapped mental agony, then being overwhelmed by emotions, leading to feeling out of control and to self-harm to relieve the feeling of loss of control, resulting in feeling better until grief or guilt reactions starts the cycle again.

My mother did not self-harm, but I think when I was a child she didn't distinguish me from herself. Most of the destructive behaviours in 'flipmode' were verbal and I don't think she was aware of what was happening to her or to us.

My mother could not cope with loss or a member of her family moving away. It seemed that was the trigger for her distressing behaviour towards my father when I was applying for jobs at the end of the systems analysts course, and towards my brother when I went to Albuquerque, and towards me in the weeks before my father died.

There was no malice in my mother, and I understood at an early age that she was distressed, tortured at times. I'd been influenced by my experiences with her, but I don't think I was traumatised by my childhood experiences. I do regret my teenage decision not to have children, but it was right. I think the moderate congenital hearing impairment had a bigger impact on me than my mother's behaviour as it affected my education and socialization throughout primary and secondary schooling.

Four years after my mother's death Audrey and I arranged to have lunch at a cafe on The Quay at Exeter. It was her turn to drive. I'd walked over to her house, rung the doorbell, and found her to be her usual cheerful self. We chatted while driving to The Quay. As she parked, her whole manner towards me changed. She became quite argumentative. By the time we'd walked to the cafe it had become difficult to elicit any reasonable response from her to anything I said.

I knew Audrey was diabetic, and as we sat down at the cafe and started looking at the menu, I began wondering if it was something about diabetes which was affecting her. I voiced that concern, which fortunately was overheard by a woman at the next table who had diabetes. She suggested Audrey ate something straight away rather than wait to order a meal. Soon after Audrey had had a drink and eaten some bread she reverted to being my cheerful friend, and picked up the conversation on the topic we had been discussing before she became argumentative.

I had not been with a diabetic experiencing a hypoglycaemic episode before. Was that what had happened to my father when he was staying in Scotland? Was it the start of whatever it was that resulted in the changes in him?

Clinical Psychologist C had not closed his file on me, but we had little contact. I emailed him asking:

> 'to be put in touch with someone who can give me some information about non-insulin dependent diabetes and support as I see if it is possible that this was a possible cause of the changes in my father during the last months of his life. I did not have the interest in health then that I have now, and with the problems with my mother then perhaps it was not managed properly.... I know that I cannot have definite answers but what happened then has affected me since. It is about gaining understanding so that I can really accept in a way that enables me to move on'.

Clinical Psychologist C's e-mailed reply suggested I looked on the Internet and no support was offered. I didn't discuss the situation with an expert, but Pauline did on my behalf. From the information she gave me it is likely untreated diabetes was at the root of my father's health problems during the last months of his life.

My father was a loving, stable presence who put his family first. It was only while writing these memoirs I understood why my father uprooted us from Swindon and the life he had been born into. I think leaving the family home and leaving Morrison & Masters were major losses to him. He seemed to have dealt with it by sealing it away, as his parents were rarely mentioned, and I only gleaned snippets of what his and their lives in Wiltshire were like. I regret my Father died before reaching that age when there would be time to reminisce.

Almost three decades after my Father died I met John, a Freemason, to whom I showed the photograph of my paternal grandfather. The records held by the Library and Museum of Freemasonry in London showed my grandfather had become a Freemason when he was twenty-two years old and remained actively involved throughout his life.

John told me about Freemasonry and their values and charitable work, both for fellow Masons and their dependents as well as for non-Masonic charities. I was told Freemasonry is not a religion, but encourages the religious approach of every persuasion to all problems in life, acknowledging it is only through the love of God for his people that human happiness of any sort can be achieved. It is only through Faith that we can find the courage to face the storms of life.

These were the values my grandfather had instilled in my father, and he in turn had passed on to Andrew and me. My faith may be unconventional but it is strong, and has carried me through the challenges since my father died.

15

Stuck Grief

SHORTLY after my mother's funeral I contacted Edward. I wanted to know what he'd said to Veronica. He told me she'd 'forced it out' of him, but I never did discover what she had been told. Over the following months I tried unsuccessfully to contact Edward, and I was receiving offensive telephone calls and letters from Veronica. In one letter she asked if Ted was the father of any of my children. I was in my mid-40s coming to terms with the fact I would never have children. In the next letter, she asked me to promise to marry Ted when she divorced him so people would know why she'd divorced him, but first she had to check what her financial position would be. On receipt of that letter I wrote to Dr A. I wished to pass to a responsible person the burden I felt of having believed, rightly or wrongly, for all those years that Edward was an abused husband. I didn't want a reply from Dr A, just an acknowledgement that he'd received my letter.

It was only with hindsight I understood the effect on me of Edward's silence and Veronica's letters and phone calls in the period following my mother's death. Instead of being able to think about my father, I would find myself getting trapped in a black hole in my head with Edward's voice and a conviction he was suffering at Veronica's hands. Sometimes it would just be an engulfing blackness, a lonely place, as if I was cut off from everyone and everything, including God.

I recall shouting at God, 'I don't care how bad you make it. I know you can't cut me off.'

I learnt in that black place to recall, and then use, the teachings of Dr Vasant Lad about pain. I remembered his words, 'It is not your pain; it is part of the world's pain.'

Late one evening I watched a television programme about domestic violence and women who abused their male partners. I cried all through the programme and next morning rang the helpline number. I was told the helpline was for men only. After a brief explanation of my circumstances an appointment was made for me to have a conversation with Les Davidson of M.A.L.E., a confidential advice line for men in violent relationships. The organisation was amongst the first to recognise that men can be victims of domestic violence. Its aims included providing a point of contact and initial help for male victims and their children.[1]

I had two long telephone conversations with Les, one about my father, and the other about my relationship with Edward. Les sent me information and suggested I read *Abused Men: The Hidden Side of Domestic Violence* by Peter W. Cook.

The conversation about my father helped me begin to get out of the blackness and the impossibility of grieving the loss of my family. I still had much work to do on myself but Les had listened. Someone had confirmed that my mother's distressing behaviour when in 'flipmode' did not make her a bad person, and in some circumstances it is possible to love someone even when you don't like or understand their behaviour.

I learnt from Les that my father was not the only husband and father who'd taken on the lone task of providing stability for his family. That conversation set me on a mission to find out more about men who experience domestic abuse.

Talking with Les about Edward definitely changed my thinking. He explained to me likely scenarios of the men, their abusing wives, and the men's mistresses. The mistress can either be a crutch or a genuine relationship. When it is a crutch it is kept very secret. When it is genuine the man is seen with the mistress and they interact with others, though they may not be presenting themselves as a couple. When the man finds a genuine relationship he has difficulty trusting enough to move fully into it because of the damage from the abuse, and often because of an extremely strong wish to help and protect his wife. The mistress has to demonstrate a high degree of tender, loving care and allow more time for him to take the actions he wants to.

My attempts to contact Edward failed. My letters to him were returned unopened and I believed Veronica was doing that as it seemed the same typewriter was used to redirect the envelopes as had been used for some of her letters to me. I wrote to Dr A, but received no reply from him. I also wrote to one of Edward's children and to his business partner, but both letters came back with no comment other than that any further letters would be returned unopened. That was when I decided to write to Edward's sister, who was a doctor, and a handful of people who knew Edward in the town where he lived. Before doing so, I wrote to Edward a few times and to Dr A to tell them what I intended to do if I did not hear from Edward. The letters I'd sent to Edward were returned unopened. So I posted the letters to his sister and friends.

It was a long letter. I mentioned the TV programme on domestic violence against men and its effect. I asked the recipients to keep an open mind if they hadn't come across the problems such men have, and about why Ted and Veronica and I did what we did. I explained about my conversation with Les and how when relationships end in the manner mine did the mistress gets stuck in the grief process unless the man gives adequate explanations to her unanswered questions. I outlined some of the story and how the relationship ended. I ended my letter by saying I did not want the recipient to be a go-between or to engage in correspondence, that human relationships change and I could accept that, my feelings for Edward had not changed and that I certainly did not want to spend time with him if he no longer wanted to know me. I explained that because of the length and nature of our friendship I needed to know why he no longer wanted to know me. I concluded the letter by asking the recipient if they knew anything which might help settle for me whether or not Edward had been truthful with me.

I received a short letter from one recipient indicating he had no knowledge of anything referred to in my letter. One letter was passed to Veronica, and on which she wrote comments in the margin before sending it to Pauline. I no longer have that letter, but my recollections of the comments were that she did not accept there was any truth in what I said.

My emotions continued to be confused. I have little recollection now of the details except for one evening when I was brushing my teeth before going to bed. I stopped brushing my teeth, and with the toothbrush in my clenched fist started stabbing at my chest. I put the toothbrush down and went downstairs to the kitchen and fetched a kitchen knife. I don't know how long I sat in the bathroom with that knife or if I had any real intention to harm myself.

Around midnight some part of me observed me sitting in my bathroom with a knife, and asked, 'What do you think you're doing?'

I put the knife down, went into my bedroom and phoned Samaritans.

Suicidal thoughts continued on and off for another couple of years. I did not feel I would act on them, as I believed, and still believe, there is some form of life that continues after the death of the body, even if we don't know what form such life takes. I also believed the emotional torment would not die with my body. I think the suicidal thoughts arose when I felt utterly helpless about, or overwhelmed by, a situation. I was the problem, so ending me would solve the problem. When not too engulfed by suicidal thoughts, I tried to observe them as an experience. That way it was harder for them to get a firm hold.

I wanted Edward out of my head but could not keep him out of it. Our relationship had started and continued because of my belief he was an abused spouse. I seemed to be incapable of walking away from the situation as I thought he was experiencing abuse and wouldn't speak with me in his previous friendly manner. My attempts to communicate with Edward produced a few letters from him but I didn't believe they were written free of Veronica's influence as I was also receiving letters and phone calls from her.

A year after my mother's death, Ted wrote to me telling me to laugh at my situation. The morning I received that letter I was working on an online Open University course *You, Your Computer and the Internet* and was following instructions to use a drawing programme. The exercise we were given was to draw cartoon faces. I drew two faces, one bearing a resemblance to Ted and the other to Veronica. I then added speech balloons with comments that were sarcastic, not humorous, and printed them onto card. Foolishly I posted the cartoon postcards to Ted and Veronica.

The next morning I acknowledged to myself how stupid I had been. I sent a letter to them in which, as far as I can recall, I apologised. I shredded all the correspondence from, and copies of my letters to Edward, Ted and Veronica, their family and acquaintances since my mother's death. I knew there was nothing I could do to reach Edward. That, I thought, was the end of whatever had been going on since Veronica's phone call the previous year before my mother had died. I did not hear any more until two weeks later, when the police were hammering on my door.

The police visit was the catalyst that crystallised my wish to tell the family story, but my anger was the trigger for an obsessive desire to find out what I had been involved in.

The North Devon police officer who'd dealt with Ted and Veronica's complaint did phone me on the Sunday morning after the police had delivered their verbal warning. He explained he was not allowed to tell me anything Ted or Veronica had told him, and that the police had no further interest in the matter unless Ted or Veronica contacted them if I ignored the warning.

It was in the weeks following the police visit that I resolved to try to understand more about professionals' reluctance to talk about abuse. I knew it was important not to sink into myself, but it was difficult to motivate myself when I didn't seem to have the ability to talk with anyone about issues that mattered to me and my perception of the problems I was having. I was angry Edward had not spoken to me, but at the same time I felt he was not acting freely.

I made an appointment with a solicitor, whose attitude was

the police must be correct and there was nothing to discuss. It was early afternoon and my impression was that he'd consumed too much alcohol at lunchtime.

Following that unsatisfactory meeting, I made an appointment with a partner at the firm of solicitors where I worked when I was lodging with Ted and Veronica. That interview was a different experience. It soon became apparent the solicitor had an understanding of men experiencing domestic abuse and he treated me with courtesy and respect.

He gave me a copy of the *Protection from Harassment Act 1997*. We discussed Section (2) of the Act which provides,

'... The person whose course of conduct is in question ought to know that it amounts to harassment of another if a reasonable person in possession of the same information would think the course of conduct amounted to harassment of the other'.

We also discussed the defence in Section (3)(c),

'that in the particular circumstances the pursuit of the course of conduct was reasonable'.

I was told there was no case law to give guidance on the Act's interpretation by the courts as the Act had been in force for less than two years. We decided being a test case would be far too expensive!

Eighteen months after my mother had died, Gilbert, the vicar who had conducted my mother's funeral service, became aware I was not coming through the bereavement process and invited me to visit him for a talk. After I'd seen him a couple of times he offered to speak with Ted. Gilbert suggested the three of us met at Gilbert's house.

On the day of the meeting I walked there across the university campus and reached the end of road where Gilbert lived at the same time as Ted drove around the corner. He stopped and offered me a lift which I accepted. He took my hand in the old familiar way he had done so many times before. I became optimistic we would talk and I would get the information to enable me to move on if Edward really did not want to know me any more.

When we were settled in Gilbert's study, Edward produced a letter he had written and was not willing to talk at all. Why didn't Edward tell me he was alright if he was alright? If he wasn't alright, I felt he knew me well enough to know I was not going to be silent until I had discovered what I had been involved in and what had been said to the police.

I started corresponding with the police. It was a process of slowly extracting pieces of information. The correspondence started with the local police station who had dealt with the complaint. They told me both Ted and Veronica were seen, and if I needed more information I should contact their Data Protection Act office. That office would give me no information without Ted's and Veronica's consents. Ted's consent on its own was not sufficient.

My next police correspondent was an inspector at the Barnstaple police station. He wrote that a formal complaint which would've warranted an in depth police investigation was not made. He explained that the purpose of the police visit was to make me aware that my correspondence with Ted and Veronica was causing them distress, and if my actions were to continue it may have amounted to a criminal offence. He accepted it would have been better if the visit by the police had been made earlier in the evening.

Six months later the same officer wrote, 'Information about you receiving assistance of a psychiatric nature was passed to officers at the time but the exact details were not known.' I asked Ted and Veronica about this. Veronica indicated she did not know the difference between a psychiatrist and a psychologist. I had never been referred to a psychiatrist. My contact with Clinical Psychologist A in North Devon and with Clinical Psychologists B and C arose after difficult circumstances which had connections with Veronica or Ted.

I'd continued sending postcards and letters to Veronica and Ted as I was still unable to get my emotions settled. I would have liked them to have gone back to the police as I felt that would result in the resolution I needed. I thought it unlikely they would as it would have revealed whether I was right in thinking they had given a limited picture when making their complaint.

My correspondence with the police continued, concluding with a letter from the Chief Constable to my MP, which explained that due to the passage of time it was not possible to establish reliably what information was given.

My continued communications with Ted and Veronica culminated in a series of meetings with Mary, a family therapist. Initially, she saw Veronica. I refused to attend the planned meeting with Mary and Ted until Veronica and Ted had withdrawn the police complaint, which they did.

The meetings with Mary and Ted were unsatisfactory. Ted and I had lunch together afterwards, when he told me that he and Veronica were afraid of what I might say. He agreed there should be a further meeting with Mary after I had seen her on my own. I met with Mary and then, I believe, she saw Ted and Veronica together. After that meeting, Mary telephoned me to suggest I meet Ted in a pub. I decided she had not grasped the situation, didn't demonstrate she had any understanding about the possibility men could be victims of matrimonial abuse, and couldn't get beyond me being 'the other woman'.

Three years after the police visit Veronica gave her consent and I was sent a copy of the police log of the initial visit by the police to Veronica and Ted, and also of the second visit made to them on the day of the Guild meeting to confirm I had been warned. The police log did not refer to the unofficial part of my relationship with Edward.

Seven years after Veronica wrote asking me to promise to marry Ted I found a letter written by Dr A to Dr B on my medical notes. The letter was dated shortly after the one I'd sent Dr A about having believed Ted was an abused husband.

Dr A's letter said I was causing a lot of trouble to one of his patients, with emotional blackmail, letters, presents, phone calls, etc. His patient especially asked him to make sure Dr B knew, and Dr A wrote he was only too happy to do what his patient had asked. Dr A continued that his patient had mentioned I was seeing someone called Harry and had asked if Dr B would make sure Harry knew what was going on. Dr A invited Dr B to get in touch if he felt like having a talk about 'this stormy' relationship. Dr A added he had a very stressed chap but had tried to say everybody seemed to be doing their best.

I was shocked when I saw the letter. I sent a copy of it to Dr A asking who his patient was and what he was alleging. Dr A's single sentence reply was 'I am under no obligation, and I am dutybound not to reveal the name of my patient'.

I asked Dr A to either withdraw the accusation of blackmail contained in a letter or to substantiate it. I had a reply from the practice manager which said, 'I regret that we can be of no further assistance to you with this matter and your letters will not be answered.'

I took the matter to ICAS (Independent Complaints Advisory Service for National Health Service Patients) who wrote to the Professional Standards Office at the General Medical Council asking them to investigate whether, in writing such a letter, Dr A had breached the professional standards that are expected of the medical profession.

The GMC made no comment as according to their rules if more than five years has elapsed since the events giving rise to the allegations (i.e. Dr A writing the letter), then they will only proceed with a complaint if to do so was in the public interest.

ICAS also wrote to Dr A's practice manager, requesting an apology. The practice manager replied that Dr A and she were both sorry that the letter caused offence, but that was not the intention, as it was a letter to a known colleague to try and meet the expressed needs of another patient at his request. The practice manager added that at the time it seemed appropriate to share the information confidentially between GPs.

When the letter from Dr A was discovered, I sent a copy of it to Dr. B, who was no longer my GP. He replied that he did not regard the letter as confidential information between GPs and told me there was no particular reason why that letter had not been shared with me.

I continued writing long letters and sending them to Ted and

Veronica, and copies to the General Medical Council to place on the file they had by then closed. I could not conceive of Ted requesting his GP to write such a letter to my GP. It took more than two years before Ted wrote to me saying he did not know that Dr A had written to Dr B until I sent him a copy of Dr A's letter. Ted's letter ended by saying, 'Obviously, therefore, I was in no position to sanction either the sending of the letter or indeed its contents.'

I knew my relationship with Edward had ended long ago, and I was not hankering after that. It had been over a decade since I decided not to see him, but my emotions continued to be troubled. My release from the tangled emotions came some six months after Ted's letter denying knowledge of Dr A's letter to Dr B. I was doing an exercise in a distance learning tutorial on Emotional Logic.[2]

Emotional Logic is not a therapy but a logical method of understanding one's emotional patterns, and the meanings and useful purposes of emotions. It can be used to release the energy trapped in emotional whirlpools and move forward. My eureka moment was when I realised I was asking for the impossible. I wanted Edward to tell me, either that he was alright, or he did not want me to care at all that he was not alright. And only he could tell me that.

In the months after my mother's death, I had become trapped in a vicious circle arising from telephone calls and letters from Veronica and silence from Ted. The police visit reinforced my belief that Veronica was influencing him. Les Davidson of M.A.L.E. had been right, my grief process over Edward had become stuck and I had needed answers to my questions.

The eureka moment gave me understanding and I accepted I would never get the answers. I had doggedly pursued my quest, written a ludicrous number of letters, learnt something about domestic violence by men's partners, and finally found closure to my relationship with Edward. All that he means to me is peacefully in my heart. I can think about him now, and what we shared gives comfort rather than pain.

It was only whilst editing this book I understood the influence my desire to support my father, when he wished to live in a separate house but continue to love and support his family, had on my actions and emotions regarding Edward. The writing process gave me the distance and perspective I needed to see the complex grief processes following my parents' deaths.

16

Untangling Threads

TWELVE years after my mother's death I was sitting at home with Dr E and Community Matron A. We'd been talking for half an hour about the difficulties I'd been experiencing with my feet and eyes when Peter unexpectedly walked in through the patio door.

'Oh! Sorry. I'd left the discs on the table when I took your computer yesterday,' he said to me.

'Hello. This is my GP and Community Matron,' I said to Peter.

'This is Peter', I said, turning back to Dr E. 'He fixes my computer.'

'Hello,' said Peter.

'Peter seems to understand my health problems. My input and output devices are defective and I need a new mother board, or should I say, CPU nowadays.'

'Yes, but you're a bit more complicated than a computer,' laughs Peter as he picks up the discs from the table. 'I'll get your computer back to you in a day or so with Windows 7 installed and everything running again.'

'Thanks.'

'I think we'd better wait until we hear from the consultant before doing anything,' Dr E says as she stands up.

I'd had my second brain scan four months earlier. At the hospital they indicated the consultant would write to my GP within a month. He'd referred me for a 24-hour ECG. Both results should have been with my GP well before she made the rare home visit. I waited another month before phoning the consultant's secretary to ask when I would be given the results. She told me the consultant had written to my GP with the results three months previously and no follow up appointment had been made for me. It seemed the jinx on my healthcare hadn't been exorcised.

Over the previous decade the tangled knot of my healthcare tightened with each new practitioner to whom I was referred. The details of my experiences might be of interest to a researcher investigating patients' experiences and ways of improving the system, but will make monotonous reading in this yarn. The entanglement of the threads relating to my physical, emotional, cognitive and psychological health was hard to unravel.

When my mother died I was in regular contact with Dr B and Clinical Psychologist C, both of whom I regarded as exemplars of their professions. What neither they nor I knew were the distortions, incomplete or overlooked information on my medical notes; the notes to which they had access, but which at that time I wasn't allowed to read.

During the last year of my mother's life, I'd had optic neuritis and other undiagnosed health problems. I knew from my training with CRUSE that bereaved people are likely to suffer more health problems in the first year of bereavement, so I'd expected it to take at least nine to twelve months for me to recover my health. Before her death I'd decided to take a year's sabbatical whereby I could stay at home, organise the seminar for Dr Lad and keep the mail order and information side of Ayurvedic Living ticking over until I was ready to resume my work. I'd use the twelve months to indulge myself in studying and reading.

Dr Lad's seminar in 1998 was due to be held four months after my mother died, but he withdrew at short notice due to unexpected circumstances. That, plus my health problems, meant it was no longer feasible to continue running Ayurvedic Living as a company. The company was wound up, but I kept Ayurvedic Living as an information service for those new to Ayurveda.

My health did not improve as I had anticipated. There was nothing specific; I just had a series of niggling physical problems and the distress of stuck grief. With hindsight I realised I should have withdrawn from any contact with Clinical Psychologist C and referred myself to CRUSE. Their councillors couldn't have worked with me whilst I was seeing another counsellor or a psychologist.

Dr B was aware of my continuing distress. Two years after my mother's death he told me that if there was anything he could do to help he would personally put in whatever time it took to get me through my distress. Sadly he left the practice to work for the Commission for Health Improvement in London before there was time for me to take up his offer.

I was diagnosed with multiple sclerosis nine months later. The incident that resulted in the diagnosis happened when I was pushing a trolley around a supermarket doing grocery shopping. Pains in my legs became so unbearable I abandoned the trolley in the middle of an aisle and went home. The next day I saw my GP, Dr C. He examined my legs, stuck pins in my feet and tapped my knees.

'I'm going to refer you to a neurologist,' he said.

'Are you thinking anything other than MS?' I asked.

'No,' he replied.

'I need practical help now. I don't want to wait to see a consultant', I said.

'All right, I'll refer you to the MS nurse.'

The jinx lost the referral letter delaying the home visit by the MS nurse for a few weeks. She spent an hour with me and listened to my catalogue of symptoms over the previous three or four years.

'Yes, you've had many of the typical problems MS brings. You'll now see the neurologist at the neuro-rehab clinic and also the physiotherapist and occupational therapist there. I'll invite you to the next course I run for those newly diagnosed with MS', the MS nurse told me.

Neurologist A at the rehab clinic was everything I could want in a consultant, but he worked within a system that restricted his choice of treatments.

'Funding for disease modifying drugs for MS is not available in the Exeter area, but change is afoot and it will be in six months. I'm working out how to recall all my MS patients, and will see you again then', he explained.

I did not see the letter which Neurologist A wrote to Dr C after my appointment until four years later. In his letter he said he suspected there had been neurological symptoms prior to the brain scan I had when I had optic neuritis. He noted that there had been a number of stressors in my life and that I attributed many of my earlier symptoms to stress rather than anything else. He summarised many of these symptoms and commented that I gave a rather imprecise account of them and tended to make light of them. His opinion was that I had secondary progressive multiple sclerosis. He felt relapses were still very active and as such I would, perhaps, be a candidate for Beta Interferon [a disease modifying drug] when the situation about the availability of such drugs became clear.

But the jinx reappeared and I was not recalled as promised but referred to him by a locum GP two years later.

During those two years Occupational Therapist A did sterling work with me and arranged a wheelchair, a four-wheeled walker and a walking frame. She gave me the gift of a positive attitude to managing disability. She worked with a person-centred model – people are not disabled; it's all about understanding what a person wants to do and the restrictions the illness and environment places on them and what can be done to ameliorate the restrictions or adjust the goals so things that can be achieved.

Before I received the appointment to see Neurologist A I had a relapse which left me unable to walk. It happened suddenly on a Sunday afternoon in January. I called an ambulance as my right side had given out and I could not raise my hands above shoulder level, and the pains in my head were terrible. The paramedics were great, but they decided I'd be better left at home rather than on a hospital trolley as there were no available hospital beds, it being January. A nurse called later to bring a commode and left me in bed with a glass of water on the bedside table and told me someone would come the next morning.

I was confined to the upstairs of my house for three months as there was no downstairs toilet until the extension to my house had been completed. The waiting time to see Neurologist A was four months. But the jinx was back. Thirteen days before my appointment I received a letter telling me the appointment was cancelled as the consultant had moved to another hospital and if I still wanted to see a consultant I should contact my GP.

Four months elapsed before the appointment with Neurologist B. It did not get off to a good start. I was taken there in my wheelchair by a volunteer driver. He wheeled me into the consulting room and before he could leave the neurologist had ignored me and was questioning the volunteer as if he was my husband.

'Okay', she said after he'd left the room. 'What medication are you on?'

'None.'

After that the appointment deteriorated. She gave me the impression that all MS patients must be on medication otherwise they're not cooperative. We discussed some of my symptoms and I was given another appointment twelve months thence.

With hindsight I realised no one had picked up that disease modifying drugs had never been discussed with me.

Neurologist B's letter to my GP, which I saw eighteen months later, discussed whether or not my condition had deteriorated so that disease modifying drugs were no longer appropriate. The letter also mentioned 'the psychological issues'. That thread, I learnt when I saw my notes, was the culprit tightening the tangled knots, but let's stay with the physiology thread and not get diverted.

The following year I saw Neurologist B again, but failed to engage her in a conversation that would help me understand and manage the problems I was having. I felt I had not been fully diagnosed and not everything I was experiencing was MS.

By then I was managing MS without medication and regularly seeing two experienced complementary therapists who helped with mobility, pain relief and my general wellbeing. I obtained nutritional advice from a third therapist. I'd read more about MS and disease modifying drugs and other medications often used in

MS. I did not wish to take medication until I had a doctor with whom I could talk and who would discuss side effects and interactions with me. I was afraid that if I started on medication before being satisfied I'd been fully and correctly diagnosed I would never understand the picture and be dealing with side-effects of medications, and that might be worse than the symptoms they were designed to treat.

Something was wrong with my healthcare but I did not know what. By 2004 regulations had been changed and patients were allowed to see their notes. With the help of the Patient Advice and Liaison Service (PALS) I read my GP notes and changed GP.

Dr D accepted it was reasonable for me to have a phobia about doctors. We discussed which neurologist I should be referred to and chose one who specialised in sorting out the physical and psychological components of a patient's experiences and finding appropriate treatments.

Neurologist C was newly arrived in Exeter and when I googled his name I found his inaugural lecture at The Peninsula Medical School was to be delivered a week or so before my appointment with him. I went to his lecture with Pauline, and afterwards I was optimistic I'd receive a full and accurate assessment of what was going on with me.

I was to be disappointed again. He confirmed I had MS. The scores on a cognitive test were satisfactory. He referred me back to Neuropsychologist A who is part of the knotted psychology thread in this yarn. Neurologist C's referral letter to Neuropsychologist A mentioned post traumatic stress, a new factor for her to consider.

The person who accompanied me to the neurology appointment told me afterwards she thought I'd misheard a number of the questions. I had forgotten about my hearing impairment, as I had become accustomed to asking for information to be repeated. That strategy only worked if I realised I had misheard or misunderstood. It was not a useful strategy when asked random questions during an appointment with a consultant.

Soon after that I was referred for hearing aids by the Rehabilitation Officer for Visual Impairment as she had noticed I was having hearing problems as well as the sight problems she was assessing. The waiting time to see an audiologist was two years. The hearing tests confirmed the earlier results and I was given digital hearing aids.

Using the aids was a nightmare, as when I did use them all sorts of reactions happened with my nervous system which were not connected with my hearing. I was referred to a senior audiologist who was brilliant in his determination to uncover problems with my hearing aids' settings. I saw him regularly over a period of months and kept a diary for him of my hearing experiences. He discovered the aids were amplifying what I could hear instead of what I couldn't hear. He had to adjust the aids' factory settings as my hearing loss was not the usual one associated with growing older. At times the hearing aids were useful, but it seemed I had developed an intermittent super-sensitivity to sound which triggered neuropathic pain and strange sensations in my body and slowed my thinking.

A saga in the physiology thread concerned my feet. That saga started when I was confined upstairs and continues as I write seven years later. There were three separate problems with my feet in addition to MS. The pain from the non-MS ailments was amplified due to the nerve damage caused by MS. That resulted in more spasms which affected the alignment of my hips and spine and added to the difficulties I had walking. And again I was failing to communicate effectively with my GP or those to whom I was referred.

The psychology thread is entwined with the emotional and cognitive threads in this yarn. Those three threads blurred into one when they encountered the health services and are swept to the mental health services where the detail gets lost. It is too easy for diagnoses to be generalised into depression or anxiety. In my case the holistic picture was lost and what was really going on was dismissed. It took me a while to untangle the knots and to do so I needed the perspective I gained when editing the first draft of the manuscript of the previous chapters of this book. Until then I had not seen the detail of my life laid out in chronological order and the interactions of aspects I had taken for granted.

The distortions that ended up on the files about me held by the mental health services originated from the brief encounters I had with Dr A after he'd referred my brother to the psychiatric hospital in Bournemouth. Dr A put the word "depressed" on his hand written notes and emphasized it, not by underlining it, but by drawing a box around it so it stood out on the page. Other notes related to problems I was having communicating with my mother. His notes did not include the context of what was happening in my life when he made his notes. Those notes were handed on to Dr B, who first met me on the morning after I'd been told my brother's body had been found, the worst morning of my life. Dr B's notes record my subsequent visits to him and are dominated by one or two lines about my mother, though at one point he wrote and underlined, 'Watch for depression'.

A couple of years after my brother's death Dr B, with my consent, referred me to the mental health services. With hindsight I understood I'd been re-shocked by emotional resonances triggered by how Edward looked on hearing his friend's son had been killed in the car crash. The re-shocking sent my emotional state back to how it was the day my brother's body was found. Sadly Dr B's referral letter to Community Psychiatric Nurse A did not reflect that. The nub of his letter said, 'The main issue with Judith has been really disastrously negative relationships with her parents. She is a damaged individual, spiritually and in her personality but she is intellectually very formidable …' Later in his letter he wrote, 'the issues for her now are trying to create a personal identity and trying to reassess the concept of family which she had held in a very conventional sense. She is also disengaging herself forcibly from her mother to try and avoid the influence which she sees her mother producing over her, which is almost completely negative.'

I did not see that referral letter until PALS intervened when Dr D became my GP. The referral letter by Dr B to the mental health services explained to me why my medical team had not assisted me in having contact with my mother. It also lead me to read Clinical Psychologist C's file where I discovered he had written to Neuropsychologist A when I was diagnosed with MS. Further incomplete, misleading information and opinion about my circumstances was passed on.

Clinical Psychologist C wrote to Dr B every nine months or so during the four years before he referred me to Neuropsychologist A. His letters indicated that I'd sort myself out for a while and then go backwards. His letters mentioned difficult relationships. He was aware of part of the story about my relationship with Edward. The visit by the police to give me a verbal warning confirmed to him (and others) that I must've been the one at fault. By the time he wrote to Neuropsychologist A he told her that I had had 'a very bizarre and pathological upbringing' which had left me extremely damaged with a fear about expanding my life and activities from their restricted level. He added 'in many ways the diagnosis of MS has given her an alternative identity'.

I had a meeting with Neuropsychologist A before I'd seen any files. The meeting was ten days after I'd had a vivid dream. It was one of those dreams where it seemed I felt my brother's physical presence. In the dream I was unbelievably distressed. My brother had his arms around me and my head rested against his chest. I was sobbing uncontrollably into the brown Aran jumper my mother had knitted for him.

'What's the matter? Tell me what's happened', my brother said.

'I can't. I can't. It's too awful, too awful', I said in my dream.

I woke up in the same distressed state I was in the dream. I phoned Samaritans. The lady on the other end of the line waited until my sobs subsided.

'I killed my father and my brother', I blurted out. 'No. No. I didn't actually kill them; I couldn't get doctors to listen to me. I tried but they wouldn't listen.'

I managed to describe to that lady the pain inside me and about my failures to get help for my mother as well.

I tried talking with Neuropsychologist A about the distress I felt over my family, but she told me the appointment was to discuss whether or not I wanted standard cognitive tests. I declined the tests as I did not think my management of MS would be helped by having them, and cognitive problems had not then become a problem for which I was seeking help. As already mentioned the cognitive tests were arranged subsequently by Neurologist C. I'd refuse to see Neuropsychologist A when I was referred back to her by Neurologist C. My refusal came after I'd read my notes and I'd failed to engage Neuropsychologist A in sorting out the incorrect information about me on her file.

Since ending my contact with Neuropsychologist A I have tried not to talk to doctors about the details of my past. Eventually I realised it was too complex and it seemed to me the system was fixated on blaming everything on my childhood.

A year or so later I was allocated a place, funded by the health services, on a pilot course of what was to become Emotional Logic. It hasn't been mentioned on my medical notes even though it is Emotional Logic that can be credited for settling the emotional side of my life and giving me a perspective on the need to balance my endocrine system. So far I have failed to engage any doctor in a discussion about the role hormones have on my health.

The pilot course was called *Adjusting to Change: The Stepping Stone Approach to Unrecognised Grieving*. The information on the handout entitled 'How Chronic Stress Affects Physical Health and Disease' hit me between the eyes and helped me make sense of my own health. On that handout post-traumatic stress disorder was linked to a whirlpool of emotions connected with Shock and Denial. The handout went on to explain that

> 'shock is associated with the release in the body of high levels of adrenaline and stress-related steroid hormones. In the short-term these hormones prepare the body's chemistry for rapid survival action when faced with danger. However, when repeatedly or continuously released, they start to hinder the way the immune system works'.

The course included a lay-person's explanation of the 'day/night swing of the immune system' and the role of adrenaline.

The post-traumatic stress Neurologist C had mentioned was not connected with my childhood but with my dealings with doctors and my inability to communicate with them since my father had been taken ill in Edinburgh. I was being re-shocked every time I felt I was not being listened to when it was more than likely I was right or had useful information that was being ignored. My interpretation of my case was that re-shocking released adrenaline, but during my childhood living on 'red alert' probably meant there had been a continuous drip of adrenaline, and that my body had adapted to abnormal levels of hormones. The bereavement process after my mother died should have allowed my body to adjust, but the re-shocking over my medical care and the stuck grief had prevented that.

At times I had experiences probably akin to going through 'cold turkey'. I've only read about 'cold turkey' as a process addicts can go through on withdrawal of the substances their bodies had adapted to. I found Peter A. Levine's book, *Waking the Tiger: Healing Trauma*, helpful in understanding my experiences. It gave me an acceptable explanation of my 'cold turkey' like symptoms, and that helped me distinguish them from the problems with my nervous system which I believed were MS related. Classifying any of my symptoms according to Ayurvedic lifestyle principles helped me manage them.

The cognitive thread in my story has caused me most distress and as yet has not been discussed comprehensively with me. It interacts with hearing impairment and sight problems, and may have been over-looked as I have academic qualifications and continued studying and researching topics that interest me, and I appear articulate when I meet health professionals.

My studying and reading sabbatical year after my mother died was extended, and lasted for more than a decade until studying was no longer feasible due to the difficulties MS brought. I didn't finish the Open University *You, Your Computer and the Internet* course. Towards the end of the course health problems prevented me completing the final assignments. I attempted other courses with the Open University but failed to complete any of them. I had contact with their support unit for people with disabilities and was impressed at the help available. They introduced me to voice recognition software so I could continue to use my computer during the spells when my fingers refused to type, but the software was inefficient when my speech was slurred.

I was unhappy losing the ability to complete structured study. I set myself the challenge of completing six Level 1 introductory courses with the Open University. I finished all six but knew my days of pursuing my interests though studying a topic in depth were over. There was a spell where I could not take in any information unless I was simultaneously hearing what I was reading. At other times I was getting too many of the difficulties I'd encountered at Exeter University to make studying worth the effort. Cognition and sight problems are a common part of MS, but I did not have the ability to convey to anyone that I thought there was something else also affecting me.

The mental health trust had three files about me. I asked for the files to be destroyed or put beyond the reach of clinicians. To me, it was a reasonable request but one which completely baffled the system. I spent four years corresponding with the mental health trust including with their clinical director. I didn't get a clear answer from anybody as to why my request couldn't be achieved. At one point I was told the files had to be kept in case my relatives wanted to sue the mental health trust!

Matters were concluded when a manager from the mental health trust made a home visit. She told me all their records had been computerised and files put into long term storage. Only the last contact would be on the computer for any future clinician to view. She confirmed that if I was referred again to the mental health services no incorrect information should be included in any assessment. But she did not explain how they'd ensure all information was correct.

I requested a copy of what was on the computer and received the notes made by Community Psychiatric Nurse B following a home visit shortly before I transferred to Dr D. I had had another relapse which affected my feet, legs, hands, and bowel control and was having problems with my eyes. I was being told my wish not to go out was due to anxiety until Occupational Therapist A visited.

'I wouldn't want to go out either if I had those problems', she commented.

The community psychiatric nurse's summary of my mental health, both its history and current situation, demonstrated to me how the complexity of my story and the mismanagement of my healthcare cannot usefully be summarised. In her summary the 'presenting problem' was anger, frustration and confusion, but she did not deal with the 'presenting problem'. Her conclusion read, 'A 51 year old lady with severe physical disabilities and a history of poor relationships who currently denies having any mental health problems, none appear to be evident through assessment'.

Before the records were computerised I was told I could put a note on my files. I placed extracts from two books I had read during my extended sabbatical. The first was from Muhammed Yunus's auto-biography, *Banker to the Poor*. When writing about his parents he mentioned the mental affliction which affected his mother. His father was the one,

> 'who shone brightly through this whole sad reality of life ... He adapted himself to the situation with grace and fortitude and created a surprising normality for the family within this chaos.'[1]

The second note I put on my mental health file was an extract from Pauline Boss' book *Ambiguous Loss: Learning to Live with Unresolved Grief*. Her book deals with situations where lack of information or understanding prevents closure being achieved following loss. She writes,

> 'The inability to resolve such ambiguous losses is due to the *outside* situation, not to internal personality defects. The outside force that freezes the grief is the uncertainty and ambiguity of the loss.'[2]

In her book she explains that those affected by ambiguous loss may be misdiagnosed when they seek treatment, as ambiguous loss, even in healthy people, can cause symptoms similar to common, diagnosable physical or mental illnesses. Boss wants doctors to acknowledge that uncertainty or ambiguity in connection with loss can undermine health, and for them to check ambiguous loss isn't a factor affecting their patients.

Those extracts are now locked away in long term storage and were never discussed with me.

When Dr D retired I did not see a GP for about eighteen months. I was in yet another phase of poor communications about my health except with Occupational Therapist A and the manager of PALS, who spent a year telling me to be patient as she anticipated I would be allocated a community matron once the pilot schemes ended and anyone with long term, complex needs could ask to be referred to a community matron. She was right.

Community Matron A has made all the difference to the management of my health and disabilities. For over two years I have been talking to the same person. The continuity and expertise she provides has improved my healthcare and enabled me to discuss details of my health a GP would never have time to hear about. Community Matron A visits me at home and I have email contact with her. I talk with her and she talks with my GP.

As I recovered from a series of excruciating pains and odd problems with visual processing she facilitated, through my GP, my request to see Neurologist D and request another brain scan. She accompanied me to the appointments with Neurologist D.

Before John and I met we both used Dragon NaturallySpeaking voice activated software and Peter looked after our computers. John and I formed an informal computer club where we share our limited knowledge about computers. The morning Peter returned my computer with Windows 7 installed, John's laptop would not start. Peter looked at it, unplugged it from the mains and removed its battery. He then started it knowing it would not start without any power. He replaced the battery and turned the computer on in the normal way and it started and was fine. John and I were puzzled and asked him what he was doing.

'Sometimes the laptop gets confused when it shuts down. Trying to start without any power clears the problem. It's quite a rare problem', he explained.

When I woke up next morning what Peter had done to John's computer was on my mind and resonated with something I'd read a few years previously when I was doing an Open University course. The book, *Where Wizards Stay up Late: The Origins of the Internet* was still on my bookshelves. I thumbed through it until I found the section at the end of Chapter 4 headed 'The Bug'. It wasn't John's computer I was thinking about, but maybe 'The Bug' was the analogy I was looking for to explain to my doctor what I was experiencing and why I had to lie down frequently for twenty minutes with a mask over my eyes. And it wasn't a mental health problem.

The Bug was a synchroniser bug. The book's authors explained that a computer has to have a means of regulating its many functions synchronously. They wrote,

'In a communications system, messages arrive unannounced; signals interrupt the machine asynchronously. Like a telephone call in the middle of dinner, an incoming packet shows up on its own schedule ... and says, "Take me now".' [3]

A computer has to be designed to handle such interruptions. Synchroniser bugs are unusual but when the computer's operating system doesn't respond properly to an incoming call a computer can crash leaving only a ghostly trace for the computer diagnostician to find. Perhaps a crash caused by a synchroniser bug happened because the synchroniser or computer had gone into a metastable[4] condition, and being barely stable, confusion arose.

Before my appointment with Neurologist D, Community Matron A suggested I had an eye test. During the test I closed my eyes every time the optician changed the lenses to prevent weird sensations and dizziness. He commented that my visual processing seemed to be affected in a manner often associated with dyslexia.

Whatever was going on with my visual processing it seemed to trigger other problems if not managed well. I had ceased watching television, avoided looking at websites where there was movement on the screen and was having great difficulties when in a moving vehicle.

I don't know what the physiological equivalent is to a computer's synchroniser, but there must be some neurological and biochemical means of managing the huge volume of inputs and outputs from the brain. Perhaps a metastable brain state triggers emergency and survival functions to kick in causing physiological symptoms that have similarities with normal flight/fight responses, including a racing heart.

Over stimulation of my brain and nervous system, often caused by pain and processing visual and audio stimuli, and the resulting metastable state of my brain distressed me until I found the 'synchroniser bug' explanation. My incomplete, layperson's hypothesis is that by lying down blood flow to my brain increases which helps clear spent neuro-chemicals and boosts the oxygen supply, and brain activity is reduced because I'm resting and have covered my eyes.

Being asked questions during a 'synchroniser bug' attack makes my symptoms worse. I've yet to see a health professional during such an attack to know if I'll handle their questions better now I have the synchroniser bug hypothesis. The hypothesis is helping me prevent and manage attacks better.

Neurologist D was straight forward and informative. He discussed the results of my brain scan with me and gave me a brief tour of the images of my brain on his computer screen. He said the scan was unequivocal evidence of MS. He also said it showed no other problems. He confirmed I was in the progressive stage of MS and urged the necessary changes to my accommodation are done sooner before it becomes too late.

In the note I'd given to him at the beginning of the appointment I asked about my cognition, communication and sight problems and neuroplasticity. He referred me to the hospital psychology team and Occupational Therapist A for further investigations. I left the appointment feeling optimistic that the jinx in my healthcare had finally been exorcised.

17

Examining the Yarn

IT IS hard to say why the records of my health became complex and did not serve my best interests. It was, perhaps, a combination of failings within the health and social care systems and some issues being too taboo to talk about. Nothing in my family's background was appalling expect the abuse my mother experienced as a child.

Many aspects of my and my family's health could have been managed better if a patient-centred approach to health and social care had been available. Distortions on my medical notes accumulated due to failings: failures to assess correctly my circumstances, my abilities and the richness of my inner life; failures in treating my parents, my brother and myself as a loving family; failures to communicate accurate information; failures to tell me subjective, unsubstantiated opinions; failures to take into account conflicts of interests between myself and other patients. In addition to these failings, a general diffusion of responsibility within the system resulted in exacerbating the normal life experiences of illnesses and bereavements encountered by my family.

When I was at school, children who had difficulties with reading and writing were more likely to be labelled as careless, lazy and stupid and told to try harder than be assessed as having special educational needs. Had I been so assessed the congenital hearing impairment should have been discovered. Was it the cause of the dyslexic type problems I had or were there other factors? I was blessed to have two primary school teachers, Mother John and Miss Courtney, who laid sound foundations. My wish to keep abreast with my brother's achievements was sufficient incentive for me to try as hard as I could. With hindsight learning double entry bookkeeping taught me to take more care than I would have done, because if I didn't balance the books I knew I'd have to find my mistakes and correct them, a skill I transferred to my education and work.

I have a love of words, but as I'd struggled so much I didn't discover that until the short courses with the Open University. I thoroughly enjoyed their introduction to Shakespeare and the two writing courses. When studying Sanskrit in America, the charts of mouth positions helped compensated for my hearing impairment.

At the time I did not understand why I'd refused to go to The College of Law to study for the Law Society's Part II exams. When I edited the first draft of the manuscript of this book I saw the connection between the hearing impairment and the feeling I had of being cut off in some sense when in social groups. I could cope with face-to-face interactions if there was no background noise but I didn't cope in environments such as a court or classroom. I instinctively knew I would not pass my exams if I went to college. In doing the correspondence course I'd removed the difficulties the hearing impairment caused.

A symptom connected with dyslexia is a discrepancy between apparent intelligence and performance at reading, writing and spelling. During my decade's reading sabbatical I read an article entitled 'Skills for the Future' by Tom West in which he wrote

> "… it is now becoming increasingly clear that often people with great visual-spatial or other non-verbal talents have 'extraordinary brains' – brains that seemed to be optimised to do tasks other than those which are normally called for in conventional word dominated educational systems. And I will also argue that – contrary to what we have been taught – for an increasing number of tasks these non-verbal talents and skills are compatible or superior to the conventional academic talents and skills." [1]

I think the dyslexic-type experiences at school and cutoffness contributed to my determined nature and the ability to connect unrelated topics in creative ways. Fortunately by the time I'd left school I'd developed good coping strategies. Perhaps the hearing and dyslexic type problems turned out to be a blessing as they helped shape my brain and my outlook on life.

The few hours I spent waiting in casualty in Edinburgh in my late twenties changed my life. It marked the beginning of a series of situations I didn't know how to handle and for which I failed to find relevant help. Thirty years later I'm still astounded at the lack of common sense and the inhumanity shown by the system to my father and his family that evening and during the days he remained in Edinburgh. If he couldn't remember he had relatives he probably couldn't remember he was diabetic. The first question the doctor at the hotel asked me was whether I was the patient's daughter. That information should have stayed with my father, and no decisions made without me being consulted and informed. The doctors who treated him should have ensured they had all the information that was easily available to them.

Once my father was back at home in Sidmouth the system was again hindering obtaining the health care my family needed. Neither of my parents were well, both were incapable of helping themselves or each other, but they were each the other's next-of-kin. I suppose it was patient confidentiality or convention that prevented their GP letting my brother or I be involved. When I read my medical notes I realised I regarded myself as a patient of the Sidmouth practice as I had not registered with a doctor in Exeter when I bought my house there. The only time I'd been to the Sidmouth surgery was five years earlier for a sick note for my employer when I had flu. Had I been in the habit of seeing a doctor I might have asked the GP for help for myself but it never occurred to me.

A few weeks later I encountered the insensitivity with which the system handled matters before my father's death in the coronary care unit. Again it was only while writing this book I realised that my father had been left in a side room with no nurses and no bleeping equipment because he was dying. There was no need for my mother to see a doctor unless he wished to explain that to her[2]. The trainee nurse had been compassionate towards me; I should have asked for a chaplain after I'd phoned my brother.

Neurologist C was correct about post traumatic stress. For more than two decades following my father's death I'd had recurring dreams about trying to leave Edinburgh and never finding my way out of the city.

I am still mystified by how mental health services work. I do not understand why a full assessment of one's physical health is not made before a GP makes a referral and this information passed on and also given to the patient. Otherwise it should be the first thing done by the mental health services. The symptoms of physical ailments should not be turned into mental health problems.

The mental health assessment should distinguish between cognitive abilities, emotional factors and normal reactions to life experiences. Again these should not be turned into mental health problems but appropriate advice given on adjusting to or managing one's circumstances.

Care should be taken before and after a referral to assess and ameliorate the social consequences of a mental health referral. One's family should be consulted and involved, where feasible, before decisions are made and throughout any treatments.

I think it was negligence that the results of my first brain scan were not passed to Clinical Psychologist C. Even if the system prevented me being diagnosed with MS at that time it should have been taken into account to see if it was relevant and influencing other aspects of my health. Clinical Psychologist C knew about the hearing tests and once it was known the impairment was congenital it would have been a good idea to have explored what, if any, of my problems stemmed from that. I also think it was wrong that Clinical Psychologist C didn't insist I received bereavement counseling before attempting anything else.

With hindsight I should have referred myself to CRUSE after Andrew died. Had I done so, there would probably have been no reason for Dr B even to have considered a referral. Sometimes a person needs encouragement to seek counselling. There were many occasions following deaths in my family when my ability to make sound decisions about my welfare was frozen.

Whilst I was marooned upstairs with the MS relapse when the extension was being built I asked CRUSE for counselling about my emotions over the death of my little sister whom I only knew through my parents' distress.

During that relapse different care workers from an agency were visiting daily. As it was January it was often dark when they arrived. Although I was expecting them, hearing strangers coming upstairs to my bedroom resulted in some sort of distressing flashbacks. The mantra in my bedroom from all who came was, 'Talk with your doctor', which I did on his one and only visit. He listened, grunted, looked at the clock on my bedside table and declared he was late for a meeting.

During the previous year I had been receiving silent telephone calls. The Saturday before the relapse the police had given permission for my phone line to be monitored but I could not put that in place with the phone company until the Monday. That morning the commode, Zimmer frame and wheelchair beside my bed forced me to admit I was disabled and no longer capable of doing the Ayurveda Lifestyle work I'd so enjoyed. Instead of having my phone monitored I changed my telephone number.

Whilst the flashback phase lasted I was having problems sleeping, and spent most nights doing Sudoku puzzles and talking with Samaritans, who were brilliant. I knew it would not help if I talked about my past and what was needed was to get me back into the present and for me to stay in the present to give myself a chance to go to sleep. I was given the telephone number of Samaritans Exeter Branch and instructed to say my name and that I had MS. Often we talked about gardening and the raised beds I was planning once the building work was finished. I call Samaritans the fourth emergency service, being there twenty-four hours a day and for whom no topic is too taboo to talk about.

Had an accurate assessment been made of my physical health and cognitive and emotional circumstances it should have been apparent that Cognitive Behaviour Therapy was not the most appropriate route for my mental health care.

Although the report on the hospital file about my first brain scan concluded 'the overwhelming impression was demyelinating disease', I was not diagnosed with multiple sclerosis. By convention, such a diagnosis was made only after two clinical episodes had been recorded.[3] Dr B was correct to speak with me about the results of the brain scan, but I doubt he knew what was written on the hospital file. Perhaps if he had, we would not have dismissed MS as a distant probability.

I did not agree with Clinical Psychologist C when he wrote to Neuropsychologist A that the diagnosis of MS had given me an alternative identity. I never needed an alternative identity – the one I had was alright by me – but bereavement counselling after my father's and brother's deaths would have helped.

Multiple sclerosis is a degenerative, neurological disease, a constant companion making demands that cannot be ignored, but can be managed. MS affects everyone who has it differently, as symptoms depend upon which areas of the brain and spinal column are affected by the lesions or scars in the myelin sheath, the insulation covering the nerves.

When I was diagnosed I was influenced by the numerous conversations I'd had in the mid-1990s with people with terminal illnesses or serious chronic conditions who wished to see Dr Lad, by memories of MS patients in the long stay ward I visited on Wednesday afternoons when I was sixteen and the approach at The Yoga for Health Foundation towards disabilities. I wished to make the best use of whatever active life I still had, and I didn't want to spend my time and energies seeking a cure that had yet to be found and successfully trialled. That was probably why I neglected to ensure I was recalled to discuss and be prescribed disease modifying drugs. I threw my attention and energies into managing MS and making unsuccessful attempts to continue my work.

One of the short Open University courses I did was an introduction to writing poetry. I wrote a poem summarising how MS altered my life.

When was the trial? What were the offences?
The sentence? Referred for life, never feel well.
Nerves demyelinated. No kin to tell.
Walking disabled. Distorted senses.
Drunkenly coordinated. Spoke unclearly.
Career extinguished. Space invaded
By unknown carers. Friendships faded.
Housebound, dependent, fatigued, aged early.
Grieve the death of life's potential. Crawl
Through crystallized scars of life's emotions.
Delve deeper, uncover life's secret haul,
Tear exhumed gems cleaved from oceans.
Turn full circle. All is primordial sound,
A unifying pulse, the multiversal ground.

When I came home from Dr C's surgery on the day he had referred me to the MS nurse, Maurice, my builder, was in the process of ripping out my kitchen prior to refitting it.

'I've just seen my GP. He thinks I've got MS', I said

'Well, the pavement at the top of your garden is level with your kitchen floor', said Maurice casually.

That was the first of much practical advice from Maurice over the next decade which has enabled me to remain in the house I bought when I went to university. For four months he continued telling me how I could have a new entrance before he convinced me to go ahead, make the entrance and cease struggling up the steps to my front door.

As soon as the entrance was completed I had more problems with my legs and I needed to use a wheelchair indoors. Alterations had to be made to my house as my kitchen wasn't big enough for a wheelchair and I needed a downstairs wet-shower room and toilet. Occupational Therapist B from Adult Community Services gave Maurice and me advice to help us plan the extension to my house which was built the following year. I had another relapse before it was finished and that was the one when I was confined upstairs for three months.

The next relapse, soon after the extension was finished, was when Community Psychiatric Nurse B visited me. I was also referred then to Adult Community Services because I didn't want to go out. Those involved with my health and social care thought I was not going out because I hadn't been out. Perhaps they were thinking there was a danger I would become agoraphobic. Occupational Therapist B was my Adult Community Services' care manager as he had been the last person from the service to have had contact with me. We were sitting in the extension and chatting about my circumstances.

'If you could have anything, what would you wish for?' he asked me.

I didn't reply immediately. In my mind's eye, standing behind him I could see my father and Gordon, one of my father's friends from Rotary.

'If they were here,' I thought, 'they'd sort this nonsense out.'

I can't remember what I replied to Occupational Therapist B, but I remembered I was still a solicitor. The Solicitors Benevolent Association would help me. I didn't want money from them I wanted a brain, or rather the ability to organise practical assistance to adjust to the realities I faced and how I wanted to manage my health and life.

When I googled the Benevolent Association, Jeremy, whom I had known when he was training and who had known my father, was the person to contact. Since then Jeremy has kept a pastoral eye on me, and is my safety net should the 'synchroniser bug' disrupt my functioning for too long.

It is impossible to untangle how hearing, language problems and my experiences in childhood with my mother interacted and shaped my character, influenced my life and affected my reactions to some of my life's challenges. When combined with bereavements and MS in my adult life they all played a part in the loss of my legal career, my experiences with Ted and Veronica and my behaviour which they found distressing. And no doubt they all contributed to numerous episodes of the 'synchroniser bug'.

With the insights gained since I found the synchroniser bug analogy I recalled two phrases that had been in use since my mid-thirties. The first, 'Playing catch up', I'd used after a period when I hadn't managed to do all I should have done and was attending to priorities only. Following such an episode I'd have to catch up with the non-essentials. After MS was diagnosed 'Playing catch up' changed to 'Being on survival mode' to get by, and there was rarely energy to play catch up afterwards. With hindsight I realised that was how my active life slipped away to MS.

The second phrase was used by Edward after I had been particularly quiet and had returned to being my normal self.

'Oh, you're back again', he'd comment.

Were those early episodes of MS or the 'synchroniser bug'? Was that the beginnings of changes in my cognitive abilities and the reason for my failure to complete the taxation correspondence course when I lived in Barnstaple?

I can't remember with which doctor I tried to discuss MS and cognition.

'It would be unusual for MS to start with cognitive problems,' he commented.

And that was the end of the conversation.

I found more information when I was doing the final assignment on the Open University course, *Beyond Google*. For the final assessment, students answered a question they'd written. My question was whether there was any evidence that reflexology benefits those with MS. When doing my research for the assignment I discovered the National Institute for Clinical Excellence's Guideline for people with multiple sclerosis. It contained comprehensive information about MS including how it can affect the different aspects of cognition.

Six months into my reading and studying sabbatical I'd attended a weekend course, *Introduction to Permaculture*.[4] I was hooked and had a reading list that would keep me engrossed for a long time. I was blessed that at the time MS was diagnosised I'd just started a *Permaculture Design* course.

Permaculture is applied common sense, and on the course we were looking at principles for designing systems that are sustainable, environmentally sound and economically viable. We were working with and learning from nature. It was not about going back to the past but using the best of the old and the new. A phrase from the course that stayed with me was 'the solution lies within the problem'. Permaculture principles can be applied to managing one's own life and home, to community projects of all descriptions and beyond.

The design course filled the months between seeing Dr C when he referred me to the MS nurse and the beginning of her course for those newly diagnosed with MS. Nothing could have been more beneficial for me in those months. In addition to being inspired and stimulated I learnt a new skill that was invaluable when managing MS and planning changes to my house and garden.

In addition to Permaculture and Ayurveda lifestyle principles I use Emotional Logic as another tool for managing daily life. Cognitive Behaviour Therapy and Emotional Logic both provide means for dealing with unhelpful thoughts and emotions. The former is dealing with habits of thinking, so if emotions follow on from thoughts, developing new ways of thinking may enable the emotions to settle down. But perhaps that is not the whole story and emotional habits can generate unhelpful thoughts. The hypotheses upon which Emotional Logic is based, claims thoughts may arise from self beliefs created by patterns of emotional processing. Such patterns can form before there is language to describe emotions or experiences giving rise to emotions. Either way, thoughts and emotions are entwined and both models offer useful skills to change or manage destructive thoughts or emotions, but I found Emotional Logic's methods of discovering one's emotional patterns more useful.

Emotional Logic's model integrates physiology, some main stream mental health conditions and everyday feelings and behaviours. Emotional Logic is a life skill and not a therapy so can be used by just about anyone to help manage their own health and relationships.[5]

Both my mother and I had traumatic experiences in childhood. Perhaps preverbal and nonverbal processing of such experiences set up unhelpful self beliefs, from which patterns of emotions, thoughts and behaviours could be triggered by resonances later in life. Once we were adults, layers of experiences, thoughts and emotions would make it impossible to lay bare the underlying cause or causes and it would probably be irrelevant anyway.

I like Pauline Boss' view in *Ambigous Loss* that some reactions are not due to internal, personal defects. More openness in society and a willingness to talk about taboo topics, especially by those working in health and other public services, would help end emotional poverty, cheer up society and reduce the national bill for mental health services.

In addition to self-help management I would like to use the best from the allopathic system of healthcare. I am excited by the understanding and developments emerging from research over the last twenty years.

Ayurveda, Emotional Logic and Permaculture are energetic systems which understand and suggest ways to manage one's subtle and not-so-subtle, personal energies and circumstances. These either enhance or disturb one's wellbeing. Soon energetic systems will not be seen as complementary or alternative. The film *The Living Matrix: The New Science of Healing*[5] shows scientific theories behind healings and gives a perspective on what healthcare could become.

My parents were part of the vanguard bringing these changes to humanity. I am blessed they sowed seeds of curiosity in me and I was given opportunities to pursue my own path and gain a growing understanding of the potential for every person to evolve unto 'our highest good'.[7]

Afterword

When I studied psychology at the end of the 1980's the degree course included issues relating to the nature -v- nurture debate. In Ayurvedic terms this is the relationship between prakruti and vikruti, one's constitution and daily life experiences. In allopathy, it is the growing understanding about the genome and epigenetics, one's genetic inheritance and factors that activate or deactivate that inheritance.

Ayurvedic lifestyle principles can be described as practical, elemental epigentics for the layperson. It is a cost effective form of preventative medicine and self management.

Those who use Ayurveda's teachings in their lives know the difference they themselves can make to their wellbeing. Using energetic systems does not exclude the allopathic system, any more than using allopathy excludes complementary medicines. It is about the sensible use of the best of both, and taking the right actions at the right time.

APPENDIX 1

The White Eagle Lodge

www.whiteagle.org

'A worldwide organisation based on profound, yet gentle philosophy. Through White Eagle's teaching we are encouraged on a path of love, tolerance and service towards all life; towards the development of inner peace, and the awareness of our eternal, spiritual nature'.

THE 'white eagle' is a symbol of spiritual vision, and The White Eagle Lodge, founded in 1936, was set up in order to bring to ordinary people the vision of the spiritual life in which we live, and which gives us life. Through becoming increasingly aware of this interpenetration of matter and spirit, we learn that death is not the end, but a return home to a greater reality; and that we can, each through our own spirit, be instruments of healing and peace for the world.

'White Eagle, who spoke through the mediumship of Grace Cooke, describes himself as a spokesperson for a wiser Brotherhood in spirit, who help humanity to understand their true spiritual nature, and to grow in wise love for all life. Always encouraging, loving and strong, he is a friend to thousands of people all over the world and a spiritual guide in a path of gentle unfoldment. Thus he has taught us a safe method of meditation, how to pray with acceptance, how to serve others through healing and through the radiation of the Christ light, and how to lead a life where love – the motivating force of the cosmos – is the key-note. Through White Eagle's teaching we learn that love works, because it is the power and wisdom behind all, and how to bring that love to bear in all our ordinary, daily encounters.

'The White Eagle Lodge is non-profit making, non-proselytising, and has great respect for all religions and spiritual groups. For example, White Eagle has referred often to the inspiration and wisdom of Buddha, as well as other spiritual teachers and masters. When he uses the word "Christ", therefore, he is not limiting what he means to the Christian tradition. Instead, he uses it in its ancient and mystical sense, as the divine essence of the Light – God. Through White Eagle, the Lodge also sees God as both "mother" and "father". It is with great respect for the angelic influence and for animal life that the White Eagle's teaching also helps us to work for an end to cruelty, and for harmony in and with our natural world'.

Extracts from The White Eagle Lodge's website
(Reproduced here with permission)

APPENDIX 2

The Aetherius Society

www.aetherius.org

WHEN I was researching these memoirs I contacted The Aetherius Society who suggested I read *Contact with the Gods from Space: Pathway to the New Millennium* by George King as an introduction to the principles of The Aetherius Society. I also read *The Twelve Blessings: The Cosmic Concept,* as it was a book I knew was important to my mother.

There was much in *Contact with the Gods from Space* to which I could see my mother related. My mother was reading material from The Aetherius Society in the 1960s, when CND demonstrations were often in the news. She believed it was vital to pray for the world, not only to prevent the threat of destruction to the planet, but also to prevent distortions on subtle or etheric levels from atomic explosions affecting cosmic energy held in a 'state of potentiality', which would be grossly harmful to future manifestations in the Cosmos in ways we cannot imagine.

The literature also referred to a new era, unfolding from the beginning of the twenty-first century, as a time when similarities in the message of unconditional love in the world's religions will emerge, and science and religion will again merge as the search for the ultimate Truth continues.

The Twelve Blessings may be challenging to a conventional Christian. It refers to Jesus Christ as the Master Jesus, and extends The Sermon on the Mount into 'the most advanced realms of mystical wisdom'[1] The first eight Blessings cover aspects of life that can be found easily within daily comprehension, but the last four Blessings relate to concepts so vast that I find any true understanding to be beyond my intellectual faculties. I interpret the underlying message as one of selfless, loving service by all Beings at every level of attainment in the journey of evolution back to the Absolute.

I think time and contemplation is necessary to gain a full appreciation of the Society's teachings, and each person will respond to them according to their individual background and beliefs, and the manner in which they came across them.

The first draft of this Appendix about The Aetherius Society included quotes from George King's books. My request for permission to use such quotes was declined by the Society. In the reply to my e-mail requesting permission, a director of The Aetherius Society said;

> 'Your mother clearly believed that we should all send out energy to the world through concerted, directed prayer. That commitment to service to humanity – Karma Yoga – is the core of The Aetherius Society's teachings and activities'.

---

[1] *The Twelve Blessings: The Cosmic Concept* as given by The Master Jesus, p6

APPENDIX 3

The Supraconscious

A copy of handwritten notes found
in papers of the late J. Duncan Morrison.
(The original source is not known.)

The use of the power of the Supraconscious is based on a seven-point hypothesis:

1. The Supraconscious is constantly amenable to control by the power of suggestion.
2. The Supraconscious is incapable of independent reasoning by the process of induction.
3. The power of the Supraconscious to reason deductively from given premises to correct conclusion is practically perfect.
4. The Supraconscious is endowed with perfect memory.
5. The Supraconscious has absolute control of the functions and conditions of the body.
6. The Supraconscious has the power to communicate by means other than the recognised channels of the five senses.
7. The Supraconscious is capable of intuition and perception of the laws of nature.

SUMMARY OF HYPOTHESIS

1. Power of Suggestion.
2. Independent Reasoning Impossible.
3. Deductive Reasoning Perfect.
4. Perfect Memory.
5. Absolute Control of Body.
6. Power of Communication.
7. Intuition.

   (Suggestion, Reasoning, Memory, Control, Communication, Intuition)

Preparation for sleep
1. Physical relaxation.
2. Mental concentration, then relaxation.
3. Recite the points of the hypothesis.

Suggestion to the Supraconscious
1. Relax, and open communication channel.
2. State positive thought and express a positive.
3. Repeat until single expression is sufficient.

The Supersense
1. Utilize 'hunches'.
2. Keep a small notepad.
3. Record day and night.
4. Consider thoughts at night.

'Mind and Matter'
1. Allow positive thoughts to be created and 'soaked in'.
2. Reverse negative thoughts.

The Happiness Habit
1. Make happiness a habit.
2. Banish monotony.
3. Develop a Happiness Maximum.

Visualisation
1. Positively affirm health.
2. Avoid disharmony.
3. Visualise perfect health, vitality and happiness.
4. Avoid upset, panic and worry.

New Psychological Laws
1. Destroy anxiety.
2. Look forward.

Use of the Hidden Power
1. Make an affirmation.
2. Visualize it in the mind's eye.
3. Project it (e.g. to part of the body).
4. Use curatively.
5. Nullify doubt.
6. Accept distraction from habitual thinking.
7. Destroy or reverse negative desires.

'Night work'

Encourage the Supraconscious to work at night and when the conscious is asleep or otherwise occupied.

The Supraconscious is a vast storehouse of knowledge. This vast accumulation of wisdom and knowledge never pauses and never ends.

The Supraconscious, unlike the limited Conscious Mind, always knows how to put together facts so that they lead to correct conclusions. It is like an immensely powerful but extremely compact computer, with a vast library of information ready for use but needing proper programming.

The Supraconscious remembers everything. The conscious mind feeds information to the Supraconscious and may then forget it. The Supraconscious never forgets.

The Supraconscious is the secret of the 'hunch' that sometimes guides us – and it can be developed into a constant and dependable guide.

The Supraconscious can bypass the limited Conscious Mind, and take absolute control of the function and conditions of the body.

The Supraconscious is the key to achievement and betterment.

The gift of the Supraconscious – or more accurately its directed use – is effective in healing, learning, influencing and improving.

The Supraconscious can be controlled. The way to control it is by the use of suggestion. Mind Power is a power for health by right thinking. Mind Power can turn the ill into the well, the infirm into the active, and the miserable into the happy.

Happiness is a habit and like all habits it can be developed. It is as easy to develop as any other habit.

There are hidden powers – magic powers – within the brain, within the Supraconscious.

The power can be tapped, used and made to work.

The secret is old – and upon its age depends its certainty.

The Supraconscious is a powerful superior and 'upper level' thinking machine. Its powers are 'above' and 'beyond'.

The Supraconscious is the root of the mind's power.

In the Supraconscious lie outstanding power and vast wisdom. All these powers and this wisdom are there to be used. They need only to be tapped.

APPENDIX 4

Ayurveda –
The Science of Life

Ayurveda is a comprehensive, energetic medical system. It has its roots, like yoga, in the Vedas of ancient India, but has evolved over millennia to be relevant in the twenty-first century as a healing modality.

Searching the term 'ayurveda' on the internet will give a plethora of results, which can be overwhelming when new to a topic.

I suggest starting with:

- The Ayurvedic Institute's Online Resource Centre a developing resource, including articles written by Dr Vasant Lad. (www.ayurveda.com)

- Dr Claudia Welch's site (www.drclaudiawelch.com)

- Information about Dr Robert Svoboda and his books is on his website www.drsvoboda.com.

- For information about Dr Swami Shankardev Saraswati, see the Satyananda Yoga website (www.satyananda.net), and for his books and CDs and e-courses, see www.bigshakti.com.

APPENDIX 5

In Celebration of Andrew's Life

*From the service at
The Crematorium, Exeter*

Thank you for joining us this afternoon and for dressing in a way that is appropriate to celebrate Andrew's life and his passing into a world of freedom and brilliant colour.

Many people underestimate the spiritual strength of the 1960s. We created the widest generation gap imaginable. The full significance of this generation gap is not yet fully appreciated. After the limbo period between the ages of Pisces and Aquarius the tide began to return in the 60s. A quiet revolution had begun. Togetherness became the key. We began to realise what a harmonious world could be like and set about building the foundations.

Now you may think I am a dreamer but I wasn't the only one.

IMAGINE[1]
Lennon – Record

Andrew, a child of the 60s, chosen to incarnate and to heal the world so that a Golden Age could follow. We have all been entrusted with a sacred task. But first we each have to clear our karma/residue of the past. This comes in the form of our responses to lessons/challenges imposed upon us. The greatest test usually is to shake clear of some of the values and traditions of the past and find an inner peace.

The Teacher 'Black Elk' says this about Inner Peace,

> 'The first peace, which is the most important, is that which comes from within the soul of men/women when they realise their relationship, their oneness, with the universe and all its powers, and when they realise that at the centre of the universe dwells Wakan-Tanka (God – Supreme Energy), and that this centre is really everywhere; it is within each of us. This is the real peace and the others are but reflections of this.
>
> 'The second peace is that which is made between two individuals.
>
> 'The third is that which is made between two nations.
>
> 'But, above all, you should understand that there can never be peace between nations until there is first known that true peace, which is within the souls of men/women.'

Andrew understood that truth – he didn't rush about in a vain spiral of experience that so many of us do. He found deep spirituality within. Those of us who have studied his astrological chart understand that this was a most important part of Andrew – his reason for being here. This amazing grace or inspiration that comes from the heart.

AMAZING GRACE
Sung by the Congregation

Amazing grace! How sweet the sound
That saved a wretch like me!
I once was lost, but now am found;
Was blind, but now I see.

'Twas grace that taught my heart to fear,
And grace my fears relieved;
How precious did that grace appear
The hour I first believed.

Through many dangers, toils and snares,
I have already come;
'Tis grace hath brought me safe thus far,
And grace will lead me home.

The Lord has promised good to me,
His word my hope secures;
He will my shield and portion be,
As long as life endures.

Yea, when this flesh and heart shall fail,
And mortal life shall cease,
I shall possess, within the veil,
A life of joy and peace.

The world shall soon dissolve like snow,
The sun refuse to shine;
But God, who called me here below,
Shall be forever mine.

When we've been there ten thousand years,
Bright shining as the sun,
We've no less days to sing God's praise
Than when we'd first begun.

John Newton (1725–1807)

Address by Stuart Neil

Thank you all very much for your help during this last week. You have helped to enable me to know a very special person. I was never fortunate enough to have met Andrew when he was around, and I feel that through speaking to each of you in turn I have got to know him and to know this very special being.

You'll note several phrases I say concerning him. You will probably recognise them from what you have been telling me.

You describe him as a tall, looming, kindly, inoffensive chap. He was highly intelligent with a very quick mind and an almost photographic memory, and he used to sum people up quickly. He was also very private, a very private person, genuine and extremely methodical. He was charming and fun to be with, and very popular with his colleagues at work. This "fun to be with" came up most of all when he went out to dinner, one of his favourite pastimes. He was a good conversationalist and combined with his ability to get on so well with people and to sum people up, and the fact that he was knowledgeable on virtually any subject you could hold a conversation on, made him an extremely agreeable companion.

His was a thoughtful, quiet life, making few demands on others. He used to care for his mother and visit her quite frequently, and latterly looked after her affairs. He made very few demands on others because he was a quiet, considerate person. He wanted to be so and not to impose on others. I think this came out particularly strongly with the discovery of his illness. He had an arterial problem and was aware of this and had been, Judith feels sure, for some time. It showed itself in the way he conducted himself in the last couple of years. He gave up his job, he stopped driving and he put his affairs very straight; so straight that it is as if he knew that one day he knew he would not be with us.

It was typical of Andrew; he told nobody about this and yet the only time it was mentioned he would say, "No one can tell me anything I don't know already".

He had, has, a very deep spiritual link with Judith; one of those unique links usually only found with twin souls. They did not need each other's physical presence. They had a rapport that covered distance and this was very useful, very helpful and very supportive for both of them, as during their early life they were mutual friends and became very close to each other. They supported each other as much as they possibly could, even to the extent that when Andrew was first to go to kindergarten school he did not fancy going on his own and so Judith went as well.

This closeness and support held them together through all their trials, tests and challenges. He was immensely proud of Judith's achievements and her courage to achieve, especially through the last few years when she has taken on quite daunting tasks. And he gave all his love and support and put his energy behind what she was doing. He learnt the Ayurveda way and approved.

This relationship with Judith is the second peace, that between two individuals, peace beyond physical presence, eternal peace.

> Most of you will remember his whimsical
> smile and dry subtle wit,
> his good sense of humour and great sense of fun.
> Think of the mischievous sparkle in his eyes
> as we surround him with our love and think
> of him for a few moments.
>
> ANDREW,
> We surround you with all our love.
> This time the cocoon was slow to open
> The silken thread of life was wound very tightly around you.
> Now the restrictions are finished, the karma is done.
> Now you are free, open your wings and fly.

> If I should die and leave you here a while,
> Be not like others, sore, undone who keep
> Long vigils by the silent dust and weep.
> For my sake turn again to life and smile,
> Nerving thy heart and trembling hand to do
> Something to comfort other hearts than thine.
> Complete these dear unfinished tasks of mine,
> And I, perchance, may therein comfort you.'
>
> Anon.

When I was a small boy and I'd come in having fallen in Granny's garden, she always used to say, 'I do not worry about you, only the good die young.'

Bobby, my wife, had a cousin who lived with the family, who was almost a brother, Carlton. He was the nicest person you could wish to meet, generous and kind and loving, just like a brother. I don't think she could have imagined anyone nicer. Carlton died when he was 32 of renal failure. He had had difficult times; he had problems throughout his twenties, but it had not affected him. When he died my wife could not understand why. She went to her church and asked why and did not feel that she was given a satisfactory answer. She could not understand why the good die young, the nice people die young and the nasty people grow old. Over the next few years she began to look more and more into this and think more about this. She was a nurse at the time. She eventually built up her own new age philosophy, for want of a better description, in which she could understand why these things happen. Now she runs a charity[2] for people who have physical problems, but also from the spiritual point of view. Death meant that this little sister began to think and then dance and then sing and now perhaps begin spiritually, as well as physically, to heal the world.

Andrew died at 41, seemed very young, but I think he had fulfilled his task here this time. It is a life well done. And his influence has not finished on this earth. He understands and approves of the Ayurvedic teachings and from his new position of freedom he will be able to transmit love and positive energy of the universe through his closeness to Judith into her efforts to bring this understanding to many. Thereby fulfilling Black Elk's third peace, the healing of nations.

'Shall the day of parting, be the day of gathering
And shall it be said, that my eve was in truth my dawn?'

Kahlil Gibran

So now, as all darkness, sorrow, negativity has fallen away, there is only love and light and colour – a new beginning. Time for everyone to dance in celebration, especially little sister.

DANCE LITTLE SISTER[1]
The Rolling Stones – Record

---

[1] For copyright reasons the words of *Imagine* and *Dance Little Sister* can't be reproduced here. The words can be found by a search on the internet.

[2] The Quiet Mind Centre www.quiet-mind.org

Bibliography

Benjamin, Harry (1936 reprinted 1955) *Everybody's Guide to Nature Cure.* Health for All Publishing.
Bennett, Glin (1987) *The Wound and the Doctor: Healing, Technology and Power in Modern Medicine.* Secker & Warburg.
Boss, Pauline (1999) *Ambiguous Loss: Learning to live with unresolved grief.* Harvard University Press.
Burns, David D. (1989) *The Feeling Good Handbook*, Penguin.
Cook, Peter W. (1997) *Abused Men: The Hidden Side of Domestic Violence.* Praeger.
Hafner, Katie et al (1996) *Where Wizards Stay Up Late: The origins of the internet.* A Touchstone Book.
King, George (1996) *Contact with the Gods from Space: Pathway to the New Millennium.* The Aetherius Society.
King, George (1958) *The Twelve Blessings: the Cosmic Concept as given by The Master Jesus.* The Aetherius Society.
Lad, Vasant (1984) *Ayurveda, The Science of Self-Healing: A Practical Guide.* Lotus Press.
Leslie, Anita (1975) *Francis Chichester.* Hutchinson of London with Hodder & Stoughton.
Levine, Peter A. (1997) *Waking the Tiger: Healing Trauma.* North Atlantic Books
Moore, Thomas (2004) *Dark Nights of the Soul: A Guide to finding your way through life's ordeals.* Gotham Books. p. 105.
Morrison, Judith H. (1995) *The Book of Ayurveda: A Guide to Personal Well-being.* Gaia.
VanHowten, Donald. (1996) *Ayurveda and Life Impressions Bodywork.* Lotus Press.
Yunus, Muhammad (1998) *Banker to the Poor: An autobiography of Muhammad Yunus, founder of the Grameen Bank.* Aurum Press.

Notes

Chapter 3 Schooldays
[1] Benjamin, Harry, *Everybody's Guide to Nature Cure* p. 17.
[2] Leslie, A. *Francis Chichester*. Stoughton.

Chapter 6 Out of Control
[1] Reproduced with permission from Jonathan Neville, Derek Neville's son, by email 14 October 2007.

Chapter 9 University
[1] www.whiteagle.org/healing/introduction.htm. Accessed 10/04/08.
[2] Bennett, Glin, *The Wound and the Doctor: Healing, Technology and Power in Modern Medicine.* p187.
[3] Ibid. p299.

Chapter 10 Wide Horizons
[1] Dr Vasant Lad, quoted in *Dhanvantri* in *Ayurveda News*, Vol. 3:1, 1994.
[2] These concepts may be difficult if they are new to you, and I am not attempting a description of Ayurveda or its philosophy here. See Appendix 4 for sources of information about Ayurveda.
[3] Morrison, Judith H., *The Book of Ayurveda: A Guide to Personal Well-being.* p. 27.
[4] Lad, Vasant, *Ayurveda: The Science of Self-Healing.* Lotus Press, p. 17.
[5] *Ibid.*
[6] Morrison, Judith H. *ibid.* p. 20.
[7] Morrison, Judith H. *ibid.* p. 56.
[8] Morrison, Judith H. *ibid.* p. 186.
[9] Houston, Vyas, *Sanskrit and the Technological Age.* www.americansanskrit.com/read/a_techage.php (Accessed 4.5.08).
[10] VanHowten, Donald *Ayurveda and Life Impressions Bodywork.* p. 2.

Chapter 14 No Diagnoses
[1] www.siara.co.uk accessed 13.09.04.

Chapter 15 Stuck Grief
[1] Mens' Advice Line www.mensadviceline.org.uk.
[2] Emotional Logic Centre www.emotionallogiccentre.org.uk.

Chapter 16 Untangling Threads
[1] Yunus, Muhammad, *Banker to the Poor: An autobiography of Muhammad Yunus, founder of the Grameen Bank.* p35.
[2] Boss, Pauline *Ambiguous Loss: Learning to live with unresolved grief.* p10.
[3] Hafner, Katie et al, *Where Wizards Stay Up Late: The origins of the internet.* p133.
[4] Metastable - a state of stability that is barely stable. Metastable states may be easily stimulated to become unstable.'
www.icknowledge.com/glossary/m.html. Accessed 4/1/11

Chapter 17 Examining the Yarn
[1] QED: Dyslexia BBC Education p16
[2] Help is more likely to be available now. See dyingmatters.org.
[3] Conventions have changed. Now a patient would be informed they experienced a clinically isolated episode. See www.mssociety.org.uk and www.mstrust.org.uk
[4] See www.permaculture.co.uk and www.permanent-publications.co.uk
[5] *Emotional Logic Home Study Program* (2010). See www. emotionallogiccentre.org.uk
[6] See www.thelivingmatrixmovie.com
[7] With acknowledgement to Derek Neville (See Chapter 6)

www.ingramcontent.com/pod-product-compliance
Lightning Source LLC
Chambersburg PA
CBHW060502090426
42735CB00011B/2078